Contributions to Finance and Accounting

The book series 'Contributions to Finance and Accounting' features the latest research from research areas like financial management, investment, capital markets, financial institutions, FinTech and financial innovation, accounting methods and standards, reporting, and corporate governance, among others. Books published in this series are primarily monographs and edited volumes that present new research results, both theoretical and empirical, on a clearly defined topic. All books are published in print and digital formats and disseminated globally. This book series is indexed in Scopus.

Pengguo Wang

Integrating Earnings Forecasts, Valuation, and Return Prediction

A Unified Framework

Springer

Pengguo Wang
Xfi Centre
University of Exeter
Exeter, UK

ISSN 2730-6038 ISSN 2730-6046 (electronic)
Contributions to Finance and Accounting
ISBN 978-3-032-05909-3 ISBN 978-3-032-05910-9 (eBook)
https://doi.org/10.1007/978-3-032-05910-9

This Springer imprint is published by the registered company Springer Nature Switzerland AG
The registered company address is: Gewerbestrasse 11, 6330 Cham, Switzerland

About the Book

Applying fundamental accounting numbers in a functional form to determine equity value and predict future stock returns in practical investments is challenging. Not only do future earnings and book values governed by conservative accounting principles jointly characterize uncertain cash flows but an investor's required rate of return used in calculating the present value of future cash flows is unobservable. This monograph explores the impact of accounting conservatism on these value attributes and establishes a formal connection between future earnings and the intrinsic value of equity, grounded in linear valuation principles. The primary goal of this work is to introduce a simple and practical methodology for valuing equity (and an enterprise). It equips investors and analysts with tools for forecasting future earnings, estimating intrinsic values, and deriving a plausible proxy for expected returns—all within a unified framework.

Contents

1 Introduction 1

2 The No-arbitrage Assumption and the Dividend Discount Model 7
- 2.1 No-arbitrage and Stochastic Discount Factor 7
- 2.2 The Risk-adjusted Discount Rate 9
- 2.3 Value of Equity 11
- 2.4 The Connections Between Accounting Fundamentals and Stock Value 14

3 Earnings-based Valuation Models and Effects of Conservatism 17
- 3.1 The Residual Income Valuation Model and Linear Earnings Information Dynamic 17
- 3.2 Conservatism Effects on Earnings-based Valuation 19
  - 3.2.1 Example 1: The Effect of Depreciation on Valuation 23
  - 3.2.2 Example 2: Valuation Under Inflationary Conditions 24
  - 3.2.3 Example 3: The Effect of Speed of Recognition of "Good" News and "Bad" News on Valuation 25
  - 3.2.4 Example 4: The Effect of Smoothing a Growing Income Stream 27
  - 3.2.5 A Combination of Conditional and Unconditional Conservatism 28
- 3.3 The Effects of the Expected Net Present Value of Future Investment Opportunities on Future Earnings and Valuation 29
- Appendix 35

4 Future Earnings and the Intrinsic Value of Equity 37
- 4.1 Analysts' Forecasts of Earnings, Model-based Forecasts, and Accounting Fundamentals 37
- 4.2 One-year Ahead Earnings and Intrinsic Value 38
- 4.3 Future Earnings and Intangible Assets 41
- Appendix 43

5 Incorporate Market Information in Valuation of Individual Firms and Predicting Returns 45
5.1 Intrinsic Value of Equity and Stock Price 45
5.2 Use Analysts' or Model-based Forecasts of Earnings to Value Individual Stocks 46
5.3 Valuation Multiples 49
5.3.1 The Intrinsic Linkage Between Equity Value and Value Drivers 50
5.3.2 A Synthetic Price Multiple and Its Estimation 52
5.4 Use Analysts' or Model-based Forecasts of Earnings to Predict Stock Returns 53
5.5 Application of Industry Information in Valuation and Predicting Returns 59
5.5.1 Estimation of Portfolio Level Valuation Parameters 59
5.5.2 Predicting Individual Stocks' Returns 65
5.5.3 Using Information Dynamics to Estimate Value and Predicting Stock Returns 75
5.6 Application of Synthetic Price Multiples 86
5.6.1 Data Description 86
5.6.2 Estimation of Industry-year Information Dynamic Parameters and Cost of Equity Capital 87
5.6.3 Synthetic Price Multiples: V/e_1, V/B and V/e 91
5.6.4 The Synthetic Price Multiples and Actual Price Multiples 95
5.6.5 Valuation Bias and Inaccuracy 99
5.6.6 Prediction of Stock Returns 101
5.6.7 The Synthetic Price Multiples of ESG Stocks 104

6 Enterprise Valuation in a Unified Framework 107
6.1 Articulation Between the Valuation of Invested Capital and the Forecasting of Abnormal Operating Earnings 107
6.2 Using a Proxy for Current Value of Invested Capital in Forecasting Future Net Operating Profits 110
6.3 Incorporating Explicitly R&D, SG&A and Intangible Assets in Information Dynamic 111
6.4 Valuation of Invested Capital 112
6.4.1 Estimating the Key Industry Value Drivers in a Unified Framework 113
6.4.2 Estimating the Present Value of Future Investment Growth 115
6.5 Applying Valuation Multiples 116
6.6 Estimating Directly the Weighted Average Cost of Capital (WACC) 118
6.6.1 Forecasting of Firm-year Specific Operating Income 120
6.6.2 Industry-year Specific WACC, Growth Rate and Other Valuation Parameters 121

6.6.3 Estimating the Firm-year Implied Weighted Average Cost of Capital 121
Appendix 122

Bibliography 125

Chapter 1
Introduction

This monograph addresses equity (enterprise) valuation and aims to provide practical tools for investors and financial analysts. We initially focus on an all-equity firm and adopt an approach to valuation similar to that carried out by fundamental analysts, attributing a market value of equity to the reported accounting values of equity, along with forecasts of future earnings and growth. It attempts to forecast future earnings, estimate intrinsic values, and derive a proxy for expected returns within a unified framework. It offers indicators of temporary mispricing and expected returns to investors in real-time.

The value of an asset equals the present value of all expected future cash flows generated from the asset. Equity valuation is fundamentally based on processing accounting information. Since investors and analysts place more weight on accounting earnings than on cash flows, forecasting future earnings becomes paramount in equity valuation. However, accounting earnings are governed by accounting principles, particularly the principle of accounting conservatism, which remains a pervasive guiding constraint in recognizing asset values and income. An over-cautious depreciation policy, the expensing of investment in research and development or human capital, the ignoring of holding gains in the nominal value of assets subject to inflation, and the early recognition of "bad" news and the delayed recognition of "good" news are all examples of conservatism that postpones the recognition of economic income and assets values. It is necessary to clarify the role of accounting in valuation.

Accounting records business transactions. Intuitively, accounting practices should not alter a company's intrinsic value, although the information they produce can influence market perceptions and, consequently, asset prices. For example, stock prices tend to be more volatile during earnings announcements. Business communities, regulators, standard-setters, and investors often discuss good or bad accounting. Good accounting can help management assess the company's performance, make strategic decisions, and plan for future growth. Good accounting ensures accountability and transparency and assists creditors and lenders in

P. Wang, *Integrating Earnings Forecasts, Valuation, and Return Prediction*,
Contributions to Finance and Accounting,
https://doi.org/10.1007/978-3-032-05910-9_1

evaluating the company's ability to meet its financial obligations. It meets legal and regulatory requirements set by governing bodies, such as tax authorities or financial regulators, and ensures compliance with accounting standards. However, from a valuation perspective, we argue that there is no inherent good or bad accounting if we do not consider market frictions, as long as accounting is persistent over time, such that the implied value drivers, including the long-run growth rate of future earnings and the cost of capital, are meaningful. The primary reasons for this are that book value and earnings jointly represent cash flows and are presented collaboratively in valuation. In a more conservative accounting, or the measure of conservatism increases, from a technical point of view, the weights attached to book value and earnings in valuation increase mechanically. For a going concern, valuation involves accounting numbers for many future years. We may also need to "undo" accounting conservatism at some point in the future. If an asset is over-depreciated, for instance, it will be under-depreciated at some future date, as a reversing process exists. Earnings conservatism and balance sheet conservatism may also interact or offset each other in different ways and they may dilute the other's impact in valuation (Pope and Walker, 2003).

Future earnings can be generated from current and future investments or result from "undo"accounting conservatism. Accounting defers earnings recognition under uncertainty, resulting in expected future earnings. We, therefore, investigate how accounting is reflected in the earnings dynamics. This monograph develops within a linear framework, where one-period ahead earnings are linearly related to their fundamental determinants. It can be regarded as a first-order approximation. More complex nonlinear relationships between economic variables are beyond the scope of this work. They are best addressed, for example, using advanced machine learning techniques, which have proven to be more adept at handling such complexities. However, our explicit structural relation between future earnings, values, and the cost of capital still guides the application of machine learning in this aspect.

Insights from reverse engineering in equity valuation models suggest that the intrinsic value of equity is one of the key determinants of future earnings. It is evident in the existing empirical literature that stock prices as a proxy for intrinsic values lead to future earnings. Our models suggest that the one-period ahead earnings can be written in terms of the "normal" earnings measured by the cost of equity multiplied by current book equity, the goodwill measured by the difference between the intrinsic value and book value, the persistence of current residual earnings, and abnormal growth in book values reflecting accounting conservatism. Focusing on the one-year ahead earnings, effectively moving the equilibrium forward to just one period ahead, we can assume a flat term structure of discount rates in valuation. It does not rule out the possibility that the discount rates and expected one-period ahead earnings change when new information arrives in the future.

Stock price and its intrinsic value are co-integrated over time in an aggregate efficient market, even if the daily stock price may not equal its intrinsic value. However, the property of co-integration has rarely been formally used in earnings or cash flow estimations, hence equity valuation. We use stock prices as a proxy for the intrinsic value to estimate future earnings. We assume market efficiency at the aggregate market or industry level, although we admit that financial markets may not be efficient at the individual firm level. It justifies the use of information included in stock prices in earnings forecasting by running cross-sectional or industry panel data regressions and obtaining portfolio valuation parameters, such as the long-run industry cost of capital and growth rate, through a reverse engineering approach. We estimate the intrinsic value of each individual firm based on these portfolio-level long-term value drivers, the persistence of current earnings, the degree of accounting conservatism, and the firm's current accounting fundamentals. Analysts and investors often use industry benchmark valuation multiples to inform their decisions (Walker and Wang, 2003). Our valuation models enable us to identify cross-sectional variations across companies within their industry and determine the deviation of an individual firm's price multiple from its industry norm.

The cost of capital and expected return have been used interchangeably in the literature, but they are not the same. The investors' required return or firms' cost of capital can never be observed. It is a concept based on intrinsic value. Although the expected return at time $t + 1$ is unobservable at time t, the return can be discernible when it is realized. It can be calculated from the trading prices of the asset at time $t + 1$. Unlike estimating an individual firm's implied cost of equity capital, which is the discount rate that equates the present value of future expected cash flows to the stock price, we use stock prices as a proxy for intrinsic values in cross-sectional or industry panel data regressions of future earnings to estimate the portfolio's long-run valuation parameters, such as the cost of capital and growth rate. That is, we focus on the production market in earnings regressions rather than the capital market in returns regressions. We show that the implied returns from our models can be written in terms of these long-run valuation parameters and fundamental ratios, such as the portfolio's long-term growth, dividend yield, the one-year ahead (abnormal) earnings growth-to-price, the (abnormal) book-to-price, and a conservatism measure-to-price. In contrast, almost all asset pricing models utilize currently available market-wide stock prices (or returns) as input. Lee et al. (2021) suggest that factor-based expected-return proxies (ERPs) are the least reliable in both cross-section and time series compared with characteristics-based ERPs and the implied cost of capital (ICCs) in terms of measurement-error variance. Characteristic-based ERPs are the most reliable in the cross section and ICCs are the most reliable in time-series. While motivated and implemented in different ways, characteristics-based models estimate the predictive relations between firm characteristics and future returns from historical data and then apply the estimates to current characteristics to capture expected future returns (see Lyle and Wang, 2015, Penman and Zhu, 2014, 2022). Each variant is constructed as a linear combination of firm characteristics, where the weights are estimated by historical cross-sectional regressions of realized returns on those characteristics. Unfortunately, the existing literature is inconclusive on the origin of the predictive ability of firm characteristics. It is unclear whether a proxy is for an unobserved macroeconomic risk factor or mispricing. Unlike characteristics-based models that estimate the coefficients of an unknown number of characteristics, we first use a reverse engineering technique from earnings regressions to estimate a few key value drivers simultaneously. Then, we apply the estimates to a few fundamental accounting ratios to capture expected future returns. In essence, our approach combines characteristics-based ERPs and ICCs to estimate the proxy for the expected returns. An important appeal of the approach is that it is not dependent on factor sensitivities or coefficients of characteristics estimated using noisy historical realized returns.

We also extend our equity level analysis to the enterprise level. We forecast future operating earnings, estimate the intrinsic enterprise values, and derive the expected enterprise cost of capital in a unified framework. They can be applied in settings involving ownership transition, IPOs, and M&A activities. We can analyze whether value is created or destroyed from public to private ownership and vice versa.

In summary, each chapter is connected by a central idea that the value of equity (enterprise) and forecasts of future (operating) earnings are intrinsically linked in a simple linear fashion. Consistent with a long-standing capital market practice, the key to implementation is to use benchmark industry averages of parameters in valuing an individual company within the industry. Importantly, all relevant industry-level valuation parameters are estimated simultaneously in the model setup. It results in forecasting the one-year ahead (operating) earnings, valuation of equity (enterprise), and return predictions, all being in a unified framework. This approach contrasts with the traditional discounted cash flow (DCF) methods, where investment practitioners and DCF model users often forecast future cash flows (dividends or earnings) and estimate a discount rate separately. For example, to determine equity value, they apply current and future accounting numbers (e.g., forecasts of earnings) by assuming a discount rate. To determine the required rate of return from a stock, on the other hand, they apply a CAPM-style factor model or a characteristic-based model based on current accounting numbers and other non-accounting information, assuming that the current stock prices reflect all available information at the time.

The monograph is largely based on my personal exploration of equity valuation, conducted in collaboration with co-authors. I am deeply indebted to my mentors and coauthors, David Ashton, Peter Pope, and Martin Walker, whose guidance and expertise have profoundly shaped my understanding of valuation techniques. I am also sincerely grateful to my coauthors, Mark Tippett, Ken Peasnell, Wei Huang, Richard Harris, and Ryan Peng, for sharing their invaluable knowledge throughout this journey. Special thanks go to James Ohlson and Stephen Penman for their kind advice and for generously sharing their insights, which have enriched my research. I am equally appreciative of the encouragement provided by my colleagues, Mark Clatworthy, Collin Clubb, Christina Dargenidou, Alan Gregory, Xiannan He, Zhigang Huang, Vicky Kiosse, Xin Ma, Stuart McLeay, John O'Hanlon, Enrico Onali, James Sefton, Kenth Skogsvik, Andy Stark, Jamie Stevenson, and Chengli Zheng, as well as my students, all of whom motivated me to bring this manuscript to completion. I take full responsibility for all errors. This monograph serves as a vital resource for my teaching, particularly for MSc students in Investment and Finance and PhD candidates. More importantly, it offers practical insights for investment practitioners and academics, including fund managers involved in stock selection, business managers navigating mergers and acquisitions (M&A), IPO activities, evaluating competitors, and corporate managers in capital budgeting decisions, as well as other strategic decision-making. Additionally, it provides tools for antitrust regulators to estimate the risk-adjusted cost of capital but avoid relying on historical stock returns. Researchers can use the proxy for expected returns in asset pricing model settings, as well as for an economic outcome that depends on institutional features, securities regulation, transparency, corporate governance, and accounting attributes.

Chapter 2
The No-arbitrage Assumption and the Dividend Discount Model

A financial asset is expected to generate future cash flows. The asset's present value is linked to the riskiness associated with the future cash flows in a specific manner in the capital markets. The concept of no-arbitrage plays a central role in this linkage. The dividend discount model (DDM) follows the no-arbitrage assumption in the capital markets. It is the fundamental pricing model; ultimately, all equity valuation models must reconcile with it.

2.1 No-arbitrage and Stochastic Discount Factor

Generally speaking, there are two types of arbitrage opportunities (see, e.g., Luenberger, 1998): (1) an investment generates an immediate positive reward without any future commitment; (2) an investment has no initial cost but has a positive probability of generating a positive payoff and no probability of generating a negative payoff. The process of exploiting arbitrage opportunities is also a process of destroying them. Arbitrage opportunities will be self-destructed in an efficient capital market. Several important financial theories, such as derivative securities pricing, are built on this insight. Therefore, it is plausible to assume that the capital market is free of arbitrage opportunities in the valuation of assets.

The concept of arbitrage-free builds a bridge between the future payoffs from an asset and its current market value. The assumption of no-arbitrage is equivalent to the existence of a stochastic discount factor (also called the pricing kernel or state-price density) m, such that the value of any asset at time t satisfies

$$V_t = E_t[\frac{m_{t+1}}{m_t} y_{t+1}], \tag{2.1}$$

P. Wang, *Integrating Earnings Forecasts, Valuation, and Return Prediction*, Contributions to Finance and Accounting,
https://doi.org/10.1007/978-3-032-05910-9_2

where $E_t[.]$ is the expectation operator conditional on information at time t, m reflects investors' beliefs and risk aversion, and y_{t+1} is payoff from the asset at time $t+1$ (see, e.g., Feltham and Ohlson, 1999, Duffie, 2010).

The future payoffs are uncertain for any risky assets and are not observable at the current time. If future payoff y_{t+1} is known at time t or there is no uncertainty, the covariance term in Eq. (2.1) equals 0, and we have $1/E_t[m_{t+1}/m_t] = \frac{y_{t+1}}{V_t} = R_f$, the gross risk-free return, where $r_f = R_f - 1$ is a risk-free rate. Since R_f is typically greater than one, the payoff y_{t+1} sells "at a discount", $V_t = y_{t+1}/R_f < y_{t+1}$.[1] It follows that a stochastic discount factor must satisfy $E_t[\frac{m_{t+1}}{m_t}] = 1/R_f$, the reciprocal of R_f. Equation (2.1) implies that

$$V_t = \frac{E_t[y_{t+1}]}{R_f} + cov_t[\frac{m_{t+1}}{m_t}, y_{t+1}]. \tag{2.2}$$

In asset pricing, an investor is modeled by a utility function $u(.)$ defined over current and future values of consumption c. A typical discount factor between t and $t+1$ can be written as: $\frac{m_{t+1}}{m_t} = \beta\frac{u'(c_{t+1})}{u'(c_t)}$, where β captures the investor's impatience (a subjective discount factor), $u'(.)$ is the first derivative of $u(.)$, and c_t represents aggregate consumption at date t (see, e.g., Cochrane, 2009). The marginal rate of substitution of time $t+1$ consumption for current consumption is determined by the relative marginal utility from consumption between t and $t+1$.

Our knowledge of stochastic discount factors (SDFs) highlights the evolution of asset pricing models.[2] As Karolyi and Van Nieuwerburgh (2020) point out, "the end goal should be that we arrive at an SDF that comes closer to achieving the mean-variance efficient portfolio and that the SDF be economically interpretable." Campbell and Viceira (2002) argue that "the power-utility property of constant relative risk aversion is inherently attractive and is required to explain the stability of financial variables in the face of secular economic growth." If we choose a discount function that is consistent with a constant relative risk aversion (CRRA) utility function $u(c_t) = c_t^{1-\lambda}/(1-\lambda)$, where λ measures the degree of relative risk aversion, then it follows:

$$\frac{m_{t+1}}{m_t} = \beta\frac{u'(c_{t+1})}{u'(c_t)} = \beta(\frac{c_{t+1}}{c_t})^{-\lambda}.$$

In other words, the stochastic discount factor reflects an investor's impatience and degree of risk aversion. For our analysis, we further assume that the logarithm of

[1] Note that R_f can be less than 1 when the economy is in a deep recession or financial crisis, like the global COVID-19 pandemic period starting from the beginning of 2020.

[2] With the findings of more candidates for risk factors and applications of machine learning (ML) in asset pricing, exploring the properties and implications of the SDF is an ongoing task. It is apparent from Lucas Jr (1978)'s consumption-CAPM-based SDF, Campbell and Cochrane (1999)'s habit-based SDF, Barberis and Huang (2008)'s prospect theory-based SDF, and Epstein and Zin (2013)'s recursive utility SDF.

growth in consumption follows a random walk with a drift: $ln(c_{t+1}/c_t) = g+\epsilon_{m,t+1}$ or

$$c_{t+1} = c_t e^{g+\epsilon_{m,t+1}}, \tag{2.3}$$

where $\epsilon_{m,t}$ follows a normal distribution $N(0, \sigma_m^2)$.[3] In general, we also expect that the growth of consumption increases with the payoff, i.e., $cov_t(\epsilon_{m,t+1}, y_{t+1}) > 0$. If we let the impatience parameter $\beta = \frac{1}{R_f}e^{\lambda g - \frac{(\lambda\sigma_m)^2}{2}}$, then we have a specific form of discount factor:

$$\frac{m_{t+1}}{m_t} = \frac{e^{-(\lambda\sigma_m)^2/2}}{R_f} e^{-\lambda\epsilon_{m,t+1}}. \tag{2.4}$$

Equation (2.4) and the Stein's Lemma together imply that[4]

$$cov_t(\frac{m_{t+1}}{m_t}, y_{t+1}) = \frac{e^{-(\lambda\sigma_m)^2/2}}{R_f} cov_t(e^{-\lambda\epsilon_{m,t+1}}, y_{t+1}) = \frac{-\lambda}{R_f} cov_t(\epsilon_{m,t+1}, y_{t+1}) < 0.$$

It follows from Eq. (2.2) that

$$V_t = \frac{E_t[y_{t+1}] - \lambda cov_t[\epsilon_{m,t+1}, y_{t+1}]}{1 + r_f}. \tag{2.5}$$

While $E_t[y_{t+1}]$ is the expected risk payoff, and $E_t[y_{t+1}] - \lambda cov_t[\epsilon_{m,t+1}, y_{t+1}]$ is the expected future certainty equivalent payoff. The model uses a risk-free rate to discount the certainty equivalent payoffs. A meaningful valuation implies that $E_t[y_{t+1}] > \lambda cov_t[\epsilon_{m,t+1}, y_{t+1}]$.

Different marginal utilities over consumption make valuation an investor-specific matter. By assuming homogeneous preferences, a representative investor or a marginal investor sets prices in aggregate terms.

2.2 The Risk-adjusted Discount Rate

Equation (2.2) is a more general form of Eq. (2.5). The first term is the asset's value in a risk-neutral economy, where the discount rate is the risk-free rate. The covariance term is the risk adjustment. It can also be written as

---

[3] Although we assume normality for mathematical expediency, we regard it as a first approximation to a general mean-variance analysis of risk. Indeed, most of the commonly used econometric algorithms adopt a variance minimization approach, but where tests of significance involve correcting unspecified error terms for non-normality.

[4] The Stein's Lemma (see, e.g., Ingersoll, 1987): If Y and Z are bivariate normal random variables and $f(.)$ is a differentiable function, then $cov_t(Y, f(Z)) = E_t[f'(Z)]cov_t(Y, Z)$.

$$V_t = \frac{E_t[y_{t+1}] + R_f cov_t[m_{t+1}/m_t, y_{t+1}]}{R_f} \equiv \frac{E_t^*[y_{t+1}]}{R_f}. \tag{2.6}$$

where $E^*[.]$ represents the expectation based on the risk-neutral probability. $E_t[y_{t+1}] + R_f cov_t[m_{t+1}/m_t, y_{t+1}]$ is the expected future certainty equivalent payoff or cash flow (see, e.g., Rubinstein, 1976). That is, we use a risk-free rate to discount the certainty equivalent payoffs. This expected future certainty equivalent payoff should be less than the expected risk payoff in general.

Equation (2.6) can be rewritten as

$$V_t = \frac{E_t[y_{t+1}]}{R_t}, \tag{2.7}$$

where $R_t = 1 + r_t$, and

$$r_t = r_f - \frac{R_f}{V_t} cov_t(\frac{m_{t+1}}{m_t}, y_{t+1}). \tag{2.8}$$

In Eq. (2.7), risk adjustment is achieved through a risk-adjusted discount rate.

Equation (2.5) is a special case, which can be rewritten as

$$r_t = r_f + (1 + r_f) \frac{\lambda cov_t[\epsilon_{m,t+1}, y_{t+1}]}{E_t[y_{t+1}] - \lambda cov_t[\epsilon_{m,t+1}, y_{t+1}]}. \tag{2.9}$$

This is the risk-adjusted discount rate or risk-adjusted rate of return, which equals the risk-free rate plus a risk premium. Since investors are generally risk-averse, they require compensation for bearing risk so that they will use a high discount rate, $r_t > r_f$. Hence, riskier assets have lower prices than equivalent risk-free assets. The risk premium depends on the risk of future payoff (y_{t+1}) and its correlation with the market as well as investors' risk attitude (λ). Different investors may have different views on the future payoffs of different assets. Equation (2.7) shows that risky payoffs must be discounted by the risk-adjusted rate.

In summary, the no-arbitrage assumption implies that the current value of a stream of future uncertain cash flows has two alternative expressions. It is equal to either the present value of expected future cash flows discounted at a risk-adjusted rate as in Eq. (2.7) or the sum of the stream of future certainty equivalent expected cash flows discounted by the risk-free rate as in Eq. (2.6). In principle, the notion above can be used to price any security, including derivative securities.[5]

[5] In option pricing, we introduce a risk-neutral probability to deal with the covariance term or risk, and discount the option's payoffs by the risk-free rate.

2.3 Value of Equity

For common equity holders, the total theoretical payoffs at time $t + 1$ is $y_{t+1} = (V_{t+1} + d_{t+1})$, where d_{t+1} is "net dividends" or dividends for convenience, and V_{t+1} is ex-dividend equity value at time $t + 1$. "Net dividends" consist of three components, including cash dividends, share repurchases, and new share issuance (or rights issues). The new share issuance is effectively negative dividends.

Future payoffs or cash flows belong to capital providers. However, different capital providers, such as shareholders and debt holders, may use different discount rates based on the risk assessment associated with their future payoffs. In this context, the risk-adjusted discount rate or the required rate of return helps investors decide if an investment is worth the cost. That is the minimum possible rate that would attract investors to invest. Because equity shares are viewed as a residual after contractual interest payments to debt holders, debt holders often require a lower rate of return than shareholders. These required rates of return from capital providers are the cost of equity capital and the cost of debt capital from a company's point of view. The intrinsic value of equity or the present value of cash flows associated with equity shares must be determined by the corresponding cost of equity capital as a discount rate.

From Eq. (2.7), equity value can be written as

$$V_t = \frac{E_t[V_{t+1} + d_{t+1}]}{1 + r_t}. \tag{2.10}$$

That is, risky cash flows are discounted by a risk-adjusted rate. From the shareholders' point of view, r_t is the (risk-adjusted) required rate of return between t and $t + 1$.

While the required rate of return is the minimum possible rate that an investor would consider investing, the expected rate of return is what the investor can reasonably expect from that investment in the marketplace. In theory, to calculate the expected rate of return, we must base it on the probability of payoff in each possible state. In practical equity valuation, many implicitly assume that the long-run expected return equals the long-run required rate of return.

In Eq. (2.10), dividends are cash flows or cash transactions between shareholders and the company, and the discount rate changes over time depending on the risk of future dividends. By recursion, we can write V_{t+1} in terms of V_{t+2} and d_{t+2}, and V_{t+2} in terms of V_{t+3} and d_{t+3}, and so on. However, this theoretical reasoning is not applicable since both the numerator and denominator involve stochastic variables. In practical equity valuation, we make further assumptions on the discount rate. We usually assume a flat term structure for the discount rate. That is, we assume that the discount rate for all future periods is constant at time t. Unlike the assumption of a constant discount rate, when relevant information is updated, the discount rate may change to another constant rate based on all available information at the time. One can view it as the shareholders' long-term average required rate of return by holding the stock in the foreseeable future or the long-term average cost of equity capital. In other words, we assume a constant risk-adjusted discount rate (r) in equity valuation at time t. As a matter of fact, financial analysts almost always implicitly assume a constant discount rate in the practical application of absolute valuation models.

Since equity can be viewed as a going concern, we also impose a transversality condition such that $\lim_{n\to\infty} E_t[V_{t+n}]/(1+r)^n = 0$. A going-concern company is never liquidated. Accordingly, by recursion, Eq. (2.10) leads to *the* most basic equity valuation model, the dividend discount model (DDM):

$$V_t = \sum_{j=1}^{\infty} \frac{E_t[d_{t+j}]}{R^j}, \tag{2.11}$$

where V_t is the ex-dividend stock value at t, and $R = 1 + r$. It means that the most recent dividends have just been paid out, and the next dividends will be paid in one period of time. Equation (2.11) gives a fundamental valuation principle: the intrinsic value of equity shares is equal to the present value of all *future* expected dividends (cash flows) generated from the shares. It is clear that Eq. (2.11) is equivalent to Eq. (2.10) under a flat term structure of discount rate:

$$E_t[V_{t+1} + d_{t+1}] = RV_t. \tag{2.12}$$

Dividends can be total or per-share numbers. When dividends are dividends per share, Eq. (2.11) gives the value per share. If we expect a constant dividend growth rate of g for all $t \geq 0$,

$$d_{t+1} = (1+g)d_t + \epsilon_{t+1}, \; g < r, \tag{2.13}$$

Eq. (2.11) implies the well-known Gordon dividend growth model (DGM):

$$V_t = \frac{E_t[d_{t+1}]}{r-g}. \tag{2.14}$$

Although it is widely believed that the one-period ahead dividend forecasts are more accurate than the long-term forecasts, Eq. (2.14) can be invalid if the short-term growth rate is greater than the required rate of return.[6] A more realistic case is an initial or specific period dividend forecast followed by a long-run sustainable growth rate that is less than the required rate of return in a multi-period setting.

[6] One-period free cash flows to equity holders (FCFE) consist of net dividends and non-working cash may provide little insight into the company's economic performance, $d_{t+1} = e_{t+1} - (b_{t+1} - b_t)$. A low or negative FCFE may result from two possibilities. Earnings are low or negative given net changes in equity, or earnings are given and positive, but the firm has a big equity investment. Declining FCFE can signal either poor performance or investments for the future.

Suppose we have dividend forecasts for n years and a terminal growth rate of g. It follows from Eq. (2.11) that

$$V_t = \sum_{j=1}^{j=n} \frac{E_t[d_{t+j}]}{(1+r)^j} + \frac{1}{(1+r)^n}[\frac{E_t[d_{t+n}](1+g)}{(r-g)}]. \tag{2.15}$$

$E_t[d_{t+n}](1+g)/(r-g)$ in the last term is the expected equity value using a constant growth rate from the horizon forecast, $V_{t+n} = E_{t+n}[d_{t+n+1}]/(r-g)$. This, then, must be discounted back to year t and added to the present value of dividends. This means that the share is worth the sum of the present value of the dividends for the specific forecast period plus the present value of the estimated share value at the end of the forecast period. Since the continuing values usually account for more than half of the total values in practice, any small change in growth rate (g) will lead to significant changes in total values. Several scenarios exist in which a company can achieve a supernormal growth rate for a few years, after which the growth rate falls to a more sustainable level. For example, the company may have possessed a patent for several years or been among the first movers on the market. That is, we assume that the firm is out of equilibrium in the short term and moves towards long-term equilibrium over several years. Assume dividends have a growth rate of g_s in the short term, which is allowed to be greater than r, followed by g_l ($< r$) in the long term.

Since valuation involves infinite-period future cash flows, the short-term growth plays a relatively less important role. To illustrate the point, we make the following example. Suppose that a company's equity cost is 8%, and the current period dividend is 100. The dividends grow at 5% for the next five years, then they will settle down to 3% starting from year 6. The current value of equity is 2249. If the dividends grow at a rate of 2%, instead of 5%, for the initial five years to achieve the same equity value of 2249, the implied long-term growth rate will be 3.73%. Even if the difference between the growth rates in the initial five years is 3%, the difference between the long-term growth rate is only 0.73%. If we pull the long-term equilibrium forward and apply the Gordon dividend growth model, we can estimate the smoothed average growth rate of 3.4% $=$ (8% $-$ 100 $\times$ (1 $+$ 3.4%)/2249.19). This rate is implied by the information available at the current time. It changes over time as new information becomes available. The implied growth rate is 3.33% next year. It reduces to a long-term growth rate of 3% in our example by year 5, as shown in Table 2.1. The example underscores the crucial role played by estimates of the long-term growth rate in valuation.

Valuation model (2.15) can be converted into a one-period model given the long-term growth assumption. This is because we can use the backward dynamic programming algorithm to calculate the present value of a cash flow stream, as shown in Eq. (2.15). For a given cash flow stream $\{d_{t+1}, d_{t+2}, \ldots, d_{t+n}, d_{t+n}(1+g)\}$, the algorithm starts from the terminal value

Table 2.1 The implied long-term growth

Period	0	1	2	3	4	5	6
Cash flows	100	105	110.3	115.8	121.6	127.6	131.5
g_s	5%	5%	5%	5%	5%	5%	3%
V	2249	2324	2400	2476	2553	2629	2708
g	3.40%	3.33%	3.26%	3.18%	3.09%	3.00%	3.00%

$$V_{t+n} = \frac{E_{t+n}[d_{t+n+1}]}{r-g} = \frac{d_{t+n}(1+g)}{r-g}, \tag{2.16}$$

then we go one-period back to calculate V_{t+n-1},

$$V_{t+n-1} = \frac{E_{t+n-1}[d_{t+n}] + E_{t+n-1}[V_{t+n}]}{1+r}, \tag{2.17}$$

and V_{t+n-2},

$$V_{t+n-2} = \frac{E_{t+n-2}[d_{t+n-1}] + E_{t+n-2}[V_{t+n-1}]}{1+r}, \tag{2.18}$$

$$\cdots$$

Finally, we have

$$V_t = \frac{E_t[d_{t+1}] + E_t[V_{t+1}]}{(1+r)} = \frac{E_t[d_{t+1} + V_{t+1}]}{(1+r)}. \tag{2.19}$$

That is, the present value of a share equals the discounted expected one-period ahead payoffs. Moving the equilibrium forward to just one period ahead, we can assume a flat term structure of discount rates in valuation.

2.4 The Connections Between Accounting Fundamentals and Stock Value

In the DDM, equity value is the present value of future net distributions of value to shareholders (dividends and stock repurchases net of new capital contributions). In contrast, security analysis aims to understand the sources of value creation, not value distribution. Accounting numbers have been proven to be useful in analyzing value creation and its drivers. Although the DDM is the fundamental valuation model, the dividend payout is largely related to a company's management strategies and investment opportunities. Management has discretion over cash dividend payments, share buybacks, and future investments. That is why wealth distribution is more difficult to forecast than wealth creation in a competitive capital market; therefore, financial analysts pay more attention to earnings forecasts.

Assume the clean surplus accounting relation (CSR) at the equity level holds in all future periods, i.e.,

$$b_{t+1} = b_t + e_{t+1} - d_{t+1}, \tag{2.20}$$

where b_t is book value of equity, and e_t is comprehensive earnings over $(t, t+1)$. Using this identity, the special case valuation model (2.14) under the assumption of a constant long-term growth rate (g) can be rewritten in terms of the accounting fundamentals b_t and e_t as

$$V_t = b_t + \frac{E_t[e_{t+1}] - rb_t}{r - g}. \tag{2.21}$$

Unlike the dividend discount model focusing on wealth distributions, this model values the firm as a function of the accounting measure of current wealth on the balance sheet (b_t), and generation of future wealth resulting from future residual income, measured by the difference between future earnings (e_{t+1}) and capital charges (rb_t), and its growth.

Rearranging Eq. (2.21), we have that forward earnings are related to current market value, book value, the cost of equity, and growth as follows:

$$E_t[e_{t+1}] = rb_t + (r - g)(V_t - b_t). \tag{2.22}$$

In words, forward earnings reconcile to value and fundamentals by thinking of earnings as comprising two components. The first component is the cost of equity capital on book equity, the normal earnings portion; the second component is the growth-adjusted cost of equity capital (or capital-growth spread) on unrecorded goodwill. It highlights the connections between accounting fundamentals, current stock value, and future earnings. The growth rate g in Eq. (2.21) represents the long-term, sustainable rate. The one-period ahead expected earnings in Eqs. (2.21) and (2.22) must be 'core' earnings, although they are conceptually comprehensive earnings. We often observe that valuation analysts exclude transitory earnings, particularly transitory losses and unpredictable items, from reported earnings. Correcting book values and earnings for conservative accounting practices requires a strong understanding of accounting principles. Transitory earnings may affect stock prices, but they do not impact the intrinsic value of equity.

Although not directly observable, from a theoretical perspective, we can write the cost of equity by rearrange Eq. (2.21) in the following simplified model:

$$r = \frac{E_t[e_{t+1}]}{V_t} + (1 - \frac{b_t}{V_t})g. \tag{2.23}$$

Equation (2.23) highlights the fundamental link between the cost of equity capital and three variables: the forward earnings yield, the book-to-market ratio, and the growth rate in future earnings. The cost of equity is relevant either directly as an input to decision models or indirectly as an important component of realized stock returns to investors. Specifically, Eq. (2.23) suggests that (1) the cost of equity is equal to the forward earnings yield when the firm has no growth in (abnormal) earnings; (2) the book-to-market ratio may be related to future stock returns for a growth firm; and (3) information that is useful in predicting future growth (g) will likely be useful in estimating the cost of capital and predicting stock returns. It suggests that the cost of equity capital and the future growth rate are just two sides of the same coin. They should be estimated simultaneously in a systematic manner.

In summary, the concepts of the long-term growth rate and average cost of capital provide a foundation for integrating earnings forecasts, valuation, and return prediction within a unified framework. It motivates us to focus on the one-period valuation models in this monograph.

Chapter 3
Earnings-based Valuation Models and Effects of Conservatism

In the clean surplus accounting framework, the dividend discount model transforms into an earnings-based valuation model, highlighting the critical roles of earnings and book value in equity valuation. However, earnings and book value are accounting attributes governed by accounting principles. This chapter addresses the impact of accounting conservatism on the dynamics of earnings information and equity valuation. Given the inherent difficulty of forecasting earnings over multiple periods and consistent with the analysis in the last chapter, we focus on predicting one-period-ahead earnings.

3.1 The Residual Income Valuation Model and Linear Earnings Information Dynamic

Assume that the clean surplus accounting relation (CSR) at the equity level holds in all future periods. The dividend discount model (DDM) is then equivalent to the residual income valuation model (RIVM) (see, Edwards and Bell, 1961, Peasnell, 1982):

$$V_t = b_t + \sum_{j=1}^{\infty} (1+r)^{-j} E_t[x_{t+j}], \tag{3.1}$$

where V_t is the ex-dividend equity value at time t. $x_t = e_t - rb_{t-1}$ is residual income or abnormal earnings. r (= R-1) is the cost of equity capital or equity holders' required rate of return at time t. This model values the firm as a function of the accounting measure of current wealth on the balance sheet, b_t, and generation of future wealth resulting from future residual income (x_t). It avoids problems associated with the numerous non-dividend paying firms in many empirical settings.

P. Wang, *Integrating Earnings Forecasts, Valuation, and Return Prediction*, Contributions to Finance and Accounting,
https://doi.org/10.1007/978-3-032-05910-9_3

Ohlson (1995) defines unbiased accounting as an asymptotic property with respect to book value, i.e., the convergence of equity book and the intrinsic value of the stock, $V_t \to b_t$ $(t \to \infty)$ and $x_t = e_t - (R-1)b_{t-1} \to 0$ in the long run. Following this notion, Ohlson starts by forecasting abnormal earnings through a specific linear information dynamic (LID), much like the Gordon dividend growth assumption.[1] Specifically, he assumes that abnormal earnings follows an AR(1) process in a competitive production market:

$$x_{t+1} = \omega x_t + \epsilon_{x,t+1},\ 0 \le \omega < 1, \tag{3.2}$$

where $\epsilon_{x,t+1}$ is a mean zero random error term. For our purpose, we ignore "other information" in this section.

The above theoretical model assumes that abnormal earnings follow a simple dampening autoregressive process with an implied negative growth rate to reflect the expected erosion of economic rents through the forces of market competition (see, e.g., Fisher and McGowan, 1983). The AR(1) process (3.2) implies that

$$e_{t+1} + (R-1)d_t = (R-1)(b_t + d_t) + \omega(Re_t - (R-1)(b_t + d_t)) + \epsilon_{x,t+1}. \tag{3.3}$$

That is, the cum-dividend one period ahead earnings can be expressed in terms of the cum-dividend book value and earnings.

Equations (3.1) and (3.2) lead to the following equity valuation model:

$$V_t = b_t + \frac{\omega}{R-\omega} x_t. \tag{3.4}$$

This closed-form valuation model demonstrates that b_t and x_t are sufficient accounting attributes for valuation. It suggests that the coefficient on abnormal earnings is the declining-perpetuity term $\omega/(R-\omega)$. The above can be rewritten as

$$V_t = \frac{R(1-\omega)}{R-\omega} b_t + \frac{R\omega}{R-\omega} e_t - \frac{(R-1)\omega}{R-\omega} d_t. \tag{3.5}$$

It establishes a link between equity market value and book value, earnings, and dividends. Therefore, price-to-book and price-to-earnings become meaningful valuation concepts in a no-arbitrage capital market.

The cum-dividend value is

$$V_t + d_t = \frac{R(1-\omega)}{R-\omega}(b_t + d_t) + \frac{R\omega}{R-\omega} e_t. \tag{3.6}$$

[1] This essentially truncates future abnormal earnings from one year ahead, not n-years ahead in conventional multiple-stage models. It appears justified by Frankel and Lee (1998) and Lee et al. (1999).

That is, the cum-dividend market value can be expressed in terms of the cum-dividend book value and earnings.

To preserve the Modigliani and Miller (MM) dividend policy irrelevance property, Ohlson also assumes the following restrictions originating in the accounting for owners' equity: $\partial e_t/\partial d_t = 0$ and $\partial b_t/\partial d_t = -1$, indicating that dividends do not affect contemporaneous earnings but reduce the book value of equity dollar-for-dollar. Equation (3.5) then gives: $\partial V_t/\partial d_t = -1$. That is, dividends reduce market value one-for-one.[2]

One of the major problems in residual income valuation is dealing with distortions of accounting numbers produced by differing accounting policies. One such distortion that has attracted considerable attention is the principle of accounting conservatism. Both book values and earnings may not always economically meaningful because of the revenue recognition principle and accounting conservatism. It suggests that we need to restate both asset and earnings values or adjust their weights in valuation in a functional form (see Ashton and Wang, 2013a, 2015). However, first, We explore the characteristics of earnings information dynamics and valuation within the context of a biased accounting framework.

We assume the DDM and clean surplus relation (2.20) hold in the following analysis.

3.2 Conservatism Effects on Earnings-based Valuation

While much progress has been made in understanding how conservatism affects valuation, less progress has been made regarding specifying the functional dependency of these valuation weights on conservatism. Ashton and Wang (2013a) develop an analytical structure that makes strong predictions on how the weights attached to accounting variables in linear information dynamic models are affected by conservatism. They start from the premise that the essential feature of conservatism is the delay in recognizing increases in the economic value of assets. An over-cautious depreciation policy, the expensing of investment in research and development or human resources, and the ignoring of holding gains in the nominal value of assets subject to inflation are all examples of unconditional conservatism that delay the recognition of economic income and asset values. The early recognition of "bad" news and the delayed recognition of "good" news is an example of conditional conservatism (Basu, 1997), which also fits neatly into the paradigm. Hence, their general theoretical modeling approach captures aspects of both conditional and unconditional forms of conservatism (Beaver and Ryan, 2005). Their approach

[2] Ohlson and Gao (2006) argue that "without the MM dividend policy irrelevance, the value function becomes much more complicated because the policy parameters would have a direct influence on any formula that determines value. Such a possibility would almost surely exclude any practical or intuitive results, aside from the mathematical mess it would cause."

enables us to identify a linear transformation linking the hypothesized unbiased and unobservable accounting system to that of a reported system biased by conservatism.

These transformations and adjustments for conservatism result in strong predictions about the dependency on the degree of conservatism of the coefficients of the reported accounting variables in the residual income valuation model, as well as the structure of the associated information dynamics. Their empirical evidence provides strong support for the predictions of the dependency of the valuation weights on conservatism and the reformulation of the associated linear information dynamics.

Assume a reported accounting information set, $\Lambda_t = \{b_t, e_t, d_t\}$, where b_t, e_t and d_t are book values of equity, earnings, and dividends at time t, respectively. Under the assumption that the clean surplus relationship (CSR) holds, the information set $\{b_t, e_t, d_t\} \equiv \{b_t, b_{t-1}, e_t\}$, where b_{t-1} is the book value with a one-year lag. In this reporting system, the accounting is biased in the sense that the expected values of long-run book and market values no longer converge. It is presumed biased because of accounting conservatism and is the manifestation of transactions in a hypothesized unbiased but unobservable accounting system, represented by $\Lambda'_t = \{b'_t, e'_t, d_t\} \equiv \{b'_t, b'_{t-1}, d_t\}$. Note that cash flows are the same in both accounting systems. Consistent with Ohlson (1995), an unbiased system implies the expected long-run convergence of book value and market value of equity. In this system, b'_t, b'_{t-1} and e'_t are the unbiased book value and lagged book value of equity and earnings at time t, respectively. Conservatism delays recognizing increases in economic wealth in reported earnings. For example, in the case of accelerated depreciation, the recognition of the economic income stream from those assets is delayed. In historical cost accounting under inflationary conditions, the recognition of asset holding gains is delayed, while conditional conservatism usually involves the reluctance to recognize uncertain "good" news. Thus, conservatism implies that we recognize immediately only a fraction $\frac{\chi_t}{1+\chi_t}$ of the increase in wealth, i.e.,

$$e_t = e'_t - \frac{\chi_t}{1 + \chi_t}(b'_t - b'_{t-1}), \tag{3.7}$$

where $\chi_t > 0$ captures the degree of accounting conservatism. The higher the $\chi_t > 0$, the more conservative the accounting is. Under CSR, $d_t = e'_t - (b'_t - b'_{t-1}) = e_t - (b_t - b_{t-1})$, we have:

$$b'_t - b'_{t-1} = (1 + \chi_t)(b_t - b_{t-1}), \tag{3.8}$$

and

$$e_t = e'_t - \chi_t(b_t - b_{t-1}). \tag{3.9}$$

For tractability of modeling, we can assume a long-run consistency in accounting policy such that

$$\chi_t = \chi + u_t, \ \forall t, \tag{3.10}$$

where χ is a constant summary measure of accounting conservatism and u_t is an independent and identically distributed (i.i.d.) random variable with zero mean. This randomness is not driven by arbitrariness in the accounting policy; rather, the policy is consistently applied, but economic events alter the circumstances under which it is implemented. Thus, for example, in the case of accelerated depreciation, while the long-run average asset mix may be assumed to be a constant, it is likely to change from year to year. In the case of historical cost accounting, the change in the inflation rate over time induces different degrees of conservatism. In the case of conditional conservatism, the size and arrival rate of "good" news drives the stochastic nature of u_t. Thus, with the foregoing assumptions, the expected long-run solution to Eq. (3.8) implies $b'_t - b'_0 = (1 + \chi)(b_t - b_0)$. Under the assumption that long-run growth is positive, ensuring that b_0 and b'_0 are insignificant compared with b_t and b'_t, we can write book value and earnings in the unbiased system in terms of accounting observables as follows:

$$b'_t = (1 + \chi)b_t, \tag{3.11}$$

and Eq. (3.9) gives

$$e'_t = e_t + \chi(b_t - b_{t-1}) = e_t + \chi(e_t - d_{t-1}). \tag{3.12}$$

The valuation model (3.5) then becomes

$$V_t = \frac{R(1-\omega)}{R-\omega}(1+\chi)b_t + \frac{R\omega}{R-\omega}(1+\chi)e_t - \left(\frac{(R-1)\omega + R\omega\chi}{R-\omega}\right)d_t. \tag{3.13}$$

The valuation weights of book value, earnings, and dividends are now reflecting the degree of accounting conservatism. As the measure of conservatism χ increases, the weights attached to book value and earnings increase. In other words, the understated book value and earnings are compensated by the inflated weights in valuation. Therefore, from a valuation perspective, there is no "good" or "bad" accounting. While adjusting for conservative accounting in book values and earnings, as in Eqs. (3.11) and (3.12), may be complicated and require strong accounting knowledge, valuation Eq. (3.13) suggests that the complex conservative accounting effects are incorporated into the valuation weights in the intrinsic value. If we can systematically estimate the valuation weights, then adjustments on individual earnings and book values become less necessary. While forecasting and valuation are related, they represent distinct analytical processes, although more accurate forecasts of earnings generally result in more accurate valuations (see Wang, 2013). One of our primary objectives in this monograph is to explore this technique.

Under clean surplus accounting: $b_t = b_{t-1} + e_t - d_t$, the above can be written in terms of book values and abnormal earnings as

$$V_t = (1 + \frac{R\chi}{R-\omega})b_t + \frac{\omega}{R-\omega}x_t - \frac{R\omega\chi}{R-\omega}b_{t-1}. \tag{3.14}$$

Hence, unlike Eq. (3.4), $\{b_t, x_t\}$ is an incomplete information set in valuation in a more general (biased) accounting system. We need to add additional b_{t-1} (or d_t) information that controls for the influence of conservatism on the expected economic value of equity.

The cum-dividend value can be written as

$$V_t + d_t = [\frac{R(1-\omega)}{R-\omega}(b_t + d_t) + \frac{R\omega}{R-\omega}e_t] + \frac{\chi R}{R-\omega}(b_t - \omega b_{t-1}). \tag{3.15}$$

Unlike Eq. (3.6), it suggests that $\{e_t, b_t + d_t\}$ is an incomplete valuation information set for the cum-dividend value. A separate b_t or d_t information must be added to $\{e_t, b_t + d_t\}$ in valuation in a more general (biased) accounting system.

The cum-dividend value can be reorganized as

$$V_t + d_t = \frac{R(1-\omega)}{R-\omega}[(1+\chi)b_t + d_t] + \frac{R\omega}{R-\omega}[(1+\chi)e_t - \chi d_t]. \tag{3.16}$$

Under some specific conditions, such as $\frac{\partial b_t}{\partial d_t} = -\frac{1}{1+\chi}$, $\frac{\partial e_t}{\partial d_t} = \frac{\chi}{1+\chi}$, the MM dividend irrelevance property is preserved, $\frac{\partial V_t}{\partial d_t} = -1$. The model converges to the original Ohlson model in an unbiased accounting system when $\chi = 0$.

The earnings dynamic (3.3), under information set Λ'_t, then becomes:

$$\begin{aligned} e_{t+1} + (R-1)d_t = &(R-1)(b_t + d_t) + \omega(Re_t - (R-1)(b_t + d_t)) \\ &+\chi[(Rb_t - b_{t+1}) - \omega(Rb_{t-1} - b_t)] + \epsilon_{x,t+1}. \end{aligned} \tag{3.17}$$

Note that $b_{t-1} = (b_t + d_t) - e_t$, and $Rb_t - b_{t+1} = (R-1)b_t + d_{t+1} - e_{t+1}$. Therefore, unlike Eq. (3.3), $\{e_t, (b_t + d_t)\}$ is also not sufficient information set for forecasting the one-year ahead cum-dividend earnings in a biased accounting system.

Ashton and Wang (2015) develop parametric models of specific examples of unconditional conservatism, such as accelerated depreciation and historical cost accounting under inflation, as well as conditional conservatism, including the delayed recognition of "good" news. They argue that from the point of view of equity valuation models, the distinction between conditional and unconditional conservatism in Beaver and Ryan (2005) is largely irrelevant,[3] and that the manifestations of the two forms are inextricably linked. They show how a common underlying mathematical structure unites these two forms of conservatism.

[3] This does not undermine the use of the classification of conservatism in Beaver and Ryan (2005) as a conceptual framework for discussing accounting policy or the empirical classification for event studies such as those carried out by Ball and Shivakumar (2005) and Basu (1997).

3.2.1 Example 1: The Effect of Depreciation on Valuation

Feltham and Ohlson (1996) establish a link between depreciation policy and valuation weights of accounting variables. Ashton and Wang (2015) re-examine the case where the actual depreciation rate α differs from the economic depreciation rate α' such that $\alpha > (<)\, \alpha'$, corresponds to over (under) depreciation. Although the reported book values and earnings are likely biased because of accounting conservatism, they also follow clean surplus accounting: $b_t = b_{t-1} + e_t - d_t$. They assume that Λ_t and Λ_t' are related via the cash flow triple $\{Y_t, I_t, d_t\}$, where Y_t denotes cash flow from operations, and I_t represents the equity portion of the total investment, including investments in both tangible and intangible assets at time t. They start by recasting this link using stochastic difference equations linking the accounting variables in Λ_t and Λ_t' to cash flows. Specifically, they assume the following relationships hold:

$$b_t' - (1-\alpha')b_{t-1}' = I_t = b_t - (1-\alpha)b_{t-1}. \tag{3.18}$$

Here $0 \leq \alpha'$ and $\alpha < 1$. For parsimony of the analysis, they also assume I_t follows a stochastic growth path:

$$I_t = (1+g)I_{t-1} + \epsilon_t, \tag{3.19}$$

where $g \geq 0$ represents the long-run average growth rate of investments. ϵ_t is a random error term with expectation zero and assumed to be serially independent. The equations, as specified in Eqs. (3.18) and (3.19), are thus stochastic difference equations. It follows that the expected long-run equilibrium values of the unbiased book values in terms of the corresponding reported values are:

$$b_t' = \frac{g+\alpha}{g+\alpha'} b_t = \left(1 + \frac{\alpha - \alpha'}{\alpha' + g}\right) b_t. \tag{3.20}$$

Given the above relationship between book values in the two accounting systems, they also establish a relationship between the earnings in the two systems. Equating cash inflows in the two systems $e_t' + \alpha' b_{t-1}' = Y_t = e_t + \alpha b_{t-1}$, we have

$$e_t' = e_t + \frac{\alpha - \alpha'}{\alpha' + g}(b_t - b_{t-1}). \tag{3.21}$$

The clean surplus relation (CSR) implies the cash identity: $Y_t = I_t + d_t$. Equation (3.20) shows that whenever the reported accounting depreciation rate (α) is greater than the economic depreciation rate (α'), accounting is conservative: the reported book value understates unbiased book values (or balance sheet conservatism). From Eq. (3.21), we see that the reported earnings are also understated relative to unbiased economic earnings whenever accounting is conservative (or earnings conservatism).

Given the reported financial information set Λ_t, the expected value of equity becomes

$$V_t = \frac{R(1-\omega)}{R-\omega}(1+\frac{\alpha-\alpha'}{\alpha'+g})b_t + \frac{R\omega}{R-\omega}(1+\frac{\alpha-\alpha'}{\alpha'+g})e_t - (\frac{(R-1)\omega}{R-\omega} + \frac{R\omega}{R-\omega}\frac{\alpha-\alpha'}{\alpha'+g})d_t. \tag{3.22}$$

If we let $\chi_U = \frac{\alpha-\alpha'}{\alpha'+g}$, Eq. (3.22) can be written more succinctly as

$$V_t = \frac{R(1-\omega)}{R-\omega}(1+\chi_U)b_t + \frac{R\omega}{R-\omega}(1+\chi_U)e_t - \left(\frac{(R-1)\omega + R\omega\chi_U}{R-\omega}\right)d_t. \tag{3.23}$$

The parameter χ_U is a convenient summary measure of the application of this unconditional conservative policy. It is a monotonic increasing function of $(\alpha - \alpha')$. If $\alpha > \alpha'$, $\chi_U > 0$ and if $\alpha < \alpha'$, $\chi_U < 0$, while $\alpha' = \alpha$ implies $\chi_U = 0$ and the absence of conservatism. The g in the denominator is merely a convenient way of summarizing the impact of the past application of over-depreciation in the simple closed-form model.

In contrast to the original Ohlson valuation model, the weights on book value, earnings, and dividends in the modified valuation model (3.23) are now functions of the degree of conservatism, χ_U, as well as the persistence of abnormal earnings and the cost of equity capital. Consistent with intuition, Eq. (3.23) shows that as the summary measure of conservatism χ_U increases, the weights attached to book value and earnings increase.

3.2.2 *Example 2: Valuation Under Inflationary Conditions*

Ashton and Wang (2015) extend the above analysis to cover the case of historical cost accounting under inflation, which is also a form of unconditional conservatism. In the case of historical cost accounting under inflation, in addition to any possible effects of accelerated depreciation, the recognition of earnings is delayed because accounting earnings ignore the contribution from the appreciation of assets. They assume that reported earnings and book values satisfy: $b_t - (1-\alpha)b_{t-1} = I_t$ and $e_t + \alpha b_{t-1} = Y_t$. The cash flow, investment, and inflation-adjusted accounting numbers, on the other hand, are linked as in the following equation system:

$$\begin{aligned} b'_{t+1} &= (1-\alpha')(1+\eta)b'_t + I_{t+1}, \\ e'_{t+1} &= Y_{t+1} - \alpha'(1+\eta)b'_t + \eta b'_t, \\ I_t &= (1+g)(1+\eta)I_{t-1} + u_t. \end{aligned} \tag{3.24}$$

Here, η is the inflation rate, and u_t is a random error term with expectation zero and is assumed serially independent. Investment has a real growth rate of g in addition to any inflationary growth. The last term in the second equation, $\eta b'_t$, represents the holding gain on assets. In this case, inflation-adjusted book values and earnings are related to reported values by equations:

$$b'_t = \left(1 + \frac{\alpha - \alpha' + \eta(1-\alpha')}{(g+\alpha')(1+\eta)}\right) b_t, \tag{3.25}$$

$$e'_t = e_t + \left(\frac{\alpha - \alpha' + \eta(1-\alpha')}{(g+\alpha')(1+\eta)}\right)(b_t - b_{t-1}). \tag{3.26}$$

The mathematical structure of the relationship between inflation-adjusted values and reported values is identical to that in Eqs. (3.20) and (3.21), with a summary measure of the conservatism given by

$$\chi_U = \frac{\alpha - \alpha' + \eta(1-\alpha')}{(g+\alpha')(1+\eta)}. \tag{3.27}$$

It is clear that χ_U increases in the inflation rate, η. This analysis generalizes earlier results found in Hughes et al. (2004) and Ashton et al. (2011).

3.2.3 Example 3: The Effect of Speed of Recognition of "Good" News and "Bad" News on Valuation

Conservatism also arises when the firm is cautious in the recognition of "good" news in the form of an unexpected, possibly uncertain, increases in income but speedy recognizes "bad" news in the form of an unexpected, or uncertain decrease, in income.[4] Their modeling of conditional accounting conservatism echoes the assumptions underlying the empirical work in this area.

Suppose that an unbiased accounting system records a set of earnings e'_t according to

$$e'_t = \tilde{e}_t + \epsilon_t, \tag{3.28}$$

where $\tilde{e}_t$ is the "unambiguous" portion of uncertain earnings at time t and $\epsilon_t > 0$ represents "good" news or an unanticipated increase in income and $\epsilon_t < 0$

[4] It may lead to improved contracting, decreased litigation risk, and reduced information asymmetry (see Watts, 2003). An implication of this is that earnings are more positively related to current equity share returns when earnings are negative than when earnings are positive (Basu, 1997; Pope and Walker, 1999; Beaver and Ryan, 2005; Pae et al., 2005; Givoly et al., 2007; Khan and Watts, 2009; García Lara et al., 2011).

represents "bad" news or an unanticipated shortfall in income. Let $\epsilon_t = b_{t-1}\epsilon$, where ϵ is an independent and identically distributed random variable with mean zero.[5] Suppose that earnings e_t can be written as

$$e_t = \tilde{e}_t + \Phi_t,$$

where the adjustment Φ_t is used to recognize the cumulative past and current impact of good or bad news that has been incorporated in the current earnings. Assume

$$\Phi_t = \begin{cases} \delta'_t = \lambda' b_{t-1}\epsilon + (1-\lambda')\delta'_{t-1} & \text{if } \epsilon < 0 \\ \delta_t = \lambda b_{t-1}\epsilon + (1-\lambda)\delta_{t-1} & \text{if } \epsilon \geq 0 \end{cases} \quad \text{and } \lambda, \lambda' \in [0,1], \lambda' > \lambda.$$

Thus, only a fraction λ (λ') of good news (bad news) is incorporated at any time t. Under conservative accounting, the impact of any good news is recognized over a relatively long period ($\lambda < \lambda'$). The greater ($\lambda' - \lambda$), the greater the degree of accounting conservatism. When $\lambda' = 1$ and $\lambda = 0$, bad news is incorporated immediately into earnings, while good news is ignored. By recursion, δ_t and δ'_t can be written as:

$$\delta_t = \lambda \sum_{s=0}^{t-1} (1-\lambda)^s b_{t-s-1}\epsilon, \text{ and } \delta'_t = \lambda' \sum_{s=0}^{t-1} (1-\lambda')^s b_{t-s-1}\epsilon. \tag{3.29}$$

Given Eq. (3.28), e_t is related to e'_t by the following relationship:

$$e_t = e'_t + \Phi_t - b_{t-1}\epsilon. \tag{3.30}$$

To summarize the history of the incorporation of news and derive a closed-form solution, they make the simplifying assumption that the expected changes in book values occur at a growth rate of g. Given the clean surplus relationship, it follows from Eq. (3.30) that the transformation from the unbiased system to the reported accounting system can be written as:

$$e'_t = e_t + \left(\frac{\kappa(1-\lambda)}{g+\lambda} + \frac{(1-\kappa)(1-\lambda')}{g+\lambda'}\right)(b_t - b_{t-1}), \tag{3.31}$$

where $\kappa = E[\epsilon|\epsilon > 0]$.[6] Therefore, for whatever managerial incentives, the valuation effect of conditional conservatism is just like unconditional conservatism and delays in recognition of increases in economic wealth in reported earnings.

---

[5] While lagged book value may capture the size effect of a firm in $\epsilon_t = \epsilon b_{t-1}$, Eq. (3.30) below, in fact, describes the stochastic nature of return on equity (ROE).

[6] In the case of ϵ being distributed as a zero mean normal with standard deviation σ, $\kappa = \frac{\sigma}{\sqrt{2\pi}}$.

Under the assumption that long-run growth is positive, ensuring that b_0 and b'_0 are insignificant compared with b_t and b'_t, the book value in the unbiased accounting system can be written in terms of the reported book value as:

$$b'_t = (1 + \kappa\frac{(1-\lambda)}{g+\lambda} + (1-\kappa)\frac{(1-\lambda')}{g+\lambda'})b_t. \tag{3.32}$$

The resulting valuation equation is:

$$\begin{aligned} V_t = \; & \tfrac{R(1-\omega)}{R-\omega}(1+\kappa\tfrac{(1-\lambda)}{g+\lambda}+(1-\kappa)\tfrac{(1-\lambda')}{g+\lambda'})b_t+\tfrac{R\omega}{R-\omega}(1+\kappa\tfrac{(1-\lambda)}{g+\lambda}+(1-\kappa)\tfrac{(1-\lambda')}{g+\lambda'})e_t \\ & -\left(\tfrac{(R-1)\omega}{R-\omega}+\tfrac{\omega R}{R-\omega}(\kappa\tfrac{(1-\lambda)}{g+\lambda}+(1-\kappa)\tfrac{(1-\lambda')}{g+\lambda'})\right)d_t. \end{aligned} \tag{3.33}$$

We note that the mathematical structure of in Eqs. (3.31), (3.32) and (3.33) assumes the same pattern as in the previous subsection with the summary measure representing, in this case, conditional conservatism taking the form: $\chi_C = \kappa\frac{(1-\lambda)}{g+\lambda} + (1-\kappa)\frac{(1-\lambda')}{g+\lambda'}$. Hence, Eq. (3.33) can be rewritten as

$$V_t = \frac{R(1-\omega)}{R-\omega}(1+\chi_C)b_t + \frac{R\omega}{R-\omega}(1+\chi_C)e_t - \left(\frac{(R-1)\omega + R\omega\chi_C}{R-\omega}\right)d_t. \tag{3.34}$$

In this case, the policy giving rise to conservatism is attributable to the relative speeds in the recognition of future negative and positive earnings. Given the "uncertainty" of the ambiguous portion of the return on equity, the degree of conservatism depends on the "speed" with which this ambiguous portion of earnings is incorporated into reported earnings and the volatility or the arrival rate of news. Since χ_C can be written as $\chi_C = \frac{1-\lambda'}{g+\lambda'} + \kappa\frac{(1+g)(\lambda'-\lambda)}{(g+\lambda)(g+\lambda')}$, we observe that the degree of accounting conservatism increases as $(\lambda' - \lambda)$ increases. The cum-dividend value can be written in a form similar to Eq. (3.15).

3.2.4 *Example 4: The Effect of Smoothing a Growing Income Stream*

Ashton and Wang (2015) also address the impact of the policy of smoothing a growing income stream on valuation. They argue that delaying the recognition of future positive earnings is a form of conservatism. The degree of conservatism can be summarized similarly by a simple χ-parameter. Assuming that expected earnings are positive, we can think of a proportion $\rho \leq 1$ of earnings being recognized at time t, with a further proportion $\rho(1-\rho)$ being incorporated from time t-1 earnings, and so on. They thus model conservatism in the form of the delayed recognition of total earnings from the past. The model becomes

$$e_t = \sum_{s=0}^{s=\infty} \rho(1-\rho)^s e'_{t-s}. \tag{3.35}$$

Assume that there is a long-run average growth in changes for unbiased earnings:

$$e'_\tau - e'_{\tau-1} = (1+g)(e'_{\tau-1} - e'_{\tau-2}) + \epsilon_\tau,$$

where ϵ_τ is an error term with mean zero and is serially independent. Asymptotically, we have

$$e'_t - e_t = \frac{1-\rho}{\rho+g}(e'_t - e'_{t-1}).$$

Note that in an unbiased system, the long-run value of $e'_t = (R-1)b'_{t-1}$. Hence

$$e'_t - e_t = \frac{1-\rho}{\rho+g}\frac{R-1}{1+g}(b'_t - b'_{t-1}). \tag{3.36}$$

Given the clean surplus relationship $b'_t - b'_{t-1} = b_t - b_{t-1} + e'_t - e_t$, it follows from Eq. (3.36) that

$$b'_t - b'_{t-1} = \frac{(\rho+g)(1+g)}{(\rho+g)(1+g)-(R-1)(1-\rho)}(b_t - b_{t-1}).$$

Under the assumption that long-run growth is positive ensuring that b_0 (b'_0) are insignificant compared with b_t (b'_t), we have:

$$b'_t = [1 + \frac{(R-1)(1-\rho)}{(\rho+g)(1+g)-(R-1)(1-\rho)}]b_t.$$

Equation (3.36) further implies that

$$e'_t = e_t + \chi(b_t - b_{t-1}),$$

where $\chi = \frac{(R-1)(1-\rho)}{(\rho+g)(1+g)-(R-1)(1-\rho)}$. It suggests that the degree of accounting conservatism is related to future earnings growth and risk.

3.2.5 A Combination of Conditional and Unconditional Conservatism

There are several interesting observations from the analysis above. First, a weighted average of Eqs. (3.23) and (3.34) gives

$$V_t = \frac{R(1-\omega)}{R-\omega}(1+\chi)b_t + \frac{R\omega}{R-\omega}(1+\chi)e_t - \left(\frac{(R-1)\omega + R\omega\chi}{R-\omega}\right)d_t, \quad (3.37)$$

where $\chi = w\chi_C + (1-w)\chi_U$, and w and $1-w$ are the relative weights on the two forms of conservatism, suggesting that different conservative policies applied to different asset classes form a natural weighting and are inextricably connected.[7] This model is identical to Eq. (3.13).

Second, Eq. (3.37) can be written in the form

$$V_t = \left(\frac{R}{R-\omega}(1+\chi) - \beta\right)b_t + \beta e_t - \left(\frac{(R-1)\omega + R\omega\chi}{R-\omega}\right)d_t, \quad (3.38)$$

with $\beta = \frac{R\omega}{R-\omega}(1+\chi)$, emphasizing the intractability of separating balance sheet conservatism from earnings conservatism. This is also consistent with Pope and Walker (2003), who argue that balance sheet conservatism reduces the measures of earnings conservatism in valuation. Again, the cum-dividend value can be written in a form similar to Eq. (3.15).

3.3 The Effects of the Expected Net Present Value of Future Investment Opportunities on Future Earnings and Valuation

The above analysis shows that book value and abnormal earnings information set $\{b_t, x_t\}$ does not provide sufficient accounting information in valuation in a more general (biased) accounting system. The lagged book value b_{t-1} (or d_t) must be added to the valuation information set. It suggests the necessity for a balance sheet to present both the current year's book value and the previous year's book value for valuation purposes. Together, it offers a theoretical framework that builds upon prior work, identifying key drivers of intrinsic value, risk, and cost of capital. Pope and Wang (2005) extend the valuation model to a more general linear setup. Assuming that $\partial e_t/\partial d_t = 0$ and $\partial b_t/\partial d_t = -1$, and $\partial V_t/\partial d_t = -1$,[8] they show that the following valuation model holds:

$$V_t = b_t + \alpha_1 x_t + \alpha_2 b_{t-1}, \quad (3.39)$$

[7] Strictly χ should carry a time subscript since both forms of conservatism are asset or income-specific and, hence, time-dependent. However, provided that the firm's policy is applied consistently across asset classes and the long-run asset mix remains on average constant, we can interpret χ as summarizing the long-run policy of the firm.

[8] These assumptions on owners' equity play a critical role in determining the functional form of an equity valuation model.

if, and only if

$$x_{t+1} = \omega_1 x_t + \omega_2(Rb_{t-1} - b_t) + \epsilon_{t+1}, \tag{3.40}$$

where $\alpha_1 = \frac{\omega_1}{R-\omega_1}$ and $\alpha_2 = \frac{R\omega_2}{R-\omega_1}$. ϵ_{t+1} is a mean-zero error term. Under conservative accounting, both ω_2 and α_2 are positive.

Noting that $Rb_{t-1} - b_t = d_t - x_t$, Eq. (3.40) implies that dividends can be useful for forecasting abnormal earnings, even if dividends are irrelevant to valuation. Equation (3.40) is also consistent with Clubb (2013), who also examines the impacts of accounting conservatism on earnings information dynamics and valuation. Changes in earnings may reflect conservative accounting (see Penman, 2021). This line of reasoning has been investigated by several researchers (e.g., Feltham and Ohlson, 1995; Myers, 1999), arguing that accounting conservatism is reflected in the information dynamics by adding a lagged book value component with a positive coefficient increasing in the degree of conservatism. However, most empirical investigations fail to detect a positive coefficient for book value in their formulation of the linear information dynamics (e.g., Dechow et al., 1999; Myers, 1999; Beaver and Ryan, 2000; Choi et al., 2006). They report a negative value attached to either the current book value or the lagged book value in the earnings information dynamics, where only one book value is incorporated. This may not be surprising since the structure of the linear dynamics implied by the Pope and Wang (2005) theoretical valuation model involves both current book and lagged book value terms.

Based on US data from 1976 to 2010 and assuming a discount rate, $r = 12\%$ as used in prior literature, Ashton and Wang (2013a) provide empirical evidence to support the theoretical prediction that ω_2 in Eq. (3.40) is positive. The summary statistics for the parameters in the information dynamics based on firm-level time series analysis and industry panel analysis are shown in Table 3.1. The results support the model with two book value terms, with the coefficient (ω_2) having the predicted positive sign. When running rolling window regressions based on a pooled sample on the relevant information dynamics to examine the sign of ω_2, the results shown in Table 3.2 are consistent.

Furthermore, Feltham and Ohlson (1995) argue that "virtually all accounting procedures are conservative in that they do not recognize today the expected net present value of future investment project." Holthausen and Watts (2001) also suggest that information dynamic (3.2) is inconsistent with firms having positive net present value (NPV) projects. To mitigate this concern, we assume that future abnormal earnings can be generated from future nonzero *NPV* investment activities. Specifically, we have a variable G_t on the right-hand of dynamic (3.40) that captures future earnings growth. For parsimony, we assume

$$G_{t+1} = \gamma G_t + \epsilon_{g,t+1}, \tag{3.41}$$

where $0 \leq \gamma < R$ and $\epsilon_{g,t+1}$ is a mean zero random error term. We can show that abnormal earnings dynamic

Table 3.1 The estimates of the information dynamic parameters

	Model 1		Model 2	
	ω_1	ω_2	ω_1	ω_2
Panel A. On individual firm basis (firms ≥ 20 observations)				
Obs.	1087	1087	1087	1087
Mean	0.542	0.062	0.378	−0.078
St Dev	0.259	0.174	0.266	0.101
Q1	0.331	−0.035	0.187	−0.138
Median	0.560	0.065	0.379	−0.062
Q3	0.758	0.157	0.554	−0.012
Panel B. On industry basis (classification is per Fama and French, 1997)				
Obs.	48	48	48	48
Mean	0.606	0.068	0.475	−0.033
St Dev	0.110	0.048	0.096	0.018
Q1	0.533	0.032	0.413	−0.040
Median	0.620	0.076	0.459	−0.031
Q3	0.676	0.106	0.524	−0.025

Model 1: $x_{t+1} = \omega_0 + \omega_1 x_t + \omega_2((1+r_e)b_{t-1} - b_t) + \varepsilon_{x,t+1}$.

Model 2: $x_{t+1} = \omega_0 + \omega_1 x_t + \omega_2 b_t + \varepsilon_{x,t+1}$.

$$x_{t+1} = \omega_1 x_t + \omega_2(Rb_{t-1} - b_t) + G_t + \epsilon_{x,t+1}, \tag{3.42}$$

holds if, and only if, the following valuation equation holds:

$$V_t = b_t + \alpha_1 x_t + \alpha_2 b_{t-1} + \alpha_3 G_t, \tag{3.43}$$

where $\alpha_1 = \frac{\omega_1}{R-\omega_1}$, $\alpha_2 = \frac{R\omega_2}{R-\omega_1}$ and $\alpha_3 = \frac{R}{(R-\omega_1)(R-\gamma)}$. Proof can be found in the appendix. Note that the variance and any higher moments, such as skewness and kurtosis in $\epsilon_{g,t+1}$ and $\epsilon_{x,t+1}$, are not presented in the valuation function, but they may have implications on (unexpected) returns.

This is an extension to Pope and Wang (2005) by incorporating the *NPV* of future investment projects in the information system. It shows that there is a one-to-one mapping between one-year ahead forecasts of (abnormal) earnings and current stock value under our model assumptions. It demonstrates that equity valuation and forecasting future (abnormal) earnings are interlinked. Equity value is written in terms of both current and lagged book value of equity, abnormal earnings, and nonzero *NPV* investment projects. The coefficient attached to abnormal earnings is the declining perpetuity at a growth rate of ω_1. The coefficient on G_t reflects a discounted compounding growth effect, and the lagged book value coefficient represents the effect of accounting conservatism adjustment on the current book value. Since conservative accounting in our model setup results from either conservative accounting principles or the firm undertakes positive *NPV* investments, adding the lagged book value and G_t effectively "undo" accounting conservatism

Table 3.2 Estimate of ω_2 in rolling window regressions

Window	Obs	Model 1	Model 2	Model 3
1975–1995	57,398	0.044	−0.098	−0.090
t-stat		4.9	−20.5	−20.8
1976–1996	59,412	0.043	−0.101	−0.093
t-stat		5.2	−21.	−21.
1977–1997	61,358	0.045	−0.102	−0.093
t-stat		5.5	−21.9	−21.3
1978–1998	63,318	0.045	−0.103	−0.092
t-stat		6.0	−21.7	−19.8
1979–1999	65,036	0.044	−0.106	−0.093
t-stat		6.3	−23.3	(−20.2)
...				
1986–2006	73,862	0.047	−0.090	−0.073
t-stat		8.8	−19.4	−15.3
1987–2007	74,757	0.046	−0.084	−0.068
t-stat		8.7	−16.2	−13.9
1988–2008	75,311	0.042	−0.088	−0.073
t-stat		8.1	−17.0	−15.3
1989–2009	75,634	0.042	−0.090	−0.075
t-stat		8.0	−17.3	−15.5
1990–2010	76,030	0.042	−0.085	−0.072
t-stat		7.9	−15.3	−14.6

Model 1: $x_{t+1} = \omega_0 + \omega_1 x_t + \omega_2((1+r_e)b_{t-1} - b_t) + \varepsilon_{x,t+1}$.

Model 2: $x_{t+1} = \omega_0 + \omega_1 x_t + \omega_2 b_t + \varepsilon_{x,t+1}$.

Model 3: $x_{t+1} = \omega_0 + \omega_1 x_t + \omega_2 b_{t-1} + \varepsilon_{x,t+1}$.

when using current book value and earnings numbers in valuation. Equity value reflecting the present value of expected all future risky cash flows anchors on the "value of assets-in-place", described by $(b_t + \alpha_1 x_t + \alpha_2 b_{t-1})$. The two bottom-line accounting numbers, book value and earnings, are presented jointly and governed by conservative principles. They are booked because uncertainty is considered to be resolved (Penman and Zhang, 2020). G_t then characterizes all future risky growth opportunities. Peng et al. (2024) extract information embedded in G from the articulation between bottom-line accounting numbers and stock prices. Their empirical findings confirm that G is strongly associated with various proxies for expected future earnings growth and firm risk attributes. Furthermore, they show how a structural expected return model incorporating G can predict out-of-sample future stock returns and generate sizeable long-short return spreads. Wang (2023) is a special case where $\omega_2 = 0$.

Note that information dynamic (3.40) has at least two advantages in empirical applications. First, regardless of the book value or lagged book value used as a deflator, as often employed in the empirical literature, the conservatism embedded in the linear information dynamics does not affect the sign of the parameter, ω_2. Second, and most importantly, the valuation model does not require the estimation of the growth rate of book value. Explicit estimates of the growth in book values are redundant in the valuation. Note that $(Rb_{t-1} - b_t)$ can be rewritten as $(d_t - x_t)$. Therefore, dividends may be useful for forecasting future earnings, but are still value-irrelevant.

It is argued that in a competitive market, the return on equity tends to the cost of equity capital, $ROE \rightarrow r$, so one would expect abnormal earnings $x_{t+1} = (ROE_{t+1} - r)b_t \rightarrow 0$ in the long run. A legitimate question is: can abnormal earnings, $x_{t+1} = (ROE_{t+1} - r)b_t$, persist in perpetuity in a competitive market when $ROE \rightarrow r$? If not, there is a danger of over-extrapolation when applying the above valuation model. Many believe that firms will eventually earn "normal" earnings rb_t, and economic profits revert towards zero in a perfectly competitive economy (Ohlson, 1995 and Nissim and Penman, 2001). However, $ROE \rightarrow r$ does not necessarily mean that $x_{t+1} = (ROE_{t+1} - r)b_t \rightarrow 0$ if book value has a permanent growth. Even if $x_{t+1} \rightarrow 0$, it does not necessarily mean sales or earnings cannot grow. It just says $e_{t+1} \rightarrow rb_t$, but other variables, including sales, assets, and earnings, can all grow at a steady growth rate in the long run. It is the same as $NPV = 0$, which does not mean that the return of an investment is zero, but simply means that the investment earns a normal rate of return.

Allowing $1 < \gamma < R$ in Eq. (3.41), dynamic (3.42) incorporates future $NPV > 0$ investments and implies that abnormal earnings do not approach zero in the long run. It permits firms' economic profits to persist in the long run with $NPV > 0$ investments arising from competitive advantages or accounting conservatism. It may suggest that technological and aggregate demand shocks can permanently affect economic growth (Campbell and Mankiw, 1987). This is consistent with the concept of an 'economic moat', attributed to Warren Buffett. A company may have distinct advantages over its competitors, allowing it to protect its market share and profitability. It may be difficult to mimic and create an effective barrier against competition from other firms.[9] Barney and Clark (2007) also explores how firms can develop and maintain a competitive edge in dynamic markets. It allows G_t to be nonstationary, particularly in an inflationary environment. As Lo and Lys (2000) point out, "it is well known that managers hold dividends stable and tend to increase them over time, and even casual observation suggests that book value and earnings are not stationary for most companies (and tend to drift upwards)." One can view $(\gamma - 1)$ as the expected growth rate of abnormal earnings in a steady state.

[9] Morningstar identifies five primary sources of economic moats, including network effects, intangible assets, cost advantages, switching costs, and its efficiency in serving its market over competitors. See https://www.morningstar.com/business/insights/blog/markets/equity-economic-moat-ratings.

The example below shows that the property of mean-reverting on ROE can be reconciled with permanent economic profitability. The mean-reverting property implies ROE tends to the cost of equity capital in the long run, $ROE_t \rightarrow r$ $(t \rightarrow \infty)$, while permanent economic profitability means abnormal earnings have a growth rate greater than zero, or $x_t \rightarrow +\infty$ $(t \rightarrow \infty)$ even if we can write $x_{t+1} = e_{t+1} - rb_t = (ROE_{t+1} - r)b_t$. Assume $\omega_1 = 0.23$, $\omega_2 = 0.02$, $\gamma = 1.02$ and $r = 8\%$ in Eqs. (3.42) and (3.41). Furthermore, assume $b_{-1} = 500$, $e_0 = 60$, $e_1 = 65.6$, and a dividend payout ratio of 50%, which is irrelevant to the cum-dividend equity value. We have (1− dividend payout ratio) $\times r = 4\%$. We can show, say in a spreadsheet, that the linear information dynamic model is consistent with an expected steady growth rate (of 4%) for every variable, including abnormal earnings, not the assumed $\gamma - 1 = 2\%$. The equity value is a finite number, and both the DDM and RIVM models give identical equity values of 938.

We can see that ROE has a trend of approaching r, but it is a slow process and lasts a very long period, say after 300 periods. The growth of all accounting variables, including book value, earnings, and dividends, all approach a sustainable growth rate of $q \times ROE = 4\%$, where $q =$ (1− dividend payout ratio) is the retention ratio. Of course, this sustainable growth rate must be less than the cost of equity capital r since q should be less than one. If the expected growth rate is positive, even if it is less than $(R - 1)$, book value, earnings, and abnormal earnings can be big numbers in the long run.

The book value, earnings, dividends, and market value of equity in the above example are all nonstationary processes expanding at a rate of sustainable growth rate, and x is the difference between two non-stationary processes, e_{t+1} and $r \times b_t$. In mathematics, $0 \times \infty = \infty/\infty$ when the book value has a permanent positive growth. An infinite number divided by another infinite number is uncertain. In other words, abnormal earnings are not necessarily zero and can remain positive indefinitely. However, the growth rate must be less than the cost of equity capital to ensure the convergence of the valuation model. The dividend irrelevance property is also preserved in the example, as one sees that the cum-dividend stock value is constant no matter what the dividend payout ratio is.

Can the Magnificent Seven stocks (i.e., Apple, Microsoft, Alphabet, Amazon, Nvidia, Meta, and Tesla) break the classic economic rule of perfect competition and continue outperforming the mean trend in perpetuity through barriers to entry and growth options? The Magnificent Seven phenomenon of the past decade has not yet shown signs of materially reverting ROE to the mean of its industry r. Is it really different this time? If one replaces "perpetuity" with something akin to "the next quarter century, followed by the mean growth rate in perpetuity," then there is a case for arguing that Magnificent Seven-like companies could plausibly avoid reverting to the mean within reasonable investment horizons. Even if their ROEs have a trend approaching r, the dominating companies may claim a "permanent" above-average annual value addition $(x > 0)$. Assets like personal data do not depreciate quickly. They can serve to generate revenue for a long time. In the future, can you depreciate artificial intelligence that can self-repair and improve over time? Due to conservative accounting principles, financial statement information may not capture this kind of asset. It looks like we are moving into a more distinctly divided corporate world in which the digital dominator continues to take an ever larger share of the expanding value cake.

Appendix

Given information dynamic (3.41), information dynamic (3.42) implies and is implied by Eq. (3.43).

"Proof of Sufficiency" Assume Eqs. (3.42) and (3.41). The present value of all expected future abnormal earnings is a function of current abnormal earnings, lagged book value, and nonzero NPV investments. We can write it as Eq. (3.43), and then identify unique valuation parameters $(\alpha_1, \alpha_2, \alpha_3)$ in terms of $(\omega_1, \omega_2, \gamma, \mathrm{R})$. From Eq. (3.43) and clean surplus relation (CSR): $b_{t+1} + d_{t+1} = Rb_t + x_{t+1}$, we have

$$
\begin{aligned}
V_{t+1} + d_{t+1} &= b_{t+1} + d_{t+1} + \alpha_1 x_{t+1} + \alpha_2 b_t + \alpha_3 G_{t+1} \\
&= Rb_t + (1 + \alpha_1) x_{t+1} + \alpha_2 b_t + \alpha_3 G_{t+1}.
\end{aligned}
$$

The dividend discount model: $E_t[V_{t+1} + d_{t+1}] = RV_t$ and Eq. (3.41) together imply that

$$
Rb_t + (1 + \alpha_1) E_t[x_{t+1}] + \alpha_2 b_t + \alpha_3 \gamma G_t = RV_t.
$$

The abnormal earnings dynamic then further implies that

$$
\begin{aligned}
&Rb_t + (1 + \alpha_1)(\omega_1 x_t + \omega_2 (Rb_{t-1} - b_t) + G_t) + \alpha_2 b_t + \alpha_3 \gamma G_t \\
&\quad = R(b_t + \alpha_1 x_t + \alpha_2 b_{t-1} + \alpha_3 G_t).
\end{aligned}
$$

Comparing the coefficients of x_t, $(Rb_{t-1} - b_t)$ and G_t, we have the following equation system:

$$
\begin{aligned}
&(1 + \alpha_1)\omega_1 = R\alpha_1, \\
&-(1 + \alpha_1)\omega_2 + \alpha_2 = 0, \\
&(1 + \alpha_1) + \alpha_3 \gamma = R\alpha_3.
\end{aligned}
$$

Solving the above equation system, we have the valuation parameters: $\alpha_1 = \frac{\omega_1}{R - \omega_1}$, $\alpha_2 = \frac{R\omega_2}{R - \omega_1}$ and $\alpha_3 = \frac{R}{(R - \omega_1)(R - \gamma)}$.

"Proof of Necessity" Assume Eqs. (3.43) and (3.41). From Eq. (3.43), the dividend discount model, and CSR, we have

$$Rb_t + (1+\alpha_1)E_t[x_{t+1}] + \alpha_2 b_t + \alpha_3 \gamma G_t = R(b_t + \alpha_1 x_t + \alpha_2 b_{t-1} + \alpha_3 G_t).$$

Reorganizing terms and noting $\alpha_1 = \frac{\omega_1}{R-\omega_1}$, $\alpha_2 = \frac{R\omega_2}{R-\omega_1}$, $\alpha_3 = \frac{R}{(R-\omega_1)(R-\gamma)}$, we have

$$\begin{aligned} E_t[x_{t+1}] &= \frac{R\alpha_1}{(1+\alpha_1)} x_t + \frac{\alpha_2}{(1+\alpha_1)}(Rb_{t-1} - b_t) + \frac{(R-\gamma)\alpha_3}{(1+\alpha_1)} G_t \\ &= \omega_1 x_t + \omega_2 (Rb_{t-1} - b_t) + G_t. \end{aligned}$$

□

Chapter 4
Future Earnings and the Intrinsic Value of Equity

Earnings are part of sales revenue. But sales are generated from investment assets. From a shareholder's perspective, earnings should at least equal the required return of equity capital on the initial investment. From a firm's point of view, it should cover the capital charge, that is, the cost of equity capital on the book value of equity. Earnings can also be generated from the firm's goodwill and other intangible assets. Future earnings can also be affected by conservative accounting principles. Although much progress has been made in understanding how factors affect earnings generation, less progress has been made in defining the functional dependence of earnings on these factors. In this chapter, we explore the determinants of future earnings.

Given the growth component G in earnings dynamic (3.41), there is a one-to-one mapping between valuation and the forecasts of one-period ahead earnings. The specification of G becomes important in establishing the functional relationship between the two. G is expected to capture future growth, accounting conservatism, and intangible asset investments (see Peng et al., 2024).

4.1 Analysts' Forecasts of Earnings, Model-based Forecasts, and Accounting Fundamentals

Textbooks often advocate a "top-down" approach from an earnings-generating perspective in forecasting earnings. Investors need to understand business from global and domestic economic factors, specific industry factors, and firm-specific factors. Specifically, forecasting earnings starts from annual growth forecasts for sales revenues. To forecast this yearly growth rate, we could begin by estimating the current and historical real growth or organic growth and forecasting future inflation to get the nominal growth rate. We could use up to a 10-year historical average

P. Wang, *Integrating Earnings Forecasts, Valuation, and Return Prediction*, Contributions to Finance and Accounting,
https://doi.org/10.1007/978-3-032-05910-9_4

growth rate as a starting point and then make some necessary adjustments. We could also forecast sales for each line of business or consider each segment's weighted sales growth or geographical weighted sales growth rates. We can then forecast key value drivers such as profit margin and turnover ratio (using opening or average assets over a period). Each line item is often assumed to be directly linked to sales growth, or the percentage of each item to sales is constant for all future periods. We may also need to make assumptions about financial leverage. Consequently, the accuracy of forecasts has been challenged, particularly by academics who have applied some econometric approaches in earnings forecasting in recent years.

Applying some cross-sectional and time series models has been claimed to outperform analysts' forecasts, particularly in the long-term and for small-sized firms' forecasting. Those econometric models often select explanatory variables from financial statement information based on previous empirical evidence (for example, Hou et al., 2012 and Li and Mohanram, 2014). Since one of the main applications for forecasting earnings is for valuation purposes, the accuracy of long-term forecasts has important implications. One of the popular approaches to implement the RIVM is to use earnings forecasts and other fundamental accounting numbers over several years (for example Frankel and Lee, 1998, Claus and Thomas, 2001, Gebhardt et al., 2001). When applying the earnings forecasts in valuation, we often assume a constant terminal growth rate in an arbitrary forecast horizon, say 5 or 12 years. The approaches also need to specify a dividend payout policy to estimate future book values of equity in recursion. Determining the long-term growth rate has proven to be a challenge in the application of a multiple-period valuation model. Most time series and cross-sectional models overlook the market information in forecasting and ignore the interaction between future earnings and the asset's current market price. In an efficient market, prices capture all available information, including forecasts of future earnings. Harris and Wang (2019) provide evidence to show that market information helps forecast long-term and short-term earnings. They show that their model-based forecasts can beat analysts' forecasts even in the short run.

An alternative popular approach in applying the RIVM is to assume a linear information dynamic of residual income. It effectively moves the equilibrium forward to just one period ahead. However, equations such as (3.42) and (3.43) are not directly applicable since the growth component G_t is unobservable. To overcome this problem, we explore the intrinsic relationship between future earnings and market value.

4.2 One-year Ahead Earnings and Intrinsic Value

The market value of equity is supposed to summarize all value-relevant market information. In particular, the long-term growth rate of earnings and associated risk should be reflected in the market value. Assuming the dividend discount model and clean surplus accounting relation, we can show that any two of the following three statements imply the third: (1) abnormal earnings dynamic (3.42) holds; (2) equity value is given by Eq. (3.43); (3) abnormal earnings satisfy

$$E_t[x_{t+1}] = \delta_1 x_t + \delta_2(V_t - b_t) + \omega_2(\gamma - b_t/b_{t-1})b_{t-1}, \tag{4.1}$$

where $\delta_1 = \frac{\omega_1\gamma}{R}$ and $\delta_2 = \frac{(R-\omega_1)(R-\gamma)}{R}$. Proof can be found in the appendix.

While Eqs. (3.42) and (3.43) build a mapping between forecasting of future (abnormal) earnings and stock value, Eq. (4.1) explicitly establishes a precise link between stock value and the one-period ahead forecasts of (abnormal) earnings.[1] Although abnormal earnings dynamic (4.1) imply neither abnormal earnings dynamic (3.42) without valuation Eq. (3.43) nor valuation Eq. (3.43) without abnormal earnings dynamic (3.42), Eq. (4.1) can be viewed as a go-between. Combining (4.1) with either Eqs. (3.42) or (3.43) implies the other.

Compared to Eq. (3.42), Eq. (4.1) suggests that the value of future growth G_t can be inferred from accounting goodwill (the difference between the market value and the book value of the equity), current abnormal earnings and abnormal growth in the book value. It shows that the expected one-year ahead abnormal earnings can be written in terms of current abnormal earnings, book values, and stock market value. Unlike abnormal earnings dynamic (3.42) and valuation Eq. (3.43), information dynamics (4.1) expresses future abnormal earnings in terms of observables if the stock price (P_t) is a good proxy for its intrinsic value (V_t). 'Economic moat' is reflected in the stock price in an efficient market. The analytical relations above are important in equity valuation, as internal consistency can avoid a potential violation of the no-arbitrage condition, as argued in Myers (1999). They can be used to link a firm's financial performance in its product market to the capital market. It improves the practicability of the implementation of the model. In terms of earnings, Eq. (4.1) can be written as

$$\begin{aligned} e_{t+1} = (R-1)b_t + \frac{(R-\gamma)(R-\omega_1)}{R}(V_t - b_t) + \frac{\omega_1\gamma}{R}x_t \\ - \omega_2(b_t - \gamma b_{t-1}) + \epsilon_{t+1}. \end{aligned} \tag{4.2}$$

It suggests that the one-period ahead earnings can be written in terms of "normal" earnings $(R-1)b_t$, the goodwill, the persistence of current residual earnings, and abnormal growth in book values reflecting accounting conservatism. Alternatively, we have

$$\begin{aligned} e_{t+1} = &\frac{(R-\gamma)(R-\omega_1)}{R}V_t + [\frac{R(R-1)-(R-\gamma)(R-\omega_1)-R\omega_2}{R}]b_t \\ &+\frac{\omega_1\gamma}{R}e_t + [\omega_2\gamma - (R-1)\frac{\omega_1\gamma}{R}]b_{t-1} + \epsilon_{t+1}. \end{aligned} \tag{4.3}$$

[1] Note that two statements (1) and (2) above are independent without information dynamic (3.41).

Equation (4.3) is similar to the forecasting model in Fama and French (2006), which utilizes several financial ratios, including price-to-book, current profitability, dividend-to-book, and asset growth, to predict future profitability or return on equity.

Noting $b_{t-1} = b_t - (e_t - d_t)$, Eq. (4.1) implies that stock value can be written in terms of current earnings, book value, dividends and expected one-year ahead forecasts of earnings as:

$$V_t = \Psi \times e_t + \mathrm{B} \times b_t + \Delta \times d_t + \Phi \times E_t[e_{t+1}], \tag{4.4}$$

where

$$\begin{aligned} \Psi &= \frac{R(\omega_2-\omega_1)\gamma}{(R-\omega_1)(R-\gamma)}, & \mathrm{B} &= \frac{R(1-\omega_1+\omega_2)(1-\gamma)}{(R-\omega_1)(R-\gamma)}, \\ \Delta &= \frac{((R-1)\omega_1-R\omega_2)\gamma}{(R-\omega_1)(R-\gamma)}, & \text{and} \quad \Phi &= \frac{R}{(R-\omega_1)(R-\gamma)}. \end{aligned} \tag{4.5}$$

While the growth component has a persistence in information dynamic (3.41), researchers also argue that expected growth is affected by both the expectation of future economic rents and the conservative nature of accounting (see Claus and Thomas, 2001). Earnings changes may result from "undo" conservative accounting. We therefore incorporate conservative accounting in the information dynamic and explicitly partition G into a growth element associated with growth in positive NPV investment opportunities and growth resulting from variations in the degree of conservatism in reporting. We measure earnings conservatism by the difference between economic earnings, $(V_t + d_t - V_{t-1})$, and accounting earnings. Economic earnings are the sum of the change in intrinsic values and dividends over the period. Hence, we extend Eq. (3.41) to:

$$G_{t+1} = (1+g)G_t + \lambda(V_t + d_t - V_{t-1} - e_t) + \epsilon_{g,t+1}, \tag{4.6}$$

Note CSR implies that $b_{t-1} = (b_t + d_t - x_t)/R$. Rescaling G, Wang (2018) rewrite Eq. (3.43) as

$$V_t = b_t + \beta_1(b_t + d_t) + \beta_2 x_t + G_t. \tag{4.7}$$

Similar to Eq. (4.2), he shows that the expected one-period ahead earnings can be written as

$$\begin{aligned} E_t[e_{t+1}] = (R-1)b_t &+ \frac{R-(1+g)}{(1+\beta_1+\beta_2)}(V_t - b_t) \\ &+ \frac{(R-1)\beta_2 - \beta_1}{(1+\beta_1+\beta_2)}(b_t - (1+g)b_{t-1}) \\ &+ \frac{(\beta_1+\beta_2)}{(1+\beta_1+\beta_2)}[(1+g)e_t - (R-1)b_t] \\ &- \frac{\lambda}{(1+\beta_1+\beta_2)}[(V_t - b_t) - (V_{t-1} - b_{t-1})]. \end{aligned} \tag{4.8}$$

From an earnings-generating perspective, the determinants of future earnings are: (1) normal earnings generated from book assets, $(R-1)b_t$, reflecting the persistence of earnings; (2) accounting goodwill, $(V_t - b_t)$, including intangible assets, and off-balance sheet items; (3) abnormal growth in book value, $(b_t - (1+g)b_{t-1})$; (4) abnormal earnings, $(1+g)e_t - (R-1)b_t \approx x_{t+1}$; and (v) conservative accounting, measured by $(V_t - V_{t-1} + d_t) - e_t = (V_t - b_t) - (V_{t-1} - b_{t-1})$, the difference between economic earnings and accounting earnings, or changes in accounting goodwill.

The above model can be written in an equivalent model:

$$\begin{aligned} E_t[e_{t+1}] = & \frac{R-(1+g)-\lambda}{(1+\beta_1+\beta_2)} V_t + \frac{(1+g)(\beta_1+\beta_2)}{(1+\beta_1+\beta_2)} e_t \\ & + \frac{g-\beta_1+(R-1)\beta_2+\lambda}{(1+\beta_1+\beta_2)} b_t \\ & + \frac{(1+g)(\beta_1-(R-1)\beta_2)-\lambda}{(1+\beta_1+\beta_2)} b_{t-1} + \frac{\lambda}{(1+\beta_1+\beta_2)} V_{t-1}. \end{aligned} \quad (4.9)$$

This equation can be used to forecast future earnings if we use stock prices as a proxy for intrinsic values. It differs from other earnings forecasting models, such as Hou et al. (2012) and Li and Mohanram (2014), by incorporating the market value of equity as an explanatory variable in forecasting.

4.3 Future Earnings and Intangible Assets

We can further extend the growth component by incorporating investments in tangible and intangible assets, including research and development $(R\&D_t)$. This section explores the theoretical relationship between intrinsic value, future earnings, and investments in intangible assets.

Equation (3.39) shows that equity value can be written in terms of book value, abnormal earnings (residual income), and lagged book value plus G_t,,

$$V_t = b_t + \alpha_1 x_t + \alpha_2 b_{t-1} + G_t, \quad (4.10)$$

where b_t is book value of equity, $x_t = e_t - rb_{t-1}$ is abnormal earnings, and e_t is earnings. G_t represents the present value of all expected future investments at time t, reflected in the current value, but not in current earnings and (lagged) book value.

Denote Y a vector of investments in tangible and intangible assets. Say, $Y_t = (capX_t, R\&D_t, SG\&A_t, INTan_t)$, where $capX$ is capital expenditure, $SG\&A$ is selling, general, and administrative expenses, and $INTan$ is the internally generated intangibles. Assume G_{t+1} is associated with current period Y_t and lagged period $Y_{t-s}(s = 1, 2\ldots)$. For example, the current market value of equity and earnings may reflect $R\&D$ investments in the last few years. We can argue past intangible investments, e.g., $R\&D_{t-1}$ may not reflected in the current G_t yet for reasons such as being too risky, but they may be reflected in future value V_{t+1} or G_{t+1}. Similar to Eq. (3.41), we assume G_t has a long-term growth g, and

$$G_{t+1} = (1+g)G_t + \sum_{s=0}^{n} \Gamma_s Y_{t-s} + \epsilon_{t+1}, \tag{4.11}$$

where $\Gamma_s = (\gamma_{s0}, \gamma_{s1}, \ldots, \gamma_{sk})$ is a vector of parameters.[2]

The above leads to the following earnings dynamic:

$$\begin{aligned} e_{t+1} = {} & \frac{(R-1-g)}{(1+\alpha_1)} V_t + \frac{(1+g)\alpha_1}{(1+\alpha_1)} e_t + \frac{(R-1)\alpha_1 - \alpha_2 + g}{(1+\alpha_1)} b_t \\ & + \frac{(1+g)(\alpha_2 - \alpha_1(R-1))}{(1+\alpha_1)} b_{t-1} - \frac{1}{(1+\alpha_1)} \sum_{s=0}^{n} \Gamma_s Y_{t-s} + \epsilon'_{t+1}. \end{aligned} \tag{4.12}$$

Alternatively, we can write equity value in terms of accounting fundamentals and future earnings as

$$\begin{aligned} V_t = {} & \frac{(1+\alpha_1)}{(R-1-g)} E_t[e_{t+1}] - \frac{(1+g)\alpha_1}{(R-1-g)} e_t - \frac{(R-1)\alpha_1 - \alpha_2 + g}{(R-1-g)} b_t \\ & - \frac{(1+g)(\alpha_2 - \alpha_1(R-1))}{(R-1-g)} b_{t-1} + \frac{1}{(R-1-g)} \sum_{s=0}^{n} \Gamma_s Y_{t-s}. \end{aligned} \tag{4.13}$$

Suppose we use prices as a proxy for the intrinsic values. In that case, we can use a time series or cross-sectional model based on Eq. (4.12) to forecast the earnings of an individual company. Time-series approaches are feasible only if we have sufficient firm-level annual data and collinearity is not a concern. Regressing the realized earnings of an individual company at time t on all previous period earnings, book value, Y_t, and prices, we can estimate the average cost of capital $(R-1)$, growth rate (g), valuation parameters $(\alpha_1, \alpha_2, \gamma_0, \ldots, \gamma_n)$ at time t. We can then use these regression coefficients and accounting fundamentals at time t to forecast the company's earnings at $t+1$. If analysts' forecasts of earnings at time t are reliable, then we could use them as a dependent variable in regressions to estimate those valuation parameters at $t+1$. We can also use cross-sectional approaches or industry panel data, based on Eq. (4.12), to forecast one-year ahead earnings. For example, we can regress earnings at year t on the right-hand side (RHS) variables and use 10-year or 5-year data to estimate parameters: $(\alpha_1, \alpha_2, R, g, \gamma_0, \ldots, \gamma_n)$ for firms within an industry. Finally, the forecasts of one-year ahead earnings e_{t+1} can

[2] We could also consider carbon emissions or the ESG factors in predicting G_{t+1}. In Feltham and Ohlson (1996), G_t is proportional to current cash investment ci_t and $Y = 0$.

be obtained by multiplying the regression coefficients by the RHS variables at year t. We will explain it in detail in the next chapter. Using the machine learning method, we could add more variables to the RHS, which may include any variable that can be forecast relevant to future earnings.

Appendix

Any two of the following three statements imply the third: (1) abnormal earnings dynamic (3.42) holds; (2) equity value is given by Eq. (3.43); (3) abnormal earnings satisfy

$$E_t[x_{t+1}] = \delta_1 x_t + \delta_2(V_t - b_t) + \omega_2(\gamma - b_t/b_{t-1})b_{t-1}, \tag{4.14}$$

where $\delta_1 = \frac{\omega_1\gamma}{R}$ *and* $\delta_2 = \frac{(R-\omega_1)(R-\gamma)}{R}$.

Proof First, we show that Eqs. (3.42) and (3.43) imply Eq. (4.14). From Eqs. (3.42) and (3.43), we have

$$\begin{aligned} E_t[x_{t+1}] &= \omega_1 x_t + \omega_2(Rb_{t-1} - b_t) + G_t \\ &= \tfrac{\omega_1\gamma}{R}x_t + \tfrac{(R-\omega_1)(R-\gamma)}{R}\left(\tfrac{\omega_1}{R-\omega_1}x_t + \tfrac{R\omega_2}{R-\omega_1}b_{t-1} + \tfrac{R}{(R-\omega_1)(R-\gamma)}G_t\right) - \omega_2(b_t - \gamma b_{t-1}) \\ &= \tfrac{\omega_1\gamma}{R}x_t + \tfrac{(R-\omega_1)(R-\gamma)}{R}(V_t - b_t) - \omega_2(b_t - \gamma b_{t-1}). \end{aligned}$$

Next, we show Eqs. (4.14) and (3.42) imply Eq. (3.43) or Eqs. (4.14) and (3.43) imply Eq. (3.42). From Eq. (4.14), we have

$$\begin{aligned} E_t[x_{t+1}] &= \tfrac{\omega_1\gamma}{R}x_t + \tfrac{(R-\omega_1)(R-\gamma)}{R}(V_t - b_t) - \omega_2(b_t - \gamma b_{t-1}) \\ &= \omega_1 x_t + \omega_2(Rb_{t-1} - b_t) + \tfrac{(R-\omega_1)(R-\gamma)}{R} \\ &\quad \times[V_t - (b_t + \tfrac{\omega_1}{(R-\omega_1)}x_t + \tfrac{R\omega_2}{R-\omega_1}b_{t-1})]. \end{aligned} \tag{4.15}$$

If information dynamic (3.42) holds, $E_t[x_{t+1}]$ in the above equation can be replaced by $\omega_1 x_t + \omega_2(Rb_{t-1} - b_t) + G_t$. Reorganizing terms in Eq. (4.15), we have: $V_t = b_t + \alpha_1 x_t + \alpha_2 b_{t-1} + \alpha_3 G_t$, where $\alpha_1 = \frac{\omega_1}{R-\omega_1}$, $\alpha_2 = \frac{R\omega_2}{R-\omega_1}$, and $\alpha_3 = \frac{R}{(R-\omega_1)(R-\gamma)}$. That is, the valuation Eq. (3.43) holds.

If valuation model (3.43) holds, the right-hand side of Eq. (4.15): $V_t - (b_t + \frac{\omega_1}{(R-\omega_1)}x_t + \frac{R\omega_2}{R-\omega_1}b_{t-1}) = \frac{R}{(R-\gamma)(R-\omega_1)}G_t$. Therefore, Eq. (4.15) implies information dynamic (3.42): $E_t[x_{t+1}] = \omega_1 x_t + \omega_2(Rb_{t-1} - b_t) + G_t$. □

Chapter 5
Incorporate Market Information in Valuation of Individual Firms and Predicting Returns

Under the assumption that the aggregate capital market is efficient, we can use stock prices to replace the intrinsic values in Eqs. (4.3), (4.9) or (4.12) to run cross-sectional or industry panel data regressions to forecast future earnings of individual firms.[1] Specifically, we can regress time t period earnings on past (up to time $t-1$) accounting and market information to obtain regression coefficients and then carry the coefficients forward to time t period accounting and market information to forecast earnings at time $t+1$ (see Harris and Wang, 2019). We can then use the forecast earnings at $t+1$ to value the equity shares of individual firms at time t and predict one-period ahead returns.

5.1 Intrinsic Value of Equity and Stock Price

Suppose the current stock price per share is P_t. The expected one-period ahead stock return based on time t information is $\bar{r}_t = E_t[P_{t+1} + d_{t+1} - P_t]/P_t$. Alternatively, we can write

$$P_t = \frac{E_t[P_{t+1} + d_{t+1}]}{1 + \bar{r}_t}, \tag{5.1}$$

[1] Over time, the market portfolio tends to reflect available information and price assets fairly on average. Aggregate efficiency is supported by the difficulty of consistently outperforming the market after accounting for costs and risk adjustments, which lends empirical support to the success of index investing. However, the capital market is not necessarily efficient at the individual firm level, at a particular time where mispricing and anomalies can persist due to transaction costs, information asymmetry, limits to arbitrage, and behavioral factors.

P. Wang, *Integrating Earnings Forecasts, Valuation, and Return Prediction*, Contributions to Finance and Accounting,
https://doi.org/10.1007/978-3-032-05910-9_5

where P_{t+1} is the stock price and d_{t+1} is the dividends per share at $t+1$. The expected return is an ex ante concept. The above equation is consistent with the no-arbitrage pricing in Eq. (2.10) when the price equals the stock's intrinsic value per share and the expected stock return equals the investors' required return. The intrinsic value of a share is generally different from the stock price. Unlike intrinsic value, current market prices reflect current supply and demand conditions and market sentiment. However, the price of the stock and its intrinsic value are co-integrated over time, even if the daily price of the stock may not be equal to its intrinsic value (see Lee et al., 1999). Valuation models are used to estimate the intrinsic value of assets.

Although the intrinsic value of equity can be presented in terms of accounting numbers in a specific form, accounting does not impact the intrinsic value of equity, given the internal relationship between accounting fundamentals. It is much like the role of dividends in equity valuation. Accounting information, however, affects changes in stock prices. Prices are related to a (current or future) trade, determined in the marketplace, and so are stock returns. The intrinsic value of equity is determined before transactions take place.

5.2 Use Analysts' or Model-based Forecasts of Earnings to Value Individual Stocks

Ashton and Wang (2013b) and Wang (2018) develop an approach that simultaneously estimates the valuation parameters alongside the cost of equity capital and the long-term growth of earnings. The approach does not assume a specific dividend payout policy and requires only one-year ahead forecasts of future earnings for valuation. The one-year ahead forecasts of earnings are generally believed to be more accurate than multi-period ahead forecasts.

Specifically, we can use cross-sectional data or industry-year data to forecast individual firms' earnings by regressing model (4.3):

$$e_{t+1} = \delta_1 P_t + \delta_2 e_t + \delta_3 b_t + \delta_4 b_{t-1} + \epsilon'_{t+1}, \tag{5.2}$$

where $\delta_1 = \frac{(R-\gamma)(R-\omega_1)}{R}$, $\delta_2 = \frac{\omega_1\gamma}{R}$, $\delta_3 = \frac{R(R-1)-(R-\gamma)(R-\omega_1)-R\omega_2}{R}$, and $\delta_4 = \omega_2\gamma - (R-1)\frac{\omega_1\gamma}{R}$. From the four regression coefficients, we can derive the four valuation parameters $(\omega_1, \omega_2, R, \gamma)$. Since there is a trade-off between the number of variables and observations in an industry in a particular year, we can similarly use industry panel data to forecast individual firms' earnings. Valuation parameters derived from the coefficients of panel data regressions may capture meaningful time trends. These model-based forecasts of earnings for individual firms, like analysts' forecasts of earnings, can be used to value individual stocks. The estimate of stock value from valuation model (4.4) is

$$\hat{V}_t = \Psi \times e_t + \mathrm{B} \times b_t + \Delta \times d_t + \Phi \times E_t[\hat{e}_{t+1}], \tag{5.3}$$

where the information parameters $(\omega_1, \omega_2, R, g)$ are estimated simultaneously from each cross-sectional regression in year t or industry panel regression up to a particular year t based on Eq. (5.2). It essentially lets data tell investors what the implied valuation drivers are and how they intrinsically connect. It implicitly assumes that stock markets are efficient at aggregate or industry levels. Each regression generates a set of parameters. More specifically, we regress the one-year ahead forecast earnings on stock prices, current earnings, book values, and lagged book values to obtain four coefficients $(\delta_1, \delta_2, \delta_3, \delta_4)$. The one-year ahead earnings can be analysts' forecasts or model-based forecasts. We can calculate the four implied valuation weights from these coefficients: $(\Psi, \mathrm{B}, \Delta, \Phi)$.

The above analysis shows that if we only consider the bottom-line accounting information, we can perform regressions based on Eq. (4.3) to estimate the four coefficients and then infer the four valuation parameters $(R, \gamma, \omega_1, \omega_2)$. Eqs. (4.4) or (5.3) gives the estimate of the stock value. If we further consider the role of intangible assets in forecasting earnings, and our focus is on $R\&D$ only, for example, Eq. (4.12) becomes

$$
\begin{aligned}
e_{t+1} = {} & \delta_1 P_t + \delta_2 e_t + \delta_3 b_t + \delta_4 b_{t-1} + \delta_{50} R\&D_t + \delta_{51} R\&D_{t-1} \\
& + \ldots + \delta_{5n} R\&D_{t-n} + \epsilon'_{t+1},
\end{aligned} \tag{5.4}
$$

where $\delta_1 = \frac{(R-1-g)}{(1+\alpha_1)}$, $\delta_2 = \frac{(1+g)\alpha_1}{(1+\alpha_1)}$, $\delta_3 = \frac{(R-1)\alpha_1-\alpha_2+g}{(1+\alpha_1)}$, and $\delta_4 = \frac{(1+g)(\alpha_2-\alpha_1(R-1))}{(1+\alpha_1)}$. We can run cross-sectional or industry panel data regressions to forecast individual firms' earnings based on the above model.

These model-based forecasts of earnings for individual firms, like analysts' forecasts of earnings, can be used to value individual stocks. If our focus is on $R\&D$ only, the estimate of stock value from model (4.13) becomes

$$
\begin{aligned}
\hat{V}_t = {} & \frac{(1+\alpha_1)}{(R-1-g)}\hat{e}_{t+1} - \frac{(1+g)\alpha_1}{(R-1-g)}e_t - \frac{(R-1)\alpha_1-\alpha_2+g}{(R-1-g)}b_t \\
& - \frac{(1+g)(\alpha_2-\alpha_1(R-1))}{(R-1-g)}b_{t-1} + \frac{1}{(R-1-g)}\sum_{s=0}^{n}\delta_{5s} R\&D_{t-s},
\end{aligned} \tag{5.5}
$$

where valuation parameters $(\alpha_1, \alpha_2, R, g, \delta_{50}, \ldots \delta_{5n})$ are estimated from each cross-sectional regression in year t or each industry panel regression up to a particular year t based on Eq. (5.4). Specifically, we regress the one-year ahead forecast earnings on prices, current earnings, book values and $R\&D$, and the lagged $R\&D$ to obtain the coefficients $(\delta_1, \delta_2, \delta_3, \delta_4, \delta_{50}, \ldots \delta_{5n})$, $n+5$ coefficients in total. From these coefficients, we can derive the implied $n+5$ valuation parameters: $(\alpha_1, \alpha_2, R, g, \delta_{50}, \ldots \delta_{5n})$.

If our focus is on the current period information, including tangible and intangible assets, such as $(P_t, e_t, b_t, b_{t-1}, capX_t, R\&D_t, SG\&A_t, INTan_t)$, Eq. (4.12) becomes

$$e_{t+1} = \delta_1 P_t + \delta_2 e_t + \delta_3 b_t + \delta_4 b_{t-1} + \delta_5 capX_t + \delta_6 R\&D_t + \delta_7 SG\&A_t + \delta_8 INTan_t + \epsilon'_{t+1}, \tag{5.6}$$

where

$$\delta_1 = \frac{(R-1-g)}{(1+\alpha_1)},$$
$$\delta_2 = \frac{(1+g)\alpha_1}{(1+\alpha_1)},$$
$$\delta_3 = \frac{(R-1)\alpha_1 - \alpha_2 + g}{(1+\alpha_1)},$$
$$\delta_4 = \frac{(1+g)(\alpha_2 - \alpha_1(R-1))}{(1+\alpha_1)}$$
$$\delta_5 = -\frac{\gamma_0}{(1+\alpha_1)},$$
$$\delta_6 = -\frac{\gamma_1}{(1+\alpha_1)},$$
$$\delta_7 = -\frac{\gamma_2}{(1+\alpha_1)},$$
$$\delta_8 = -\frac{\gamma_3}{(1+\alpha_1)}.$$

From the eight equations above, we can infer the eight valuation parameters, $(\alpha_1, \alpha_2, R, g, \gamma_0, \gamma_1, \gamma_2, \gamma_3)$, in terms of $\delta_j (j = 1 - 8)$. That is,

$$1 + g = \frac{(1+\delta_2+\delta_3) + \sqrt{(1+\delta_2+\delta_3)^2 - 4(\delta_2 - \delta_4)}}{2},$$
$$R - 1 = g + (1+\alpha_1)\delta_1 = g + \frac{(1+g)\delta_1}{1+g-\delta_2},$$
$$\alpha_1 = \frac{(1+g)}{1+g-\delta_2} - 1,$$
$$\alpha_2 = (1+\alpha_1)\delta_3 - (R-1)\alpha_1 - g,$$
$$\gamma_0 = -\delta_5(1+\alpha_1),$$
$$\gamma_1 = -\delta_6(1+\alpha_1),$$
$$\gamma_2 = -\delta_7(1+\alpha_1),$$
$$\gamma_3 = -\delta_8(1+\alpha_1).$$

We can then estimate the value of the stock from model (4.13).

5.3 Valuation Multiples

Investors often estimate the value of a target company by a specific price multiple (P/Z) within the cross-section, where Z is a value driver, such as (operating) earnings or book value of equity (asset). Despite the widespread use of price multiples, the theoretical foundation linking certain individual multiples of the selected peers to the target company's value is weak. Bhojraj and Lee (2002) argue that the selection of a homogeneous group of comparable peers is essentially an art form. Young and Zeng (2015) emphasize that divergent accounting practices can make even very different companies appear similar. In this section, we introduce the concept of a synthetic price multiple, a valuation multiple that connects to a discounted future cash flow (earnings) model, utilizing the firm's economic and accounting fundamentals, as well as multi-drivers of value in its construction. Valuation model (4.4) builds a foundation for the construction of such a "synthetic price multiple".

Synthetic price multiples possess three distinguishing features. Firstly, when applying the synthetic price-to-forward earnings, price-to-book, and price-to-current earnings multiples on a target firm, all generate identical value estimates because they are grounded on the same discounted cash flow (earnings) model. This is in contrast to Kim and Ritter (1999) and Liu et al. (2002) who argue that price multiples based on forward earnings generally perform better than book value and other value drivers, while Nissim (2013) asserts that book value multiples generate less biased estimates than using earnings multiples in the financial sector. There is no clear support for selecting one value driver as superior to others in the literature. Secondly, a synthetic price multiple, such as the price-to-forward earnings multiple for a target company, can be expressed as an adjustment to its industry's "normal" price-to-forward earnings multiple. It incorporates the fundamental economic and accounting characteristics of the corresponding industry, including the persistence of abnormal earnings, the cost of equity capital, the growth of future earnings, and accounting conservatism. The difference between the price multiple and its industry "normal" value effectively defines a value premium. As such, generating a synthetic price multiple does not require identifying the target's peers or aggregating the peers' price multiples.[2] Thirdly, the adjustment term not only reflects the fundamental characteristics but also serves as a function of the value drivers that drive the cross-sectional variation between companies within the same industry. Specifically, it is captured by the difference between the target company's future and current return on book equity (ROE), its industry average cost of equity capital, and the difference between the target book value growth rate and its industry average growth rate. In other words, unlike the commonly used price multiples that build solely on peers' inputs, a synthetic price multiple for the target company directly connects to its value drivers, which may reflect the target's

[2] There is no consensus on aggregating the peers' price multiples in practice. Some use the harmonic mean, and others use the median of comparable companies' multiples.

superior products, better customer access, and economies of scale in the cross section. Collectively, a synthetic price multiple incorporates several economic and accounting fundamentals and, thus, can be viewed as an enhanced price multiple.

Since various value drivers are intrinsically linked in the forecasting of future abnormal earnings (cash flows), their weights in valuation reflecting economic characteristics must be jointly estimated. To systematically estimate industry-year parameters embedded in a synthetic price multiple, we derive the theoretical determinants of one-period ahead abnormal earnings in terms of current abnormal earnings, accounting goodwill measured by the difference between the market value and book value, and abnormal growth in book value under conservative accounting. We accordingly regress the expected one-period forward earnings on current earnings, current and lagged book values, and stock prices.[3] In other words, the determinants of the synthetic price multiples are jointly estimated in an internally consistent manner by explicitly focusing on the multi-dimensional fundamental economic and accounting characteristics. Therefore, a synthetic price multiple is more systematic and less subjective than the commonly used price multiples.

5.3.1 *The Intrinsic Linkage Between Equity Value and Value Drivers*

Applying the clean surplus relation (CSR) and noting $x_t = e_t - (R - 1)b_{t-1}$, Eq. (4.4) demonstrates how e_t, b_t and e_{t+1} articulate in valuation in a multi-dimensional setting. Following Penman (1996, 2013), a price-to-book ratio (P/B) of 1.0 is referred to as a "normal" P/B ratio, a price-to-earnings ratio (trailing P/E) of $R/(R - 1)$ is referred to as a "normal" trailing P/E, and a price-to-forward earnings ratio (P/E_1) of $1/(R - 1)$ is referred to as a "normal" forward P/E_1. We can establish the relation between the valuation multiples and their "normal" values below.

Three valuation multiples: value-to-forward earnings, value-to-book, and (cum-dividend) value-to-current earnings, can be written as

$$\frac{V_t}{E_t[e_{t+1}]} = \frac{1}{(R-1)} + \frac{M_1 N^T}{E_t[e_{t+1}]}, \tag{5.7}$$

$$\frac{V_t}{b_t} = 1 + \frac{M_2 N^T}{b_t}, \tag{5.8}$$

[3] This is in contrast to Bhojraj and Lee (2002) who aim to identify the best possible comparable peers and regress multiples on a set of variables shown to help predict the implied cost of capital in Gebhardt et al. (2001).

$$\frac{V_t + d_t}{e_t} = \frac{R}{(R-1)} + \frac{M_3 N^T}{e_t}, \tag{5.9}$$

where

$$M_1 = \frac{1}{(R-\omega_1)(R-\gamma)}[\frac{R(\omega_1+\gamma-1)-\omega_1\gamma}{(R-1)}, -\omega_1\gamma, -R\omega_2],$$

$$M_2 = \frac{1}{(R-\omega_1)(R-\gamma)}[R, -\omega_1\gamma, -R\omega_2],$$

$$M_3 = \frac{R}{(R-\omega_1)(R-\gamma)}[1, \frac{-(R-\gamma+\omega_1(\gamma-1))}{(R-1)}, -\omega_2]$$

and

$$N = [(E_t[ROE_{t+1}] - (R-1))b_t, (ROE_t - (R-1))b_{t-1}, (\gamma - b_t/b_{t-1})b_{t-1}].$$

The above valuation multiples have several important features. First, each of the valuation multiples is equal to its respective "normal" price multiples $\frac{1}{R-1}$, 1 and $\frac{R}{R-1}$ plus an adjustment term.[4] Second, value drivers and the fundamental characteristics of a company are intrinsically embedded in the valuation multiples. Vector $M_i (i = 1, 2, 3)$ in the adjustment terms is determined by the economic and accounting characteristics of the company. They describe the short-term competitive force of the company in the marketplace (ω_1), its accounting policy (ω_2), the long-term cost of capital ($R - 1$), and growth rate (λ) of future investment opportunities. Third, vector N in the adjustment terms contains multi-dimensional common factors in each valuation multiple. It shows that the difference between the return on equity (ROE, both the current and forward) and the cost of equity capital, $(ROE-(R-1))$, and the deviation of growth in the book value of equity from its long-term growth rate $(b_t/b_{t-1} - \lambda)$ are the key determinants of these multiples and the premium of the equity value. This finding is consistent with empirical evidence documented in Nissim (2013), which shows that conditioning the price-to-book ratio on ROE significantly improves valuation accuracy.

The theoretical foundation behind these multiples can be seen from the determinants of value premiums: $(V_t - \frac{E_t[e_{t+1}]}{(R-1)})$, $(V_t - b_t)$ and$(V_t + d_t - \frac{R}{(R-1)}e_t)$ from the rearranging of expressions in Eqs. (5.7), (5.8) and (5.9). These value premiums are determined by the risk inherited in (future) earnings and book value under conservative accounting principles and fundamental economic characteristics. Earnings are not recognized and assets are not booked unless they have a low risk (see Penman and Zhang, 2020). It tells investors to differentiate earnings released from risk and earnings still at risk. The accounting rate of return $(ROE_t = x_t/b_{t-1})$ combines earnings and book value to convey risk and value, as demonstrated in

[4] Note that the value is cum-dividend value in the value-to-current earnings multiple.

the Fama and French (2015) five-factor model and the Hou et al. (2015) q-model. The expensing of risky investments such as $R\&D$ reduces current earnings and book value, but increases the expected higher earnings of the investments in the future. Higher expected future earnings on lower current book value (relative to the cost of capital) or higher expected economic spread indicate high risk. Higher current earnings relative to past book value or a higher current economic spread indicate low risk. These are reflected in the positive and negative signs attached to the forward and current economic spreads in the value premiums, respectively. While these two periods' ROEs in vector N may vary significantly over the life of an asset, the economic characteristics embedded in their coefficients, reflecting the long-term property based on currently available information in vector M, jointly determine the value premiums. The coefficients of the forward economic spread in $M_i (i = 1, 2, 3)$ in terms of $\frac{R(\omega_1+\lambda-1)-\omega_1\lambda}{(R-1)(R-\omega_1)(R-\lambda)}$ and $\frac{R}{(R-\omega_1)(R-\lambda)}$ are positive functions of growth (λ) and persistence of abnormal earnings (ω_1). Since accounting numbers are governed by conservative accounting principles, accounting conservatism can be considered a "noise". Therefore, M_i corrects that "noise" by including the ω_2 term in constructing valuation multiples. Book value conservatism conveys risk in our model set-up via the abnormal growth in book values.

5.3.2 A Synthetic Price Multiple and Its Estimation

A synthetic price multiple is the valuation multiple when a firm's specific parameters ($\omega_1, \omega_2, R, \lambda$) on the right-hand side of Eqs. (5.7)–(5.9) are replaced by its industry parameters ($\omega_{it,1}, \omega_{it,2}, R_{it}, \lambda_{it}$). As a result, this implies that we use industry averages as a proxy for "normal" price multiples for individual firms within the industry. This is consistent with the fact that many practitioners use industry multiples as the first cut in relative valuation. It highlights the nature of the industry portfolio in a security analysis. Companies in the same industry usually compete in input and output markets, and return on equity (ROE) tends to converge to the industry mean value (Sloan and Lundholm, 2006; Penman, 2013). They tend to have similar risk profiles and, consequently, similar costs of capital (Fama and French, 1997). Considerable cross-industry variations in the level of accounting conservatism or financial reporting practices are also documented (Barth et al., 1999; Young and Zeng, 2015). Differences in sector growth rates have long been studied in the literature (Chenery, 1960; Boatsman and Baskin, 1981; Alford, 1992; Kim and Ritter, 1999; Liu et al., 2002). The multi-dimensionality of comparable companies suggests the usefulness and importance of industry groupings.[5] Therefore, when

[5] Intuitively, using valuation parameters estimated from a portfolio of firms with greater homogeneity should generate more accurate estimates of the firm-specific parameters. While in theory, we can estimate valuation coefficients in a finer portfolio formation or form portfolios based on firm characteristics such as book-to-market and size, we may end with a limited number of observations in portfolios for cross-sectional regressions (see Wang, 2018). Therefore, there is likely a trade-off between finer portfolio formation and statistical reliability in estimations.

estimating the synthetic price multiples, we use industry cross-sectional parameters $(\omega_{it,1}, \omega_{it,2}, R_{it}, \lambda_{it})$ as a proxy for the firm-year-specific parameters to characterize the target company's expected economic and accounting properties based on time t information. It allows us to examine the determinants of cross-sectional variations of the synthetic price multiples. Once we have estimated $(\omega_{it,1}, \omega_{it,2}, R_{it}, \lambda_{it})$ in vector M, we can estimate the following determinants of cross-sectional variations: the forward spread $(E_t[ROE_{t+1}] - (R_{it} - 1))$, the current spread $(ROE_t - (R_{it} - 1))$ and the abnormal growth in book values $(b_t/b_{t-1} - \lambda_{it})$ for each individual firm in industry i, and hence vector N. For convenience, we denote the synthetic price-to-forward earnings, price-to-book, and price-to-earnings multiples, V/x_1, V/B and V/x, respectively. Given the commonality of M for all firms in industry i, synthetic price multiples for firms in the industry are effectively determined by their (expected) economic spreads and abnormal growth in book values, which are components of N. Since Eqs. (5.7)–(5.9) are the same equation in different forms, we can apply any of them to value equity and generate the identical value estimate if we use a common set of $(\omega_{it,1}, \omega_{it,2}, R_{it}, \lambda_{it})$. That is, the value estimates are independent of the choice of value drivers in forming valuation multiples in our model setup. Even if forecasts of earnings are not available for privately held firms, and the conventional price-to-forward earnings ratio is not applicable, we can apply the synthetic value-to-book multiple and expect it to generate the same value as using the synthetic value-to-forward earnings multiple.

In sharp contrast to the commonly used price multiples in relative valuation, a synthetic price multiple utilizes the target firm's multi-drivers of value in construction in addition to incorporating its industry-specific accounting and economic fundamentals. Not only does the conventional relative valuation not provide clear guidance on identifying peer companies, but a possible peer's price multiple may also be completely disconnected from the target company's value drivers.

5.4 Use Analysts' or Model-based Forecasts of Earnings to Predict Stock Returns

Unlike an investor's required return or a firm's cost of equity capital, which is defined on the intrinsic value, an investor's (expected) return is defined on stock prices. Stock prices may incorporate the effects of accounting conservatism if financial statement information influences investor perceptions and expectations. However, we can use investors' required return $(V_{t+1} + d_{t+1} - V_t)/V_t$ as a proxy for the future equity return. It differs from the implied cost of equity capital (ICC), which is the discount rate that equates the present value of future expected cash flows (to equity holders) to the market value of the stock. In terms of standard financial mathematics, ICC is the internal rate of return of an investment in equity. Under the implicit assumption of a flat term structure of discount rates, the implied cost of equity capital has been popular as a proxy for expected stock returns in recent decades. ICC estimates rely on a specific equity valuation model, where risk adjustment is incorporated through a risk-adjusted discount rate. It implicitly assumes that the capital market is efficient at the individual firm level and that the current stock price accurately reflects its intrinsic value.

We can also apply the same insight to estimate the ICC for a portfolio, such as an industry ICC. The advantage of a portfolio-level analysis is that we can assume the capital market is efficient at the aggregate level. Still, it may not be efficient at the individual firm level. At the portfolio level, the growth rate ($\gamma - 1$) can be estimated simultaneously with the cost of capital. Given multi-period forecasts of earnings and dividend policy, O'Hanlon and Steele (2000) is one of the first to apply a parsimonious version of the RIVM model to estimate the ICC and the growth in residual incomes. Easton et al. (2002) and Easton (2004) apply the so-called abnormal earnings growth (AEG) model to estimate the ICC and growth of abnormal earnings simultaneously. In essence, they use the reverse engineering technique in applying the reformatted multi-period dividend discount model (2.15). Based on a one-to-one mapping between valuation and earnings forecasting in a no-arbitrage economy, Ashton and Wang (2013b) simultaneously estimates the growth rate of the present value of future investments and the ICC based on only one-year ahead forecasts of earnings on a portfolio without assuming a dividend policy.

If we define the one-period ahead return, $r_{t+1} \equiv (V_{t+1} + d_{t+1} - V_t)/V_t$, we can show that its expected value $E_t[r_{t+1}]$ equals r based on time t information in the valuation framework that built on the dividend discount model (2.12). This is because the model is developed under the assumption of risk neutrality. For example, Wang (2023) addresses a special case when $\omega_2 = 0$ in Eq. (4.4). It leads to

$$\frac{V_{t+1} + d_{t+1}}{V_t} = 1 + r + \frac{1+r}{1+r-\omega}\frac{\epsilon_{x,t+1}}{V_t} + \frac{1+r}{(1+r-\omega)(1+r-\gamma)}\frac{\epsilon_{G,t+1}}{V_t},$$

and the expected value equals $1 + r(\equiv R)$ based on time t information. Hence, the return expression above cannot be directly used to estimate the expected future stock returns. However, valuation models such as Eq. (4.4) can be used to develop a return model in terms of fundamental accounting ratios and their innovation terms, and in terms of $(R, \gamma, \omega_1, \omega_2)$, where $R-1$ is the long-term average cost of capital. He shows that

$$\begin{aligned}\frac{V_{t+1}+d_{t+1}}{V_t} &= \gamma + (R-\gamma)\frac{b_t}{V_t} + \frac{R}{R-\omega}\frac{x_{t+1}-x_t}{V_t} + \frac{R-\omega\gamma}{R-\omega}\frac{x_t}{V_t} \\ &+ \frac{R}{(R-\omega)(R-\gamma)}\frac{\epsilon_{G,t+1}}{V_t}.\end{aligned} \tag{5.10}$$

It highlights the role of variations in profitability (or changes in abnormal earnings) and the growth of future investments in describing changes in stock values. In terms of earnings, the above can be written as

$$\frac{V_{t+1}+d_{t+1}}{V_t} = \gamma + [R\frac{1-\omega}{R-\omega} - \gamma]\frac{b_t}{V_t} + \frac{R}{R-\omega}\frac{e_{t+1}}{V_t} - \frac{\omega\gamma}{R-\omega}\frac{e_t}{V_t} + \frac{(R-1)\omega\gamma}{R-\omega}\frac{b_{t-1}}{V_t} + \frac{R}{(R-\omega)(R-\gamma)}\frac{\epsilon_{G,t+1}}{V_t}. \tag{5.11}$$

If we consider accounting conservatism, we can derive stock returns from Eq. (3.43), together with Eqs. (3.41) and (3.42) as below:

$$\frac{V_{t+1}+d_{t+1}}{V_t} = \gamma + \frac{\gamma e_t - (\gamma-1)b_t}{V_t} + \frac{R}{R-\omega_1}\frac{e_{t+1}-\gamma e_t}{V_t} - [\frac{(R-1)\omega_1 - \omega_2 R}{R-\omega_1}]\frac{b_t - \gamma b_{t-1}}{V_t} + \frac{\epsilon_{t+1}}{V_t}. \tag{5.12}$$

Stock returns are expressed in terms of fundamental accounting ratios. Are accounting ratios capturing rational priced risk in a firm's future cash flows? The mainstream of asset pricing literature is clearly developed in this direction. Time series models regressing portfolio or individual stock returns on "factor mimicking portfolios" formed on the basis of accounting-based characteristics (such as book-to-price, profitability, investment growth) establish evidence on the statistical relationship between stock returns and accounting fundamentals (see, e.g., Fama and French, 1993, 2015; Hou et al., 2015).

Again, we can follow common industry practice to estimate the firm-specific expected returns. Specifically, for firm j in industry i at time t, we can use cross-sectional or industry-year specific parameters to proxy the firm-year specific parameters in Eq. (5.12). We could use 5- or 10-year industry panel data to capture the long-term trend. Note that this procedure implicitly assumes market efficiency at the aggregate industry or market level and uses stock prices as a proxy for the intrinsic values.

If we use cross-sectional or industry parameters to proxy firm-specific parameters, the proxy of the expected one-period ahead returns (or predicted stock returns) can be written as:

$$E_t[R_{t+1}] = \gamma_{it} + \frac{\gamma_{it}e_t - (\gamma_{it}-1)b_t}{P_t} + \frac{R_{it}}{R_{it}-\omega_{1,it}}\frac{E_t[e_{t+1}] - \gamma_{it}e_t}{P_t} - [\frac{(R_{it}-1)\omega_{1,it} - \omega_{2,it}R_{it}}{R_{it}-\omega_{1,it}}]\frac{b_t - \gamma_{it}b_{t-1}}{P_t}, \tag{5.13}$$

where the cross-sectional or industry-year information parameters, $\omega_{1,it}, \omega_{2,it}, \gamma_{it}$ and the time-varying industry-specific discount rate ($r_{it} = R_{it} - 1$) are estimated simultaneously as in Eq. (4.12). In other words, we employ the portfolio-level ICC technique as an intermediate procedure to estimate a firm-specific return under the assumption that the market is efficient at the aggregate level.[6]

From a more general model (4.13), the return can be expressed as:

$$\frac{V_{t+1}+d_{t+1}}{V_t}-1=g+\frac{e_{t+1}-gb_t}{V_t}+\alpha_1\frac{e_{t+1}-(1+g)e_t}{V_t}$$
$$+(\alpha_2-(R-1)\alpha_1)\frac{b_t-(1+g)b_{t-1}}{V_t}+\sum_{s=0}^{n}\Gamma_s\frac{Y_{t-s}}{V_t}+\frac{\epsilon_{t+1}}{V_t}.$$

It can also be written in term of dividends as :

$$\frac{V_{t+1}+d_{t+1}}{V_t}-1=g+\frac{(1+g)d_t}{V_t}+(1+\alpha_1)\frac{e_{t+1}-(1+g)e_t}{V_t}$$
$$+(1+\alpha_2-(R-1)\alpha_1)\frac{b_t-(1+g)b_{t-1}}{V_t}$$
$$+\sum_{s=0}^{n}\Gamma_s\frac{Y_{t-s}}{V_t}+\frac{\epsilon_{t+1}}{V_t}. \tag{5.14}$$

That is, the cost of equity capital can be expressed as the sum of the long-term growth rate of future dividends and the forward dividend yield, adjusted for abnormal growth in earnings and book value, as well as investment ratios.

If we use cross-sectional or industry parameters to proxy firm-specific parameters, we have a proxy for the one-year ahead stock return as:

$$E_t[R_{t+1}]=1+g_{it}+\frac{(1+g_{it})d_t}{P_t}+(1+\alpha_{1,it})\frac{E_t[e_{t+1}]-(1+g_{it})e_t}{P_t}$$
$$+(1+\alpha_{2,it}-(R_{it}-1)\alpha_{1,it})\frac{b_t-(1+g_{it})b_{t-1}}{P_t}+\sum_{s=0}^{n}\Gamma_{s,it}\frac{Y_{t-s}}{P_t}. \tag{5.15}$$

In the digital era, many firms, such as high-tech firms, are asset-light since intangibles and goodwill may not be recorded, and R&D investments are not

[6] In contrast, we observe that all asset pricing models follow the same basic methodology as in empirical implementations of the capital asset pricing model (CAPM). In application, one has to (1) choose a proxy for a risk-free asset (e.g. treasury bills); (2) estimate market risk premia (e.g. from capital market history); (3) estimate the firm's risk exposure to market risk. One common explanation for the failure of factor models is the inevitable use of noisy ex post realized returns and thus measurement error in forward-looking risk premia and factor betas (Elton, 1999). While asset pricing theory admits time-varying conditioning information, empirical implementations of factor models implicitly assume that factor risk premia and firm risk exposure (the 'betas') estimated from past information sets remain stable over time.

recognized. Therefore, firms with low book-to-market ratios do not necessarily have lower risk. It is expected that the book-to-market ratio will play a less significant role in explaining stock returns in some industries in the 'new economy', where intangible assets are often "off-balance sheet" and operating activities are less sensitive to the changes in the term structure of interest rates. Equation (5.15) suggests that the investment factor should include investment in intangibles, which under conservative accounting principles are often treated as expenses, reducing current profitability.

An alternative to Eq. (4.4) is that we write equity value in terms of book value, dividends, abnormal earnings, and growth term G as Eq. (4.7):

$$V_t = b_t+\beta_1(b_t+d_t)+\beta_2 x_t+G_t = b_t+(\beta_1+\beta_2)x_t+(1+r)\beta_1 b_{t-1}+G_t, \tag{5.16}$$

where G_t follows dynamic (4.6). While earnings conservatism is adjusted in the dynamic of G_t, the lagged book value term adjusts book value conservatism in the valuation model as in Pope and Wang (2005).

Assuming clean surplus accounting, Eqs. (5.16) and (4.6) imply the total one-period ahead required return:

$$\frac{V_{t+1}+d_{t+1}}{V_t} = [1+\beta_1-(R-1)\beta_2]\frac{b_t}{V_t}+[1+\beta_1+\beta_2]\frac{e_{t+1}}{V_t}+\frac{G_{t+1}}{V_t}. \tag{5.17}$$

The positive association between the book-to-value ratio (B/V) and the required equity return becomes apparent when we control forward earnings yield and the ratio of one-period ahead NPV of future investment-to-value.[7] If stock prices are a good proxy for intrinsic values, when regressing stock returns on book-to-market, and either reasonable proxies for $\frac{E_t[G_{t+1}]}{P_t}$ and $\frac{E_t[e_{t+1}]}{P_t}$, or both forward ratios are missing, one would observe that B/P is positively related to expected returns (see, e.g., Fama and French, 1992, 1993, 2006).

In parallel with the standard dividend growth model, Eq. (5.17) can be written in terms of growth, dividend yield, abnormal growth in book value, and abnormal growth in forward earnings, as well as the impact of accounting conservatism as:

$$\begin{aligned}\frac{V_{t+1}+d_{t+1}}{V_t} &= 1+g+(1+g)\frac{d_t}{V_t}+(1+\beta_1-(R-1)\beta_2)\frac{b_t-(1+g)b_{t-1}}{V_t}\\ &+(1+\beta_1+\beta_2)\frac{e_{t+1}-(1+g)e_t}{V_t}\\ &+\lambda\frac{(V_t+d_t-V_{t-1})-e_t}{V_t}+\frac{\epsilon_{G,t+1}}{V_t}.\end{aligned} \tag{5.18}$$

---

[7] Note that Eq. (4.7) implies that $V_t = (1+\beta_1-(R-1)\beta_2)b_t+(\beta_1-(R-1)\beta_2)d_t+R\beta_2 e_t+G_t$. The coefficient of book value is expected to be greater than one in conservative accounting.

It suggests that equity returns and growth are interlinked. Note that G_{t+1} is replaced by applying Eqs. (4.6) and (5.16). In particular, if we set $\beta_1 = \beta_2 = 0$, and $\lambda = 0$, Eq. (5.18) reduces to

$$\frac{V_{t+1} + d_{t+1}}{V_t} - 1 = g + \frac{e_{t+1}}{V_t} - g\frac{b_t}{V_t} + \frac{\epsilon_{t+1}}{V_t}. \tag{5.19}$$

If we use prices as a proxy for the intrinsic values of equity, Eq. (5.19) shows that B/P is negatively related to the one-period ahead return, and B/P amplifies the growth after controlling for positive growth and forward earnings yield. This is contrasts with a large body of empirical asset pricing literature. If there is no growth ($g = 0$), then B/P should not have explanatory power for expected returns. This parsimonious model suggests that book-to-market should not be viewed as an independent risk factor, nor should market-to-book (P/B) itself represent growth as commonly interpreted. The resolution of this paradox depends on the additional control variables used to explain expected stock returns, especially those capturing expected growth. In other words, the book-to-market ratio can be positively or negatively related to stock returns, depending on how we control for expected growth. Although the forward earnings yield has long been used in equity valuation by financial analysts, it appears that not enough attention has been paid to forward earnings in the empirical asset pricing literature (Fama and French, 2006; Lyle et al., 2013; Penman, 2016). Note that ϵ_{t+1} in (5.14) and $\epsilon_{G,t+1}$ in (5.18) may hold some higher moments properties, or they may involve extreme values and asymmetric returns, but their expected values can be estimated.

It is also interesting to note that Eq. (5.18) provides an alternative explanation for why current returns may be associated with future returns. It shows that accounting conservatism can cause a time-serial correlation in stock returns. Accounting conservatism understates 'true' current incomes or only recognizes a portion of economic earnings. The unrecognized portion will be recognized at a later stage and may be reflected in future returns. The conservative nature of reporting may influence investors' beliefs about future profitability when expectations of growth and future earnings are formed.

We can use the same technique to write the expected one-period ahead earnings in terms of current earnings, (lagged) book values, and (lagged) prices. We then estimate the valuation parameters $(\beta_1, \beta_2, \lambda, R, g)$. If we use cross-sectional or industry parameters to proxy firm-specific parameters, we have a proxy for the one-year ahead stock return:

$$\begin{aligned} E_t[R_{t+1}] = {} & 1+g_{it}+(1+g_{it})\frac{d_t}{P_t}+(1+\beta_{1,it}-(R_{it}-1)\beta_{2,it})\frac{b_t-(1+g_{it})b_{t-1}}{P_t} \\ & +(1+\beta_{1,it}+\beta_{2,it})\frac{E_t[e_{t+1}]-(1+g_{it})e_t}{P_t} \\ & +\lambda_{it}\frac{(P_t+d_t-P_{t-1})-e_t}{P_t}. \end{aligned} \tag{5.20}$$

In summary, proxies for the cost of equity capital using accounting fundamentals can be derived from two distinct perspectives: the characteristic asset pricing perspective and the accounting-based valuation perspective. The literature supporting these two approaches has evolved independently, with asset pricing approaches being largely agnostic about the accounting measurement origins of the accounting characteristics used to create risk factors. However, the boundary between the two methodologies is becoming increasingly blurred. Asset pricing approaches can gain new insights by understanding the principles used in measuring accounting constructs such as book value, investment, and profitability (see Ashton and Wang, 2025). Accounting principles determine how much earnings are recognized currently or, alternatively, deferred to the future. When earnings recognition is deferred until the realization criteria are met, accounting principles generate earnings growth. Further, accounting principles connect the resulting growth to risk—recognition is deferred until uncertainty about the (future) cash flows from a transaction is sufficiently resolved (Penman and Zhu, 2022). As a consequence, accounting numbers are relevant to estimating the cost of capital. They express expected returns in terms of expectations of earnings and earnings growth, so that any variables relevant in forecasting earnings, earnings growth, and risk in earnings also predict the required (risk-adjusted) return and risk in returns, if the market prices those outcomes as risky. However, they must be expressed in a specific and constrained manner to describe the cost of capital.

5.5 Application of Industry Information in Valuation and Predicting Returns

To estimate the value of a stock and predict its returns within a unified framework, we perform three interconnected steps. Firstly, we need to forecast one-period ahead earnings for each firm. It can be analysts' forecasts or model-based forecasts, such as models in Hou et al. (2012) and Harris and Wang (2019). Examples in this section utilize the widely used consensus forecasts from financial analysts. Secondly, we use the forecasts of earnings to estimate simultaneously the parameters in information dynamics from cross-sectional or industry panel regressions. Thirdly, we apply the estimates to individual firms in the industry, incorporating their firm-specific value drivers.

5.5.1 Estimation of Portfolio Level Valuation Parameters

As an example, we introduce the Ashton and Wang (2013b) model, which builds on a general linear relationship between equity value and accounting fundamentals. It is a reformulation of Eq. (4.7). In essence, they assume that the cum-dividend equity value can be written in terms of the value of assets-in-place and the present value of all future investments or the value of growth options. The value of assets-in-place is a linear function of earnings, book value, and dividends, holding property of dividend irrelevance, which implies both book value and market value are in the cum-dividend terms. Specifically,

$$V_t = \alpha_1(b_t + d_t) + \alpha_2 e_t - d_t + G_t, \tag{5.21}$$

where G_t is the net present value (NPV) of all future investment projects or the firm's growth component. The variable G_t represents the value attributed by the market to information not captured by the three accounting variables but incorporated into the market value. Because accounting numbers represent a firm's historical transactions and market values are generally considered to include the future growth of companies, G_t must reflect the nature of the growth component. Prior literature also demonstrates that the growth in G is associated with conservatism, as book values and earnings are likely to be under-reported, thereby distorting values between conservative and less conservative firms. They, therefore, partition the G_t variable into a growth element associated with growth in positive NPV investment opportunities and growth coming from variations in the degree of conservatism in reporting. They measure conservatism by the difference between economic earnings, $(V_t - V_{t-1} + d_t)$ and accounting earnings e_t or earnings conservatism. An abnormal return on equity reflects both real growth and a correction for GAAP differences between short-run forecasts of earnings and economic earnings (Easton et al., 2009). Note that clean surplus relation implies that the difference between economic earnings and accounting, $(V_t + d_t - V_{t-1}) - e_t$ is equal to the changes in goodwill, $(V_t - b_t) - (V_{t-1} - b_{t-1})$. The effects of accounting conservatism on the short-horizon forecasts of earnings will differ from firm to firm and thus affect the base from which earnings are assumed to grow in perpetuity. Conservative accounting may also influence investors' beliefs about expectations of future growth. In short, the net present value (NPV) of all future investment projects G_t characterizes the firm's growth component and reflects accounting conservatism. Ashton and Wang (2013b) and Wang (2018), therefore, assume information dynamic (4.6) or

$$G_{t+1} = (1 + g)G_t + \lambda(V_t + d_t - V_{t-1} - e_t) + \epsilon_{G,t+1}. \tag{5.22}$$

g here is the firm's expected steady-state growth rate, not the short-term growth rate of individual accounting items, such as sales growth, asset growth, or earnings growth. The growth proxies used in empirical investigations in Penman and Zhu (2014) can be considered a subset of the G growth component. Under the no-arbitrage condition, Eq. (5.21) implies that

$$E_t[e_{t+1}] = \frac{R}{(\alpha_1 + \alpha_2)} V_t - \frac{\alpha_1}{(\alpha_1 + \alpha_2)} b_t - \frac{E_t[G_{t+1}]}{(\alpha_1 + \alpha_2)}. \tag{5.23}$$

It shows that values lead earnings in the sense that values can still help predict subsequent period earnings, given equity book values and non-accounting information.

The unspecified non-accounting variable G_t presents an immediate problem in any direct application of the above model. However, Eq. (4.9) suggests that the expected one-period ahead earnings can be written in terms of $(V_t, e_t, b_t, b_{t-1}, V_{t-1})$, or: [8]

$$e_{t+1} = \delta_1 V_t + \delta_2 e_t + \delta_3 b_t + \delta_4 b_{t-1} + \delta_5 V_{t-1} + \epsilon_{t+1}, \tag{5.24}$$

where

$$\begin{aligned} \delta_1 &= \frac{R-(1+g)-\lambda}{(\alpha_1+\alpha_2)}, \\ \delta_2 &= \frac{(1+g)(\alpha_1+\alpha_2-1)}{(\alpha_1+\alpha_2)}, \\ \delta_3 &= \frac{(1+g-\alpha_1+\lambda)}{(\alpha_1+\alpha_2)}, \\ \delta_4 &= \frac{(1+g)(\alpha_1-1)-\lambda}{(\alpha_1+\alpha_2)}, \\ \delta_5 &= \frac{\lambda}{(\alpha_1+\alpha_2)}, \end{aligned} \tag{5.25}$$

and $R = 1 + r$. Assuming the aggregate capital market is efficient, we can run a regression based on the above equation at the portfolio level, using the one-year ahead analysts' forecasts of earnings as a proxy for market expected one-year ahead earnings and stock prices as a proxy for intrinsic values.

We note that equation system (5.25) provides a one-to-one mapping between five regression coefficients (δ_1-δ_5) and five valuation parameters $(R, g, \alpha_1, \alpha_2, \lambda)$. If we regress forecasted earnings on (lagged) price, earnings, and (lagged) book value terms based on Eq. (5.24), we can back out the implied cost of capital, growth rate g, and valuation parameters α_1, α_2, and λ in terms of the regression coefficients.[9] Specifically, the portfolio level implied growth rate, cost of capital, and other valuation parameters can be written as

$$\begin{aligned} g &= -1 + \frac{1+\delta_2+\delta_3-\delta_5+\sqrt{(1+\delta_2+\delta_3-\delta_5)^2-4(\delta_2-\delta_4-\delta_5)}}{2}, \\ r &= -1 + (1+g)(1+\frac{\delta_1+\delta_5}{1+g-\delta_2}), \\ \alpha_1 &= 1 + \frac{\delta_4+\delta_5}{(1+g)-\delta_2}, \\ \alpha_2 &= \frac{\delta_2-\delta_4-\delta_5}{(1+g)-\delta_2}, \\ \lambda &= \frac{(1+g)\delta_5}{1+g-\delta_2}. \end{aligned} \tag{5.26}$$

[8] We could develop a similar expression using net dividends. Note also that the model is initially developed on a total dollar basis.

[9] Alternatively, we can use GMM to estimate the parameters directly. It requires us to set an initial parameter set.

Table 5.1 Descriptive statistics for regression coefficients

	Mean	St.Dev	Min	Low Q	Median	Upper Q	Max
δ_1	0.05	0.014	0.031	0.039	0.047	0.057	0.087
	(11.34)	(2.45)	(4.77)	(9.66)	(11.21)	(13.54)	(15.2)
δ_2	0.306	0.094	0.191	0.232	0.28	0.385	0.483
	(11.37)	(2.8)	(6.88)	(9.22)	(11.09)	(12.67)	(19.77)
δ_3	0.009	0.016	−0.016	−0.005	0.007	0.019	0.057
	(0.68)	(1.27)	(−1.16)	(−0.40)	(0.72)	(1.54)	(4.24)
δ_4	0.022	0.015	−0.015	0.012	0.023	0.033	0.049
	(1.91)	(1.35)	(−1.11)	(0.94)	(1.96)	(2.77)	(4.75)
δ_5	−0.001	0.008	−0.017	−0.007	−0.002	0.004	0.017
	(−0.35)	(2.27)	(−6.38)	(−1.50)	(−0.44)	(1.03)	(3.9)
Adj-R^2 (%)	37.90	8.70	26.50	30.60	36.30	44.20	60.40

The sample in Ashton and Wang (2013b) consists of prices and accounting data in the intersection of the Center for Research in Security Prices (CRSP) and Compustat over the period 1974–2006 and the Institutional Brokers Estimate System (I/B/E/S) between 1976 and 2007. The adjusted numbers of shares outstanding, adjusted price, and adjusted dividends at the end of the fiscal year, and adjusted price of equity three months after the fiscal year-end are collected from CRSP. Relevant accounting data is collected from Compustat. Firms with negative book values are deleted. Earnings are measured as net income before extraordinary items. They use median consensus forecasts of earnings per share at the first month after the corresponding I/B/E/S-reported prior-year earnings announcements, $feps_{t+1}$. All variables used in their estimation are divided by the adjusted number of shares in issue to reduce heteroskedasticity and increase comparability across time. In constructing the data set, they omit firms in the extreme percentile of earnings, book value, price, earnings-to-price, return on book equity, size, market-to-book ratio, and leverage, and firms with a price per share less than \$1. To reduce nonstationarity and minimize the effects of endogeneity, they deflate both sides of Eq. (5.24) by the price three months after fiscal year-end to provide contemporaneity with the fiscal year-end reporting of book values and earnings.

Table 5.1 reports the descriptive statistics for the 32 regression coefficients of δ_i (i=1-5) in Eq. (5.24) based on the 32 annual estimates between 1975–2006, together with descriptive statistics of their t-values (in brackets). The sample size varies over the 32 years, ranging from a low of 600 firms in 1975 to a high of 2573 firms in 1997. The average number of annual observations is 1734. Table 5.2 summarizes the statistics of the implied cost of capital (ICC), growth rate (g), and risk premia by year and by industry. The risk premium (RP) is calculated relative to the yield on a five-year US government bond. The industry classification is per Fama and French (1997).

Table 5.2 Descriptive statistics for valuation parameters

	By year					By industry				
	ICC		g		RP	ICC		g		RP
	%	t-Stat	%	t-Stat	%	%	t-Stat	%	t-Stat	%
Average	11.24	44.84	4.2	8.3	3.83	10.79	46.74	4.21	5.01	3.1
St.Dev	2.96	11.6	1.1	2.54	2.13	1.83	40.77	2.13	3.15	1.73
Min	7.27	22.03	2.45	3.86	0.71	4.95	3.75	−2.75	−1.34	−1.93
Q1	9.2	38.21	3.51	6.4	2.44	9.99	22.78	3.51	2.74	2.28
Median	10.2	45.48	4	7.91	3.53	11.25	37.17	4.36	5.24	3.49
Q3	13.45	50.41	4.79	10.31	4.35	11.86	58.64	5.26	7.18	4.15
Max	16.86	75.11	7.65	13.4	9.87	14.83	226.58	8.86	15.25	7.16

Therefore, we can simultaneously estimate the implied cost of equity capital and growth rate at the portfolio level.[10] Regressions based on industry-level analysis give industry value drivers such as industry cost of capital and growth rate, which are often used in individual equity valuation. The above results indicate that the cost of equity capital is approximately 11% and the risk premium ranges from 3% to 4%. Ashton and Wang also find that the long-run growth is about 4.2%, which coincides with the estimate from the Board of the U.S. Congress over their sample period.

Table 5.3 details the estimates of cost of capital (and t-statistic), growth rates (and t-statistic), and risk premia on a year-by-year basis, using both the simple model without incorporating earnings conservatism (Panel A):

$$\frac{feps_{t+1}}{P_t} = \delta_1 + \delta_2 \frac{e_t}{P_t} + \delta_3 \frac{b_t}{P_t} + \delta_4 \frac{b_{t-1}}{P_t} + \epsilon_{t+1}, \tag{5.27}$$

and the extended model like model (5.24) incorporating earnings conservatism (Panel B):

$$\frac{feps_{t+1}}{P_t} = \delta_1' + \delta_2' \frac{e_t}{P_t} + \delta_3' \frac{b_t}{P_t} + \delta_4' \frac{b_{t-1}}{P_t} + \delta_5' \frac{P_{t-1}}{P_t} + \epsilon_{t+1}'. \tag{5.28}$$

We observe that the mean cost of capital, 11.2%, and risk premium, 3.8%, are virtually identical in the two models. The risk premia are reported based on five-year U.S. government bond yields as a proxy for the risk-free rate. Indeed, the correlation coefficient between our two estimates of the cost of capital from the two models and the two estimates of the equity risk premium is over 0.99. It shows that there is no material impact on valuation bias when incorporating a conservatism-adjustment

[10] The requirement to identify five parameters precludes their estimation on an individual firm basis. This would restrict us to the few firms with 30 continuous years of history. When estimating the parameters for individual firms with at least 20 observations, we found that the average cost of capital was not significantly different; however, the estimate of the long-run growth rate was significantly higher, at around 9%, which may reflect survivorship or success bias.

Table 5.3 Implied cost of capital, growth rate, and risk premium, year-by-year

		Panel A: when $\delta_5 = 0$					Panel B: when $\delta_5 \neq 0$				
		ICC		g		RP	*ICC*		g		RP
Year	N	%	tv	%	tv	%	%	tv	%	tv	%
1975	600	15.18	43.57	7.61	13.97	7.40	15.22	41.53	7.65	13.23	7.44
1976	751	15.67	30.02	5.56	7.10	8.49	15.46	22.03	5.68	7.19	8.28
1977	1048	16.83	37.35	3.99	6.04	9.84	16.86	37.22	4.19	6.07	9.87
1978	1143	15.86	49.78	3.73	6.37	7.54	15.92	38.68	3.65	5.39	7.60
1979	1144	15.97	55.14	3.90	7.65	6.46	15.99	52.42	3.91	6.80	6.48
1980	1170	16.16	46.81	5.78	13.16	4.71	16.38	43.78	5.03	9.61	4.93
1981	1243	15.18	63.54	6.09	11.27	0.93	15.19	62.70	6.00	10.40	0.94
1982	1361	14.58	60.55	4.91	10.31	1.57	14.86	62.57	5.17	10.85	1.85
1983	1409	12.56	69.94	5.57	13.36	1.77	12.31	45.99	5.78	13.40	1.52
1984	1417	12.94	73.25	5.03	12.50	0.68	12.97	75.11	5.07	12.59	0.71
1985	1499	11.74	59.62	4.81	10.15	1.62	11.74	59.65	4.97	10.50	1.62
1986	1473	10.06	36.42	2.61	4.65	2.76	9.96	34.51	2.93	5.16	2.66
1987	1502	10.11	48.51	3.58	8.52	2.17	10.17	48.20	3.37	7.11	2.23
1988	1581	11.82	55.07	4.51	8.86	3.34	11.67	50.63	4.35	8.53	3.19
1989	1567	10.89	51.29	4.38	9.16	2.39	10.95	50.33	4.37	8.28	2.45
1990	1542	11.36	61.01	3.76	8.77	2.99	10.77	48.18	2.75	5.46	2.40
1991	1597	10.38	46.08	4.15	8.76	3.01	10.42	45.41	3.84	7.43	3.05
1992	1678	10.01	49.21	4.38	10.17	3.82	9.97	48.82	4.71	10.84	3.78
1993	1848	9.36	44.59	3.78	8.94	4.22	9.36	44.74	3.92	8.62	4.22
1994	2183	10.03	50.65	3.60	7.78	3.34	10.02	49.96	3.58	7.55	3.33
1995	2451	10.26	49.58	4.87	11.27	3.88	10.23	48.76	4.72	9.96	3.85
1996	2523	9.43	54.20	3.76	9.95	3.25	9.43	53.06	3.68	8.91	3.25
1997	2573	8.54	42.52	4.01	10.77	2.32	8.54	42.77	4.08	10.28	2.32
1998	2506	8.85	41.74	3.55	8.05	3.70	8.71	37.36	3.34	6.81	3.56
1999	2330	9.68	52.90	3.92	9.61	4.13	9.38	45.55	3.34	7.14	3.83
2000	2188	9.83	58.22	5.04	14.05	3.67	9.65	52.34	4.58	10.96	3.49
2001	2313	8.06	38.78	3.83	8.87	3.50	8.30	41.82	4.08	9.86	3.74
2002	2305	8.40	35.33	3.24	5.06	4.58	8.58	38.49	3.73	6.43	4.76
2003	2317	8.25	35.73	3.23	6.37	5.28	8.27	35.84	3.40	6.32	5.30
2004	2287	7.47	27.62	2.08	3.83	4.04	7.29	26.07	2.45	4.36	3.86
2005	2245	7.70	28.35	3.34	5.89	3.65	7.70	27.84	3.55	5.81	3.65
2006	1687	7.18	22.61	2.35	3.75	2.43	7.27	22.34	2.58	3.86	2.52
Mean	1734	11.26	47.50	4.22	8.90	3.86	11.24	44.84	4.20	8.30	3.83
Med	1589	10.19	48.86	3.96	8.86	3.57	10.20	45.48	4.00	7.91	3.53

term in the information dynamics. Furthermore, the empirical results suggest that the growth rate is only slightly affected by the degree of accounting conservatism.

Wang and Huang (2015) implement the above approach to Chinese capital markets. It is widely believed that realized stock market returns have been volatile and provided a poor reflection of economic growth and investor expectations in

Table 5.4 Valuation parameters on Chinese firms: 2004–2012

	By year					By industry				
	ICC		g		RP	ICC		g		RP
	%	t-stat	%	t-stat	%	%	t-stat	%	t-stat	%
Mean	14.58	12.24	10.14	6.5	11.04	12.26	10.28	8.61	4.91	8.80
St.Dev	3.84	5.35	3.52	2.89	4.18	3.72	6.73	3.40	3.34	3.71
Min	9.51	6.84	5.65	3.6	5.56	7.85	2.74	3.98	1.42	4.49
Q1	11.53	8.03	7.20	4.69	7.74	9.54	6.02	6.78	3.17	6.14
Median	14.72	11.77	10.49	6.26	11.66	11.52	8.37	7.85	3.57	8.09
Q3	16.07	14.68	12.37	6.5	13.16	15.41	12.39	9.90	4.26	11.98
Max	20.73	24.01	15.72	13.07	16.71	18.84	28.45	14.15	12.75	15.43

China until recently. They estimate simultaneously the implied long-run growth rate and cost of equity capital for listed Chinese firms over the period 2004–2012. The descriptive statistics of the implied cost of capital (ICC), growth rate (g), and risk premium by year and industry are reported in Table 5.4. The risk premium (RP) is calculated relative to the yield on the Chinese 10-year Treasury notes. The industry classification follows that of the China Securities Regulatory Commission.

The results indicate that the implied mean growth rate in earnings is approximately 10%, and the mean implied cost of capital is around 14.6%. These suggest that the implied growth rates from companies' fundamentals align with the economic growth over the sample period and that the implied cost of capital is consistent with investors' expectations.

5.5.2 *Predicting Individual Stocks' Returns*

Wang (2018) apply model (5.20) to predict stock returns. The US data is extracted from 1975 to 2011, and the median consensus forecasts of earnings per share at the first month after the corresponding I/B/E/S-reported prior-year earnings announcements are used as a proxy of expected earnings. All total variables used in the estimation are divided by the adjusted number of shares outstanding to reduce heteroskedasticity and increase comparability across time. The sample descriptive statistics of relevant variables are reported in Table 5.5. They include price (P), book value (b), earnings (e), analysts' forecasts of earnings (feps), book-to-price (b/P), earnings-to-price (e/P), forward earnings-to-price (feps/P), market capitalization (Mktcap), and leverage (Lev).

When using stock prices as a proxy for the intrinsic values in Eq. (4.9), we can run regression:

$$e_{t+1} = \delta_1 P_t + \delta_2 e_t + \delta_3 b_t + \delta_4 b_{t-1} + \delta_5 P_{t-1} + \epsilon_{t+1}, \tag{5.29}$$

Table 5.5 Sample descriptive statistics

	feps	P	b	e	b/P	e/P	feps/P	Mktcap	Lev
N	60,170	60,170	60,170	60,170	60,170	60,170	60,170	60,170	59,744
Mean	−1.108	16.630	11.180	1.091	0.840	−0.048	−0.067	1683.0	0.884
StDev	−1.035	12.730	22.650	3.177	2.342	−0.318	−0.077	4759.0	5.718
P_1	−0.990	1.338	0.549	−3.078	0.072	−0.628	−0.193	12.02	0.000
Q1	−0.410	7.000	3.693	0.194	0.344	−0.022	−0.045	108.1	0.040
Median	−0.900	13.380	7.148	0.703	0.557	−0.054	−0.068	335.0	0.240
Q3	−1.600	22.820	12.610	1.447	0.859	−0.084	−0.094	1172.0	0.720
P_{99}	−4.550	58.750	73.990	10.020	5.524	−0.613	−0.245	23079.0	9.442

where

$$\delta_1 = \frac{R - (1+g) - \lambda}{(1+\beta_1+\beta_2)}, \tag{5.30}$$

$$\delta_2 = \frac{(1+g)(\beta_1+\beta_2)}{(1+\beta_1+\beta_2)}, \tag{5.31}$$

$$\delta_3 = \frac{g - \beta_1 + (R-1)\beta_2 + \lambda}{(1+\beta_1+\beta_2)}, \tag{5.32}$$

$$\delta_4 = \frac{(1+g)(\beta_1 - (R-1)\beta_2) - \lambda}{(1+\beta_1+\beta_2)}, \tag{5.33}$$

$$\delta_5 = \frac{\lambda}{(1+\beta_1+\beta_2)}, \tag{5.34}$$

where P_t and P_{t-1} are the contemporary stock price and lagged stock price, respectively. The regression coefficients δ_1—δ_5 are reported in Table 5.6.

Table 5.6 reports the regression coefficients (t-values) of δ_i (i=1-5) for each of the 150 industry-year portfolios based on the estimates in a two-year rolling window between 1980 and 2009. N is the number of observations in a two-year rolling window. The industry classification for the 5 industries is based on Ken French's website. Descriptive statistics are also reported, including mean, standard deviation, minimum, lower quartile, median, upper quartile, and maximum. Panels A and B report the results on a year-by-year and industry-by-industry basis, respectively. We observe that δ_1 and δ_5 are highly significant in explaining one-year ahead earnings, confirming that prices lead earnings after controlling for current earnings and book values. We also note that current earnings (δ_2) are a significant predictor of future earnings. Neither the coefficient of current book value (δ_3) nor the coefficient of lagged book value (δ_4) is statistically significant.[11] On average, five variables:

[11] It may suggest that analysts do not pay much attention to book value when they forecast net earnings.

Table 5.6 Regressing forecasted earnings on price, earnings, book value, lagged book value and lagged price

Panel A: By year, mean value for five industry

Year	δ_1	tv	δ_2	tv	δ_3	tv	δ_4	tv	δ_5	tv	$R^2(\%)$	N
1980	0.05	6.25	0.47	7.00	0.01	0.18	0.01	0.66	0.02	2.20	54.06	1682
1981	0.05	6.84	0.39	6.70	0.02	0.51	0.01	0.61	0.02	2.47	52.63	1812
1982	0.04	6.62	0.36	6.93	−0.01	−0.29	0.03	1.44	0.02	3.46	51.29	2013
1983	0.03	6.26	0.37	7.70	0.03	0.47	0.00	0.89	0.02	3.55	51.76	2284
1984	0.03	6.44	0.36	7.68	0.04	1.43	−0.01	−0.04	0.01	3.16	47.78	2411
1985	0.04	6.57	0.34	7.80	−0.01	0.10	0.03	1.26	0.01	2.87	41.19	2491
1986	0.04	6.56	0.30	6.91	−0.02	−0.57	0.05	1.96	0.01	1.53	33.29	2572
1987	0.03	5.64	0.28	6.50	−0.01	0.04	0.04	1.37	0.01	2.54	31.95	2572
1988	0.04	5.97	0.31	6.84	−0.01	0.24	0.04	1.23	0.01	2.21	32.95	2631
1989	0.03	4.75	0.29	6.66	0.02	1.18	0.01	0.63	0.02	3.26	35.22	2840
1990	0.03	4.91	0.29	6.21	0.02	0.69	0.02	0.85	0.02	4.24	38.75	2916
1991	0.03	5.92	0.29	6.40	0.00	−0.04	0.03	1.48	0.02	3.31	39.86	2942
1992	0.04	7.32	0.27	5.99	0.01	0.55	0.02	0.94	0.01	1.15	33.63	3085
1993	0.03	6.94	0.32	6.74	−0.01	0.25	0.03	1.11	0.01	2.77	36.99	3362
1994	0.03	6.19	0.33	7.24	0.00	−0.14	0.03	1.56	0.01	2.84	36.47	3761
1995	0.03	6.06	0.29	6.57	0.03	0.94	0.01	0.68	0.01	2.79	34.18	4203
1996	0.03	7.08	0.27	6.76	0.02	0.84	0.01	0.75	0.01	2.92	32.16	4549
1997	0.03	7.61	0.26	6.56	0.00	0.32	0.03	1.39	0.01	2.59	30.68	4744
1998	0.02	7.57	0.32	8.74	−0.01	−0.20	0.04	1.89	0.01	3.94	37.85	4734
1999	0.02	5.44	0.38	10.35	−0.02	−0.73	0.05	2.65	0.02	4.57	43.55	4444
2000	0.02	6.77	0.35	7.90	−0.02	−0.36	0.05	2.03	0.01	3.45	39.41	4088
2001	0.03	7.35	0.30	7.22	0.00	0.46	0.03	0.76	0.00	0.57	33.44	4058
2002	0.03	8.45	0.29	7.41	0.01	0.63	0.01	0.30	0.00	0.59	32.83	4217
2003	0.03	8.41	0.33	9.13	0.00	0.68	0.01	0.08	0.01	2.86	40.77	4361
2004	0.03	9.54	0.34	8.38	0.01	0.60	0.00	−0.04	0.00	0.18	40.1	4670
2005	0.03	8.58	0.31	7.56	0.01	0.52	−0.01	−0.19	0.00	0.42	35.82	4842
2006	0.03	7.69	0.31	7.67	0.00	0.13	0.01	0.03	0.00	0.91	33.93	4859
2007	0.03	7.28	0.34	8.81	−0.01	−0.28	0.02	0.41	0.01	2.15	37.04	4822
2008	0.03	7.58	0.32	9.20	−0.01	−0.95	0.02	1.30	0.01	2.28	34.28	4262
2009	0.03	9.50	0.28	8.49	0.00	0.14	0.01	0.23	0.01	2.03	33	4123
Mean	0.03	6.94	0.32	7.47	0.00	0.24	0.02	0.94	0.01	2.46	38.56	3545
StDev	0.01	1.18	0.04	1.03	0.02	0.54	0.02	0.70	0.01	1.14	6.72	1034
Min	0.02	4.75	0.26	5.99	−0.02	−0.95	−0.01	−0.19	0.00	0.18	30.68	1682
Q1	0.03	6.20	0.29	6.71	−0.01	−0.11	0.01	0.46	0.01	2.06	33.49	2587
Median	0.03	6.80	0.31	7.23	0.00	0.25	0.02	0.87	0.01	2.68	36.73	3910
Q3	0.03	7.58	0.34	7.87	0.01	0.58	0.03	1.38	0.02	3.24	40.60	4423
Max	0.05	9.54	0.47	10.35	0.04	1.43	0.05	2.65	0.02	4.57	54.06	4859

(continued)

Table 5.6 (continued)

Panel B: By industry, mean value for 30 years

Industry	δ_1	tv	δ_2	tv	δ_3	tv	δ_4	tv	δ_5	tv	$R^2(\%)$	N
1	0.03	8.25	0.28	6.74	0.01	0.80	0.01	0.45	0.02	3.99	40.09	20,985
2	0.04	8.34	0.30	8.57	0.00	0.07	0.02	1.21	0.01	2.01	36.30	26,202
3	0.03	8.22	0.27	7.56	0.00	−0.04	0.02	1.04	0.01	2.45	34.54	19,917
4	0.02	1.66	0.45	5.78	−0.01	−0.15	0.04	0.89	0.01	0.77	43.68	7818
5	0.04	8.21	0.31	8.69	0.01	0.54	0.02	1.11	0.01	3.08	38.20	31,440
Mean	0.03	6.94	0.32	7.47	0.00	0.24	0.02	0.94	0.01	2.46	38.56	21,272

current earnings, current and lagged prices, and current and lagged book values, together explain 38.6% of one-year ahead of analysts' forecasts of earnings.

From Eqs. (5.30)–(5.34), we can derive

$$1 + g = \frac{1 + \delta_2 + \delta_3 - \delta_5 + \sqrt{(1 + \delta_2 + \delta_3 - \delta_5)^2 - 4(\delta_2 - \delta_4 - \delta_5)}}{2}, \tag{5.35}$$

$$R = (1 + g)\left(1 + \frac{\delta_1 + \delta_5}{1 + g - \delta_2}\right), \tag{5.36}$$

$$\beta_1 = \frac{(R - 1)\delta_2 + \delta_4 + \delta_5}{(1 + g)(1 + g - \delta_2)}, \tag{5.37}$$

$$\beta_2 = \frac{\delta_2 - (\delta_4 + \delta_5)}{R(1 + g - \delta_2)}, \tag{5.38}$$

$$\lambda = \frac{(1 + g)\delta_5}{1 + g - \delta_2}. \tag{5.39}$$

Table 5.7 shows the implied long-term average cost of capital, growth rate, valuation parameters, accounting conservatism parameter, and the risk premium for each of the 150 industry-year portfolios for the 5-industry over the 1980–2009 period. The risk premium (RP) is calculated relative to the yield on a 10-year US government bond. Panels A and B report the results on a year-by-year and industry-by-industry basis, respectively. We observe that the annual mean cost of capital is 9.6% and the mean risk premium is 2.32% over 1980–2009. The estimated annual mean growth rate is 3.34%. We also note a downward trend in the cost of capital, with the average falling from 12% between 1980 and 1990 to 9.66% between 1991 and 2000, and finally to 6.48% between 2001 and 2009. While the average long-run growth is 3.95% between 1980 and 2003, the annual growth rate is not statistically different from zero after 2004. However, the risk premium exhibits an upward trend between 2004 and 2009, reflecting the fact that the risk-free rate decreases at a greater rate than the mean expected returns. This coincided with the 2008 financial and credit crisis, during which investors demanded a higher risk premium. As expected, all valuation weights on book value ($1 + \beta_1$) are greater than 1 over the 30 years. All valuation weights on earnings (β_2) are greater than

Table 5.7 Implied cost of equity capital, growth rate, valuation parameters, and risk premium

Panel A: by year, the mean value of 5-industry						
Year	(R-1)(%)	g(%)	β_1	β_2	λ	RP(%)
1980	14.710	2.190	0.157	0.722	0.037	3.283
1981	14.400	4.374	0.134	0.529	0.026	0.477
1982	13.340	3.979	0.141	0.419	0.030	0.329
1983	12.960	5.309	0.091	0.521	0.029	1.856
1984	12.080	4.605	0.053	0.503	0.022	-0.385
1985	10.780	2.901	0.115	0.401	0.022	0.165
1986	9.833	3.180	0.112	0.297	0.015	2.163
1987	10.280	3.908	0.103	0.279	0.020	1.886
1988	11.190	4.246	0.109	0.317	0.015	2.341
1989	11.340	4.525	0.075	0.307	0.026	2.850
1990	11.140	4.496	0.083	0.295	0.031	2.595
1991	10.520	4.292	0.091	0.306	0.023	2.657
1992	9.643	4.091	0.065	0.310	0.006	2.633
1993	9.355	3.317	0.115	0.453	0.018	3.485
1994	10.160	4.367	0.106	0.400	0.020	3.075
1995	10.330	4.887	0.062	0.324	0.018	3.756
1996	9.570	4.444	0.064	0.289	0.017	3.130
1997	9.202	4.660	0.087	0.262	0.014	2.852
1998	8.796	3.945	0.113	0.351	0.018	3.536
1999	9.359	4.135	0.137	0.435	0.024	3.709
2000	9.620	4.288	0.131	0.379	0.017	3.590
2001	8.166	3.682	0.065	0.346	0.001	3.146
2002	7.451	2.815	0.040	0.366	0.000	2.841
2003	7.089	2.182	0.076	0.484	0.011	3.079
2004	5.795	0.993	0.033	0.582	0.002	1.525
2005	5.426	0.557	0.013	0.477	0.004	1.136
2006	5.090	0.178	0.038	0.440	0.005	0.290
2007	5.855	0.844	0.076	0.456	0.010	1.225
2008	6.590	1.409	0.071	0.391	0.012	2.930
2009	6.706	1.285	0.042	0.347	0.009	3.446
Mean	9.559	3.336	0.087	0.400	0.017	2.320
St.Dev	2.557	1.454	0.036	0.104	0.009	1.199
Q1	7.630	2.346	0.064	0.312	0.011	1.608
Median	9.632	3.962	0.085	0.385	0.017	2.749
Q3	11.050	4.372	0.113	0.455	0.023	3.142
Panel B: by industry, the mean value for 30-year						
Industry	(R-1)(%)	g(%)	β_1	β_2	λ	RP(%)
1	10.030	3.032	0.067	0.318	0.023	2.786
2	9.827	2.758	0.076	0.347	0.014	2.588
3	8.445	2.676	0.067	0.290	0.014	1.206
4	8.905	5.012	0.135	0.687	0.013	1.666
5	10.590	3.203	0.088	0.357	0.020	3.355
Mean	9.559	3.336	0.087	0.400	0.017	2.320

zero and statistically significant at the 1% level. The conservatism parameters (λ) are always positive, with a mean value of 0.017. The Fama-MacBeth t-statistics for all five valuation parameters are statistically significant at the 1% level.

Consistent with industry practice, we can use the sample average growth rate, cost of capital, and valuation multiples as common parameters for all firms in each industry-year portfolio to derive the firm-specific one-period ahead returns. Therefore, the firm-specific implied expected one-period return IER_t at time t can be estimated from Eq. (5.20), by noting that $d_t = e_t + b_{t-1} - b_t$, as

$$\begin{aligned} IER_t &= (1+\overline{g}_{it})[1 - \tfrac{b_t}{P_t} - (\overline{\beta}_{1,it} - (\overline{R}_{it} - 1)\overline{\beta}_{2,it})\tfrac{b_{t-1}}{P_t} - (\overline{\beta}_{1,it} + \overline{\beta}_{2,it})\tfrac{e_t}{P_t}] \\ &+ (1+\overline{\beta}_{1,it} + \overline{\beta}_{2,it})\tfrac{E_t[e_{t+1}]}{P_t} + (1+\overline{\beta}_{1,it} - (\overline{R}_{it} - 1)\overline{\beta}_{2,it})\tfrac{b_t}{P_t} \\ &+ \overline{\lambda}_{it}\tfrac{(P_t - b_t - (P_{t-1} - b_{t-1})}{P_t} - 1, \end{aligned} \tag{5.40}$$

where $\overline{R}_{it} - 1, \overline{g}_{it}, \overline{\beta}_{1,it}, \overline{\beta}_{2,it}$ and $\overline{\lambda}_{i,t}$ are the long-term average cost of capital, growth rate, valuation parameters, and conservatism parameter, respectively, for firms in industry i and year t.

The 10-year US government bond yield is subtracted from the IER to compute the implied risk premium. This implied risk premium measures the expected risk premium (ERP) used in the following regression tests. To examine the (incremental) explanatory power of the implied expected return (IER) on future realized returns, the relationship between one-year ahead excess realized stock returns (i.e., one-year ahead realized returns subtracted by the 10-year US government bond yield, XRET1) on the ERP and other control variables is tested. 12-month buy-and-hold returns for each firm from April to March each year are calculated. These control variables include the unexpected return due to cash flow news, discount rate news, and conventional risk characteristics (the CAPM beta, book-to-market, firm size, leverage, term spread, and default spread). It is believed that a positive correlation between the ERP and XRET1 provides support for the validity of the IER. A valid proxy of expected return should also be consistent with established asset pricing theory (for example, Lintner, 1965; Sharpe, 1964; Modigliani and Miller, 1958). Although the true risk factors that determine expected returns are unknown or they may not be reliably estimated, as a first order approximation we can examine the relationship between the expected risk premium (ERP) and a few well-known risk proxies, such as market beta, leverage, default risk, and the market value of equity (size).

Following prior literature (e.g., Campbell, 1991; Vuolteenaho, 2002), when examining the relationship between the IER and realized future stock returns, we consider cash flow news (CFN) and discount rate news (DRN). CFN equals actual earnings per share for year $t + 1$ less analysts' forecasts of one-year ahead earnings per share or 'earnings surprise', scaled by stock price at time t. Vuolteenaho (2002) suggests that time t discount rate news proxy is a function of the time $t + 1$ change in the implied expected returns. Hence, time t discount rate news (DRN), is proxied by $(IER_{j,t} - IER_{j,t-1})$ for firm j in the analysis.[12] Following Fama and French (1989) and others, term spread and default spread are also considered. Term Spread is calculated as the difference between the 10-Year US Treasury constant maturity rate and the 3-month US T-Bill yields. The Default Spread is calculated as the difference between Moody's Seasoned Baa and Aaa Corporate Bond yields. Data on corporate bonds and US T-Bills/Bonds are obtained from the FRED database of the Federal Reserve Bank of St. Louis. Further, it may be reasonable to delete firm-year observations with the implied expected one-year ahead return less than the risk-free rate if the IER is qualified as a proxy for the expected return (Easton et al., 2009).[13] In the following analysis of the characteristics of expected return, such firm-year observations are eliminated.[14] Our interest is in the association between excess one-year ahead realized returns (XRET1) and excess implied expected risk premium (ERP). Size is measured as the logarithm of a firm's market capitalization, and leverage is the total debt divided by the firm's market capitalization as of 3-month after the fiscal year end. Total debt is the sum of long-term debt (DLTT) and short-term debt (DLC). Market beta is estimated using the market model, which utilizes the value-weighted NYSE/Amex market index return, incorporating at least 18 and up to 60 months of lagged monthly returns. The standard deviations of monthly returns are also computed using at least 18 months of data over the prior 60 months as a measure of total risk.

Table 5.8 Panel A provides descriptive statistics pertaining to XRET1, ERP, and other risk proxies. Mean and median estimates of the expected risk premium are 4.7% and 3.5%, respectively. While the median XRET1, 3.6% falls within the range of the expected risk premium, its standard deviation of 60.2% greatly exceeds the

---

[12] Note Botosan et al. (2011) argue that DRN is an economy-wide discount rate news proxy. In their analysis, DRN is measured by the one-year ahead change in the yields of the five-year treasury constant maturity as of the month the expected return estimates. If we use that measure, DRN becomes less significant, while the main results are similar.

[13] There are about 24% of firm-year observations with the IER less than the risk-free rate. This includes the IERs that declined between 2001 and 2009. Note that 31% of the firm-years in the Easton and Monahan (2005) sample (from 1981 to 1998) have values of implied cost of equity capital below the risk-free rate. This suggests that the IER is a downward-biased measure of expected return. The main results remain similar when we exclude firm-year observations with the IER less than zero, rather than using the risk-free rate. Further investigation shows that firms with IER <0 have smaller market capitalization than firms in the full sample (with median 230 vs. 335), smaller (negative) forward (forecasted) earnings yield (with median -1.3% vs. 6.8%) and much higher beta (with median 1.36 vs. 1.04). The averages of B/P are 0.84 and 3.03, respectively, for the full sample and firms with IER <0.

[14] One of the drawbacks inherent in one-period models is that they do not differentiate between short-term and long-term growth rates—the empirical growth construct is typically a long-term steady-state growth rate. This may, in turn, lead to an underestimation of the ICC at the portfolio level, similar to other firm-level ICC approaches. As a proxy of expected stock returns, the firm-level implied cost of capital is often regarded in existing literature as understating true expected returns due to model misspecification. The ICC literature also often further restricts the implied cost of capital less than zero. As a consequence, the ICCs usually show low volatilities and high Sharpe ratios. This is also a limitation of the IER as a proxy of expected return.

Table 5.8 Excess realized return, implied risk premium and risk proxies

Panel A: descriptive statistics

	$XRET_1$	ERP	CFN	DRN	Beta	Size	Lev	Term	Default
N	43,674	45,022	44,698	39,012	43,846	45,022	44,702	45,022	45,022
Mean	−0.111	0.047	−0.044	−0.012	1.058	6.014	0.699	1.685	1.095
StDev	−0.602	0.047	−0.156	0.069	0.610	1.723	1.922	1.373	0.582
p5	−0.582	0.005	−0.224	−0.106	0.213	3.360	0.000	−0.530	0.640
Q1	−0.213	0.019	−0.029	−0.023	0.614	4.753	0.060	0.580	0.690
Median	−0.036	0.035	−0.003	−0.005	0.984	5.924	0.260	1.580	0.960
Q3	−0.312	0.058	−0.004	0.010	1.395	7.182	0.714	2.840	1.180
p95	−1.008	0.135	−0.025	0.054	2.202	9.061	2.547	3.540	2.320

Panel B: returns on IER-sorted portfolios

IER quintiles	1	2	3	4	5	Q5–Q1
Mean of IER	0.073	0.087	0.099	0.116	0.179	0.107
Mean of 12 m ahead realized returns	0.087	0.088	0.096	0.111	0.174	0.087
Mean of 36 m ahead realized returns	0.366	0.404	0.393	0.425	0.566	0.201
Mean of 60 m ahead realized returns	0.750	0.796	0.810	0.899	1.216	0.466

standard deviation of ERP. Panel A also provides descriptive statistics for proxies of cash flow news, discount rate news, term spread, and default spread. CFN has a mean value of −0.044, which is statistically significantly negative at the 1% level, suggesting optimism in analysts' earnings forecasts. The mean of DRN is −0.012, which is also significantly negative, indicating an average annual decline in the IER over the sample period. The means of term spread and default spread are 1.685 and 1.095, respectively. The statistics also describe a sample where the average market risk is comparable to that of the market portfolio with a mean (median) beta of 1.058 (0.984) and a mean (median) debt-to-equity ratio of 69.9% (26%).

Table 5.8 Panel B documents IER's out-of-sample predictive ability with respect to future stock returns by sorting firms into quintiles of the implied expected return distribution at the end of March of each year. For each portfolio, the mean buy-and-hold return for the next 12 months is calculated. Hedge returns, which are the difference in returns between the top (Q5) and bottom (Q1) quintiles of IERs, are also calculated. It shows that the IER exhibits a monotonic relation with future realized returns. The difference in realized returns over 12 months between the top and bottom quintiles of IER, Q5–Q1, equals 8.7%. If the hedge returns represent the expected return effect, intuitively, the magnitude of the hedge returns should persist over time. Panel B, indeed, shows that the average realized return spreads between quintiles 5 and 1 are 20.1% for 36-month buy-and-hold returns and 46.6% for 60-month buy-and-hold returns.

Next, we examine the excess return predictive ability of the expected risk premium, ERP, at the firm level. We also investigate the cross-sectional relation between a set of conventional risk characteristics and ex post realized return. All regressions are based on a pooled sample, with year fixed effects and standard errors

Table 5.9 Regressing excess one-year ahead realized returns (XRET1) on the implied risk premium (ERP) and risk proxies

	XRET1	t-stat	XRET1	t-stat	XRET1	t-stat	XRET1	t-stat
ERP	1.83	2.62	2.15	3.66	1.55	3.52	1.51	4.6
CFN			1.23	12.77			1.35	12.68
DRN			−0.959	−4.66			−0.794	−4.34
Beta							0.018	0.46
Size							−0.022	−2.15
B/P							0.089	3.42
Term					0.039	1.28	0.034	1.04
Default					0.137	1.95	0.12	1.75
Constant	0.026	0.62	0.038	0.90	−0.178	−1.71	−0.054	−0.37
Adj-R^2	1.93%		8.02%		4.83%		11.70%	

clustered by firm and year as in Petersen (2009). Table 5.9 reports coefficients and their t-statistics (in brackets) for these regressions.

Notably, regardless of the risk proxies we control for, the implied risk premium retains significant explanatory power for excess one-year-ahead realized returns. Both CFN and DRN have significant incremental roles in explaining future realized returns. Specifically, the result of the univariate regression of excess realized returns on expected risk premium in Table 5.9 column 2 shows that ERP is positively related to XRET1 with a coefficient of 1.83, which is not statistically different from 1. The regression coefficient of the difference between XRET1 and ERP on expected risk premium is 0.83 with a t-statistic of 1.19. When we include our proxies for cash flow news and discount rate news in the regression, it reveals a strong positive relationship between excess realized returns and cash flow news and a strong negative relationship between excess realized returns and discount rate news. Adjusted R-squareds increase from 1.93 to 8.02%. This result is consistent with our expectation and with results documented in Vuolteenaho (2002) and Botosan et al. (2011). While market beta has a positive sign, it is not significantly related to excess future realized returns if book-to-market and size are included in the regression. Both term spread and default spread have the correct signs but are not statistically significant at the 5% level. The coefficient of book-to-market itself is positive and highly significant.

Given firm characteristics including growth of future investments, book-to-market, earnings-to-price, dividends-to-price and past returns are the main inputs in the estimation of the IER, we only examine the relationship between expected risk premium (ERP) and the CAPM beta, size, leverage, total risk, term spread and default spread to avoid drawing potential spurious inferences (Botosan and Plumlee, 2005; Easton and Monahan, 2016). Based on prior empirical studies on the cross-sectional determinants of returns, we expect the expected return to be positively associated with beta, leverage, the standard deviation of annual returns, and risk spreads, and negatively associated with firm size.

Table 5.10 Relation between implied risk premium and risk proxies

Beta	0.005			0.004	0.004	−0.003
t-stat	2.67			2.64	2.44	−1.41
Size		−0.007			−0.006	−0.005
t-stat		−12.39			−11.37	-9.46
Lev			0.006		0.005	0.005
t-stat			7.48		7.51	7.57
Term				0.000	0.000	
t-stat				−0.3	−0.13	
Default				0.012	0.010	
t-stat				5.37	3.05	
St.Dev						0.046
t-stat						6.24
Constant	0.043	0.088	0.043	0.031	0.067	0.057
t-stat	19.59	19.08	21.73	5.67	9.77	11.45
adj R^2	0.34%	5.94%	5.12%	2.35%	11.90%	12.10%

Table 5.10 shows that the results of univariate and multivariate regressions of the expected risk premium on market beta, firm size, and leverage are all in the theoretically predicted directions. Specifically, the expected risk premium is significantly positively related to beta and leverage but negatively related to firm size. However, when we control for total risk, there is an insignificant negative relation between the implied risk premium and beta. The total risk itself is strongly and positively related to EPR, reflecting a property that the I/B/E/S analysts' forecasts take into account more total risk than the firm's systematic risk.[15] In addition, the coefficient of beta remains very stable in magnitude, whether we use univariate or multivariate regressions, if excluding total risk. When we include the term spread and default spread into the regressions, we find that the default spread is statistically significantly related to the implied risk premium. However, the term spread shows a negative relation, though it is not statistically significant.

Although using benchmark industry averages in the valuation of an individual firm is a long-standing industry practice, grouping firms based on industry classification is known to be challenging in ensuring the homogeneity of firms. Further sorting based on firms' characteristics is a natural extension. Since the size of different firms within an industry can be significantly different and size is one of the most important characteristics of a firm, we can further group firms by size quintiles within each industry-year portfolio to infer the firm-specific IER.[16] The results in Wang (2018) confirm and strengthen the above findings.

[15] Hail and Leuz (2006) also suggest that the implied cost of capital seems to be more closely related to stock return volatility than to beta.

[16] Firms in the industry-year portfolios can also be further sorted based on firms' book-to-market ratio or their past realized returns instead of size.

The above analysis shows that the firm-specific measure of the implied expected return is intrinsically linked to commonly used financial ratios, including book-to-market, (forward) earnings yield, dividend-to-price, as well as growth and past returns. The expression yields the insight that expected returns are associated with the risk related to uncertainty about the future growth of the net present value of future investments. It provides an explanation as to why the book-to-market (B/M) ratio may help explain expected stock returns. Forward earnings yield is identified as an omitted factor in many factor models. It also demonstrates that accounting conservatism can lead to time-serial correlation in stock returns.

Note also that we estimate the unknown growth rate g at the industry-year level and plug it into the model, along with firm-specific variables, to obtain the firm-specific implied cost of capital. We could well have used an implied cost of capital and other coefficients at the industry-year level to estimate a firm-specific g if our objective is to estimate firm-specific growth.

5.5.3 Using Information Dynamics to Estimate Value and Predicting Stock Returns

Starting from linear information dynamics, Wang (2023) applies a special case of model (4.4) when $\omega_2 = 0$ to value equity value, and Eq. (5.13) to estimate equity returns. The corresponding information dynamics are

$$x_{t+1} = \omega x_t + G_t + \epsilon_{x,t+1}, \tag{5.41}$$

$$G_{t+1} = \gamma G_t + \epsilon_{g,t+1}. \tag{5.42}$$

They are the same as dynamics (3.42) and (3.41) when $\omega_2 = 0$.

The sample in Wang (2023) includes all listed securities in NYSE, Amex, and Nasdaq. Data are extracted from the CRSP monthly returns file, the Compustat industrial annual file, and forecasts of earnings from the Institutional Brokers Estimate System (I/B/E/S) from 1979 to 2015. The adjusted number of shares outstanding and adjusted price at the end of the fiscal year and the adjusted price of equity three months after the fiscal year-end are collected from CRSP. The cumulated adjustment factors for number of shares and stock price are collected from CRSP to calculate the adjusted number of shares outstanding and the adjusted price. Stock prices three months after the fiscal year-end are used to ensure that information about the prior year's financials has been incorporated into the analysts' forecasts of earnings. Relevant accounting data are collected from Compustat. Firms with negative book values (CEQ) are deleted. Earnings are measured as net income before extraordinary items (IB). One-year ahead analysts' forecasts of earnings ($feps_{t+1}$) are used as a proxy of the market's expectation of the firm's future earnings. Stock prices are used as a proxy for the intrinsic values of stocks. The median consensus forecasts of earnings per share at the first month after the

Table 5.11 Descriptive statistics of sample firms

Sample descriptive statistics									
	P_t	e_t	b_t	d_t	$feps_{t+1}$	$\frac{feps_{t+1}}{P_t}$	$\frac{e_t}{P_t}$	$\frac{b_t}{P_t}$	$\frac{b_{t-1}}{P_t}$
N	98,955	98,955	98,955	98,955	98,955	98,955	98,955	98,955	98,955
Mean	18.700	0.954	11.590	0.419	−1.199	−0.067	−0.035	0.719	0.701
St.Dev	18.740	−2.653	18.570	1.084	−1.530	−0.069	−0.142	0.659	0.707
p1	1.156	−5.190	0.465	0.000	−1.630	−0.192	−0.556	0.089	0.065
Q1	6.988	−0.139	3.710	0.000	−0.380	−0.043	−0.018	0.348	0.306
Median	13.500	−0.671	7.423	0.054	−0.900	−0.068	−0.053	0.568	0.529
Q3	23.880	−1.484	13.700	0.465	−1.660	−0.096	−0.084	0.871	0.848
p99	95.050	−9.324	74.320	3.996	−7.000	−0.255	−0.365	3.409	3.566

corresponding I/B/E/S-reported prior-year earnings announcements are used. All total variables used in the estimation are divided by the adjusted number of shares outstanding to reduce heteroskedasticity and increase comparability across time. In constructing the data set, 1% at the top and bottom stock prices, (price deflated) book value, (price deflated) earnings and dividends, number of shares outstanding, and (price deflated) analysts' consensus forecasts of earnings are deleted to avoid the influence of extreme observations. Table 5.11 presents the descriptive statistics of the sample firms. These are largely consistent with those reported in previous studies.

When $\omega_2 = 0$ in Eq. (4.3), we have

$$e_{t+1} = \delta_1 V_t + \delta_2 e_t + \delta_3 b_t + \delta_4 b_{t-1} + \epsilon_{t+1}, \tag{5.43}$$

where

$$\delta_1 = \frac{(R-\gamma)(R-\omega)}{R}, \tag{5.44}$$

$$\delta_2 = \frac{\omega\gamma}{R}, \tag{5.45}$$

$$\delta_3 = \frac{R(R-1)-(R-\gamma)(R-\omega)}{R}, \tag{5.46}$$

$$\delta_4 = -(R-1)\frac{\omega\gamma}{R}. \tag{5.47}$$

To estimate parameters (ω, γ, R), we can run cross-sectional regression based on Eq. (5.43):

$$\frac{feps_{t+1}}{P_t} = \delta_1 + \delta_2\frac{e_t}{P_t} + \delta_3\frac{b_t}{P_t} + \delta_4\frac{b_{t-1}}{P_t} + \frac{\epsilon_{t+1}}{P_t}. \tag{5.48}$$

From the regression coefficients and Eqs. (5.44)–(5.47), we can obtain (ω, γ, R). Alternatively, we can directly run nonlinear regressions in a three-year rolling window based on the equation below:[17]

$$\frac{feps_{t+1}}{P_t} = \frac{(R-\gamma)(R-\omega)}{R} + \frac{\omega\gamma}{R}\frac{e_t}{P_t} + [\frac{R(R-1)-(R-\gamma)(R-\omega)}{R}]\frac{b_t}{P_t} - \frac{(R-1)\omega\gamma}{R}\frac{b_{t-1}}{P_t} + \frac{\epsilon_{t+1}}{P_t}. \tag{5.49}$$

Table 5.12 reports the estimated parameters ($\omega, \gamma - 1$) and the implied cost of capital $R - 1$ ($\equiv ICC$) as well as their t-statistics on a year-by-year basis. The most noteworthy feature of the results in Table 5.12 is that on average, $1 < \gamma < R$, with the mean (median) of γ = 1.018 (1.017). 31 out of the 34 observed values of γ are significantly greater than 1. Only in 2006–2007, were the values of γ significantly less than 1. This suggests a lack of significant growth opportunities in the years leading up to the 2008 global financial crisis. The mean (median) of the persistence of abnormal earnings, ω, is 0.21 (0.20). These values are similar to those reported in Myers (1999). Consistent with Ashton and Wang (2013b), the cost of equity capital falls almost monotonically from a high of 14.9% in 1981 to 4.8% in 2006–2007. It was more than 10% in the 1980s and is between 4.8% and 6% after 2004. All are lower than 9% after 1992. The mean and median values are 8.3% and 7.7%, respectively. Comparing the trend of the implied cost of capital with ten-year U.S. government bond yields, we see that the cost of capital declines with the risk-free rate. The summary statistics of the estimated parameters, the persistence of abnormal earnings, and the growth rate ($\omega, \gamma - 1$) are presented in Panel A of Table 5.13.

Prior literature assumes empirically a temporally and cross-sectionally constant discount rate in model applications. To examine the impact of a fixed cost of capital on the estimation of information parameters and valuation for each firm-year, we follow the prior literature and assume a constant discount rate of 9% in the model implementation. Specifically, we run cross-sectional nonlinear regressions in a three-year rolling window with a constant $R - 1 = 9\%$ based on Eq. (5.49). We simultaneously estimate (ω, γ) each year and refer to two information parameters (ω, γ) as (ω', γ'), where the dashes denote estimates using a constant cost of capital. Panel B of Table 5.13 reports these summary statistics of the implied persistence of abnormal earnings (ω') and growth rate (γ'-1) as well as their t-statistics. We note that the persistence of the growth variable satisfies: $1 < \gamma' < R$ for all sample years. The mean and the median of the persistence of abnormal earnings (ω') are close to 0.23. In general, the magnitudes of ω' (γ') in Panel B and ω (γ) in Panel A are similar.

For comparison, we also estimate the information parameters in the sequential procedure as is normally adopted in the existing literature (e.g., Dechow et al., 1999). The procedure effectively sets G_t= 0 in estimating parameter ω, ignoring the possibility that G_t constitutes a correlated omitted variable in the information

---

[17] For a nonlinear regression, we first use (ω, γ, $R - 1$) = (0.2, 1.0, 0.09) as a starting point. These are parameter values similar to those used or reported in prior literature. The results are similar if we run regressions on an annual basis or using a five-year rolling window.

Table 5.12 Simultaneous estimation of information parameters and cost of capital

	ω	t-stat	$\gamma - 1$	t-stat	ICC	t-stat	N
1981	0.275	27.92	0.041	16.70	0.149	89.49	2174
1982	0.291	44.63	0.048	26.17	0.133	113.70	4346
1983	0.267	51.58	0.048	33.55	0.131	147.60	6606
1984	0.241	54.67	0.046	37.53	0.127	170.70	8718
1985	0.203	49.51	0.038	32.19	0.113	162.60	9164
1986	0.178	44.78	0.032	28.19	0.107	157.00	9410
1987	0.160	40.77	0.027	24.36	0.102	149.90	9600
1988	0.168	42.47	0.024	21.67	0.100	144.50	9730
1989	0.161	40.74	0.027	24.50	0.103	149.00	9867
1990	0.156	39.57	0.027	25.79	0.105	151.00	9923
1991	0.165	43.54	0.026	24.81	0.100	145.90	10,019
1992	0.157	42.12	0.024	24.00	0.093	136.40	10,324
1993	0.168	45.02	0.022	22.08	0.087	125.50	10,923
1994	0.192	51.05	0.018	17.89	0.085	124.10	12,060
1995	0.190	50.48	0.017	17.27	0.083	124.90	13,335
1996	0.181	50.53	0.017	17.76	0.082	128.90	14,532
1997	0.182	52.22	0.015	16.50	0.077	125.80	15,497
1998	0.171	50.95	0.013	15.43	0.074	123.20	15,692
1999	0.187	52.61	0.016	18.27	0.076	119.90	15,258
2000	0.203	54.34	0.016	18.12	0.076	110.40	14,402
2001	0.212	59.35	0.015	16.13	0.074	99.89	13,548
2002	0.220	63.10	0.017	17.39	0.073	93.32	12,836
2003	0.219	64.96	0.014	13.82	0.064	84.21	12,748
2004	0.230	69.56	0.009	8.88	0.057	78.40	12,899
2005	0.247	69.15	0.006	5.95	0.056	77.88	12,989
2006	0.293	74.74	−0.008	−7.18	0.048	63.02	13,135
2007	0.280	71.02	−0.006	−5.70	0.048	64.40	12,903
2008	0.205	58.45	0.005	4.85	0.056	74.56	12,599
2009	0.198	58.13	0.004	4.59	0.057	74.39	12,463
2010	0.198	57.11	0.004	4.30	0.059	75.71	12,280
2011	0.201	57.61	0.006	5.93	0.060	76.00	12,273
2012	0.236	64.68	0.003	2.77	0.057	77.77	12,291
2013	0.256	65.66	0.002	1.61	0.055	75.44	12,154
2014	0.252	57.40	0.003	2.80	0.056	65.80	9273
Mean	0.210	53.54	0.018	15.85	0.083	111.21	11,352
StDev	0.04	10.41	0.014	10.80	0.027	32.71	2918
Median	0.202	52.42	0.017	17.33	0.077	116.80	12,277

dynamics. Again, we assume $R-1=9\%$ in information dynamics (3.41) and (3.42) when $\omega_2=0$, and run regressions in a three-year rolling window. Specifically, we first estimate an unconditional value of ω from an abnormal earnings autoregression on a year-by-year basis. We then use the unconditional ω estimated to calculate G

Table 5.13 Summary statistics of information parameters estimated from different estimation procedures and alternative discount rates

	Mean	St.Dev	Min	Q1	Median	Q3	Max	FM-t
Panel A: simultaneous approach, $R - 1 = ICC$								
ω	0.210	0.040	0.156	0.179	0.202	0.240	0.293	30.39
t-stat	53.54	10.41	27.92	44.84	52.42	59.13	74.74	
$\gamma - 1$	0.018	0.014	−0.008	0.006	0.017	0.026	0.048	7.30
t-stat	15.85	10.80	−7.18	5.94	17.33	24.27	37.53	
Panel B: simultaneous approach, R˘1 = 9%								
ω'	0.228	0.057	0.142	0.189	0.233	0.274	0.357	23.25
t-stat	57.14	15.06	30.39	42.36	56.99	69.92	82.63	
$\gamma' - 1$	0.024	0.009	0.013	0.020	0.022	0.025	0.057	16.14
t-stat	22.04	4.94	12.32	18.36	22.65	25.82	31.40	
Panel C: sequential approach, R˘1 = 9%								
ω''	0.473	0.052	0.377	0.435	0.463	0.509	0.568	53.08
t-stat	24.42	5.10	8.76	21.08	25.22	27.23	33.48	
γ''	0.603	0.069	0.460	0.553	0.598	0.665	0.731	51.21
t-stat	20.79	8.02	6.66	16.32	18.86	27.33	35.70	
Panel D: compare the information parameters								
$\omega' - \omega$	0.018	0.022	−0.014	0.003	0.016	0.038	0.082	4.64
$\omega'' - \omega$	0.263	0.041	0.179	0.237	0.266	0.293	0.344	37.16
$\gamma' - \gamma$	0.006	0.012	−0.015	−0.004	0.006	0.013	0.034	2.88
$\gamma'' - \gamma$	−0.415	0.078	−0.588	−0.458	−0.427	−0.348	−0.262	−31.03

as: $G_t = feps_{t+1} - (R-1)b_t - \omega(e_t - (R-1)b_{t-1})$, and finally estimate γ from regressions based on information dynamic (3.41). We report the summary statistics of the estimates (ω, γ) in Panel C of Table 5.13. We refer to (ω, γ) as (ω'', γ''), where the double dashes denote their values based on the sequential estimates of the parameters. We observe values of ω'' and γ'' are very similar to those reported in Choi et al. (2006). The mean value estimates for the persistence of abnormal earnings and G are 0.473 and 0.603, respectively. ω'' is in a range of 0.377 to 0.568, while γ'' is between 0.46 and 0.731. While the sequential estimation procedure produces values of the persistence (γ'') of G that are significantly less than 1, in striking contrast, γ' estimated from the simultaneous estimation procedure is significantly greater than 1 in each of the sample years as reported in Panel B.

Finally, a formal comparison of parameter estimates is presented in Panel D of Table 5.13, which reports the summary statistics in differences between information parameters estimated using different discount rates and estimation procedures. It shows that both persistence of abnormal earnings and G from the simultaneous estimation procedure when assuming a constant discount rate are statistically significantly larger than those when using a time-varying discount rate, the mean of $(\omega' - \omega)$ is 0.018 and mean of $(\gamma' - \gamma)$ is 0.006. It suggests that information parameter estimates (ω', γ') may be upwardly biased when using a constant discount rate $R - 1 = 9\%$ relative to using a time-varying implied cost of capital as a discount rate. This result has implications for estimating the intrinsic value of equity, as we discuss below. Panel D also shows that the persistence of abnormal earnings is larger and the persistence of G is much smaller when using the sequential estimation procedure than when using the simultaneous estimation procedure. The mean of $(\omega'' - \omega)$ is 0.263 and mean of $(\gamma'' - \gamma)$ is -0.415.

Because the cost of capital varies by industry and competition is mainly between firms in the same industry, we can estimate the information parameters and time-varying industry-specific cost of equity capital by running industry-year regressions. This allows the information parameters to reflect variation in economic and accounting environments across industries and over years (Fama and French, 1997; Barth et al., 1999). Since some industries only have a limited number of observations in some sample years, firms are grouped into five industries based on the industry classification from Ken French's website, and regressions are run in a three-year rolling window.[18] Since the proposed approach utilizes time t information contained in stock prices, we make an out-of-sample comparison of valuation bias and inaccuracy with that in existing approaches.

Three parameters $(\omega_{it}, \gamma_{it}, R_{it})$ for industry i in year t are estimated either from a simultaneous estimation procedure or a sequential procedure. When applying a sequential procedure, we assume $R_{it} - 1 = 9\%$ for each firm-year. The persistence of abnormal earnings (ω_{it}) is the regression coefficient from 3-year rolling window regressions on an industry-year basis: $\frac{x_{t+1}}{P_t} = \omega_0 + \omega \frac{x_t}{P_t} + \epsilon_{x,t+1}$, where $x_{t+1} = e_{t+1} - (R-1)b_t$ is calculated by using realized earnings. ω_0 is the intercept term. The persistence of G (γ_{it}) is estimated from 3-year rolling window regressions on an industry-year basis: $\frac{G_{t+1}}{P_t} = \gamma_0 + \gamma \frac{G_t}{P_t} + \epsilon_{g,t+1}$, where $G_t = feps_{t+1} - (R-1)b_t - \omega x_t$, and $feps_{t+1}$ is one-year ahead analysts' forecasts of earnings. γ_0 is the intercept term. When applying a simultaneous procedure, we use information up to time t-1 and estimate $(\omega_{it}, \gamma_{it}, R_{it} - 1)$ for industry i in year t based on Eq. (5.49). We also estimate $(\omega_{it}, \gamma_{it})$ for industry i in year t by assuming $R_{it} - 1 = 9\%$ from regression on Eq. (5.49).

With different sets of information parameters estimated using different estimation procedures and different discount rates, Eqs. (4.4) and (4.5) when $\omega_2 = 0$ give different sets of intrinsic values of equity shares. Following prior literature, the extreme 1% of the model predicted values are deleted, and negative predicted equity values are set to zero (Barth et al., 1999, 2005). Moreover, the extreme 1% of bias and inaccuracy are winsorized.

Table 5.14 reports the valuation bias and inaccuracy with the theoretical coefficient of each variable in model (4.4), estimated at time t information from the sequential approach, and with the theoretical coefficients of relevant variables estimated at time t-1 information from the simultaneous approach. Panel A of Table 5.14 shows that the intrinsic value estimated from the sequential procedure understates stock price by 25.8% on average, which is similar to those reported

[18] Results are quantitatively similar when we group firms in 12-industry and running a 10-year rolling window regression.

Table 5.14 Valuation bias and valuation inaccuracy

	N	Mean	StDev	Q1	Median	Q3
Panel A: valuation bias						
R-1 = 9%, Sequential estimation	76,653	0.257	0.426	0.090	0.348	0.545
R-1 = 9%, Simultaneous estimation	76,653	−0.105	0.662	−0.340	0.064	0.323
R-1 = ICC, Simultaneous estimation	76,653	−0.099	0.593	−0.316	0.033	0.283
H0: mean of valuation bias (SIM 9%) = mean of bias (SEQ 9%), t-statistic = - 180						
H0: mean of valuation bias (SIM ICC) = mean of bias (SEQ 9%), t-statistic = - 190						
H0: mean of valuation bias (SIM ICC) = mean of bias (SIM 9%), t-statistic = - 4.06						
Panel B: valuation inaccuracy						
R-1 = 9%, Sequential estimation	76,653	0.418	0.269	0.221	0.404	0.582
R-1 = 9%, Simultaneous estimation	76,653	0.462	0.486	0.160	0.329	0.572
R-1 = ICC, Simultaneous estimation	76,653	0.413	0.438	0.140	0.295	0.518
H0: mean of valuation bias (SIM 9%) = mean of bias (SEQ 9%), t-statistic = 23.01						
H0: mean of valuation bias (SIM ICC) = mean of bias (SEQ 9%), t-statistic = − 3.06						
H0: mean of valuation bias (SIM ICC) = mean of bias (SIM 9%), t-statistic = − 35.81						

in the existing literature. On the other hand, the intrinsic value estimated from the simultaneous procedure overstates stock prices on average by 9.8–10.4% depending on whether the discount rate is assumed to be time-varying or constant. The median bias from the sequential procedure is 34.9%. In sharp contrast, it is between 3.6 and 6.5% from the simultaneous procedure. When using the simultaneous procedure and a constant discount rate of $R - 1 = 9\%$, equity value is overstated more than when using a time-varying implied cost of capital as a discount rate. This is consistent with Panel D of Table 5.13 since information parameter estimates (ω', γ') are upwardly biased relative to (ω, γ). The smallest median bias is based on the information dynamics with a time-varying industry-specific discount rate. Based on the simultaneous estimation procedure, there is no evidence of systematic out-of-sample undervaluation or overvaluation of stock prices. This also leads to high standard deviations of valuation biases relative to those from the sequential procedure. While the means of valuation inaccuracy are comparable from different estimation approaches, Panel B of Table 5.14 shows that the first quartile, median, and third quartile valuation inaccuracy using the simultaneous estimation procedure are all lower than those from the sequential estimation procedure. In particular, the information dynamics estimated from the time-varying discount rate generate the most accurate valuation. The median valuation inaccuracy is 29.7%, which is significantly smaller than 40.4% when the sequential estimation procedure is used. These results suggest that we should simultaneously estimate both information parameters (ω, γ) and a time-varying cost of equity capital when implementing earnings-based valuation models. It also indicates that G is not subordinate to the abnormal earnings in valuation.

If we use the one-year ahead analysts' forecasts of earnings as a proxy for the market expectation of firms' one-period ahead earnings and assume $\omega_2 = 0$,

Eq. (5.13) gives an estimate of the expected stock returns. That is, a proxy for the expected stock return for firm j in industry i at time t is

$$E_t[\frac{P_{t+1}+d_{t+1}}{P_t}] = \gamma_{it} + \frac{R_{it}}{R_{it}-\omega_{it}}\frac{feps_{t+1}}{P_t} - (\gamma_{it}-1)\frac{b_t}{P_t} - \frac{\omega_{it}\gamma_{it}}{R_{it}-\omega_{it}}\frac{e_t}{P_t} - \frac{(R_{it}-1)\omega_{it}}{R_{it}-\omega_{it}}\frac{b_t-\gamma_{it}b_{t-1}}{P_t}, \tag{5.50}$$

where the industry-year information parameters (ω_{it}, γ_{it}) and discount rate (R_{it}-1) are estimated simultaneously. To evaluate the usefulness of the proxy, we can follow prior literature and test whether it can predict realized future stock returns. Based on two tautologies, the log-transformed realized t+1 period returns are usually decomposed into three components: "true" expected return, cash flow news (CFN), and discount rate news (DRN) at $t+1$. Denote $R_t = \ln(1+RET_t)$ the log of the realized one-period ahead stock returns (RET_t), and $ER_t = \ln(1+MPR_t)$ the log of model (5.50) predicted returns, where $MPR_t = E_t[P_{t+1}+d_{t+1}]/P_t - 1$. When future realized cash flows or earnings are greater (less) than the expected cash flows or earnings, time t+1 realized return will be greater (less) than the expected return, all else being equal. When future discount rates are upwardly (downwardly) revised, the time $t+1$ realized return will be lower (higher) than the expected return, all else being equal. By definition, the two news components are unpredictable *ex ante*. Vuolteenaho (2002) suggests that the proxy for discount rate news should be a function of the time t+1 change in the implied expected returns and firm-specific. Hence, consistent with Easton and Monahan (2005, 2016), time t+1 discount rate news is proxied by $DRN_{t+1} = resER_{t+1}/(1-0.98\kappa)$, where $resER_{t+1}$ is the residual from the following firm level model predicted return regression: $ER_{t+1} =$ constant$+\kappa ER_t + resER_{t+1}$ and κ is the slope.[19] It captures firm-specific discount rate shocks. Cash flow news is defined as actual earnings per share for year $t+1$ less analysts' forecasts of one-year ahead earnings per share or "earnings surprise", scaled by stock price at time t. It intends to capture firm-specific cash flow shocks. Therefore, we examine the relationship between the realized one-period-ahead stock returns and the model (5.50) predicted returns after controlling for CFN and DRN. In the following regression:

$$XRET_{t+1} = \delta_0 + \delta_1 XER_t + \delta_2 CFN_{t+1} + \delta_3 DRN_{t+1} + \varepsilon_{t+1},$$

where $XRET_{t+1} = R_{t+1} - \ln(1+r_f)$ and $XER_{t+1} = ER_{t+1} - \ln(1+r_f)$ are the one-year ahead excess realized stock returns and the excess model predicted returns, respectively. r_f is the 10-year US government bond yield, δ_1 and δ_2 are expected to be close to one and δ_3 is expected to be close to minus one if the model predicted returns (MPR) are a good proxy for the expected returns. Since the proxy of expected return is measured with error, the coefficients of XER, CFN, and DRN are expected to differ from their theoretical values.

[19] To estimate the firm-level discount rate news, we delete all firms with less than 6 observations in the firm-level regressions. As a result, the sample firms are reduced from 10,759 to 4696.

Table 5.15 Relation between excess realized returns and excess model-predicted returns

Panel A: descriptive statistics								
	N	Mean	StDev	P5	Q1	Median	Q3	P95
XRET	60,688	0.009	0.420	-0.712	−0.186	0.042	0.243	0.610
XER	61,265	0.026	0.035	-0.020	0.003	0.021	0.041	0.090
CFN	61,265	−0.024	0.093	-0.164	−0.031	−0.004	0.007	0.052
DRN	56,569	0.000	0.077	-0.061	−0.020	−0.003	0.016	0.075
Panel B: fixed effect regression								
Univariate regression				Multivaiate regression				
	Const.	XER	R^2	Const.	XER	CFN	DRN	R^2
XRET	-0.027	1.410	0.014	−0.002	2.310	1.246	−0.992	0.102
t-value	-12.85	29.06		−0.93	49.3	58.35	−49.05	
Panel C: the Fama-MacBeth regression								
Univariate regression				Multivaiate regression				
	Const.	XER	R^2	Const.	XER	CFN	DRN	R^2
XRET	−0.007	0.758	0.017	0.017	1.736	1.418	−1.104	0.156
t-value	−0.26	3.73		0.66	11.53	11.84	−7.82	

Table 5.15 Panel A reports the summary statistics of the one-year ahead excess realized stock returns ($XRET$), the model-predicted excess returns (XER), cash flow news (CFN), and discount rate news (DRN). It shows that $XRET$ is much more volatile than XER. The mean of $XRET$ is much smaller than its median, while the mean and the median of XER are similar. Panel B presents regression coefficients (t-values) of the one-year ahead excess realized stock returns ($XRET$) on the model-predicted excess returns (XER). Two-way cluster-robust standard errors are used to correct for both cross-sectional and time series dependence. The coefficient of XER in the univariate regression is 1.41, which is significantly different from zero (t-statistic 29.06).[20] In the multivariate regression, the coefficient of XER is 2.31 with t-statistic of 49.3. It suggests that ER is a downward-biased measure of the expected return as documented in the ICC literature. The results in Table 5.15 are, however, in contrast with findings in Easton and Monahan (2005), who find that many popular ICC measures are negatively associated with realized returns after controlling for CFN and DRN. The coefficients on proxies for CFN and DRN are positive (1.246) and negative (−0.992), respectively, with theoretically predicted signs. In particular, the coefficient of DRN is statistically indifferent from minus one. Panel C reports the cross-sectional regression results based on the Fama and MacBeth (1973) method. We report the average estimates in the sample period. While the coefficient of XER is less (greater) than one in the

[20] Guay et al. (2011) report that the coefficients of most ICC measures are between −0.33 and 0.43 in univariate cross-sectional regressions, and they are not statistically distinguishable from zero at conventional levels.

Table 5.16 12-, 24- and 36-month ahead realized returns from the model-predicted return decile sorted portfolios

	1	2	3	4	5	6	7	8	9	10
Return	0.040	0.056	0.066	0.074	0.081	0.088	0.096	0.106	0.123	0.174
bhr1	0.099	0.112	0.129	0.132	0.145	0.151	0.159	0.177	0.181	0.228
Beta	1.245	1.172	1.074	1.021	0.978	0.947	0.956	0.994	1.033	1.093
B/M	0.510	0.518	0.535	0.560	0.584	0.627	0.664	0.719	0.810	0.993
mkcap	6.161	6.226	6.265	6.277	6.272	6.231	6.039	5.909	5.677	5.351
Sharpe ratio	0.087	0.133	0.181	0.185	0.246	0.287	0.304	0.319	0.305	0.350
bhr2	0.179	0.207	0.234	0.265	0.271	0.280	0.308	0.313	0.341	0.416
bhr3	0.268	0.335	0.372	0.405	0.436	0.437	0.463	0.505	0.540	0.621

univariate (multivariate) regression, both CFN and DRN have correct signs. They are closer to their theoretical values than those reported in prior studies.[21]

We also document the model-predicted returns' out-of-sample predictive ability with respect to future realized stock returns by sorting firms into deciles of the model-predicted return distribution at the end of each financial year in Table 5.16.

For each portfolio, the mean buy-and-hold returns for the next 12-, 24-, and 36-months are calculated, bhr1, bhr2, and bhr3. It exhibits a strictly monotonic relationship with future realized returns for all three horizons. The hedge returns, as measured by the differences in realized returns over 12-, 24-, and 36-month periods between the top and bottom deciles of the predicted expected stock returns, are equal to 13, 23.8, and 35.3%, respectively. In addition, Table 5.16 appears to suggest that the monotonic relation with future realized returns is associated with the book-to-market ratio (B/M) and firms' market capitalization (mkcap). It is also almost monotonically positively related to the Sharpe ratio, though the CAPM beta cannot explain it.[22]

It is well documented that the I/B/E/S analysts' forecasts are upwardly biased and only available for large and financially healthy firms, especially in the earlier sample years. To examine whether the underrepresented small firms and financially distressed firms affect the results in valuation bias and valuation inaccuracy, we use the Heckman two-stage correction to account for the endogeneity in this selection bias. We estimate the probability of being included in the I/B/E/S consensus forecast as a function of the control variables presented in Eq. (5.49) and firm size in the first stage. While size is assumed to affect the probability of analysts' following, it is not supposed to influence earnings per share.

Table 5.17 reports the descriptive statistics of the estimated information parameters ($\omega_{it}, \gamma_{it}, R_{it} - 1$) for industry i in year t alongside the inverse Mills

---

[21] Studies show that realized stock returns are often insensitive to discount rate news when regressing realized returns on a proxy of the expected return, CFN and DRN (Easton and Monahan, 2005; Nekrasov and Ogneva, 2011; Mohanram and Gode, 2013).

[22] It is well documented that Beta is notorious for its poor association with stock returns despite its deep theoretical appeal (e.g., Frazzini and Pedersen, 2014).

Table 5.17 Valuation bias and valuation inaccuracy with the Heckman two-stage correction

	ω	t-stat	$\gamma - 1$	t-stat	ICC	t-stat	IMR	t-stat	Bias	Inaccu.
N	130,191	130,191	130,191	130,191	130,191	130,191	130,191	130,171	71,079	71,079
Mean	0.185	23.74	0.015	6.44	0.082	55.33	0.019	2.61	−0.146	0.438
StDev	0.075	5.70	0.017	4.95	0.025	23.89	0.045	4.95	0.661	0.516
Q1	0.146	19.83	0.005	2.90	0.066	41.68	−0.004	−0.47	−0.359	0.142
Median	0.161	23.41	0.012	7.17	0.081	59.72	0.023	3.10	0.008	0.297
Q3	0.192	27.44	0.020	9.85	0.097	74.37	0.050	6.40	0.261	0.527

ratio (IMR=λ) between 1981 and 2014. They are estimated from the pooled cross-sectional nonlinear regressions on an industry-year basis by applying the simultaneous procedure on Eq. (5.49). It shows that these information parameters are compatible with those reported in Table 5.12. The mean and the median of λ are significantly positive. However, this is mainly because all λ are significantly positive from 1981 to 2003. In fact, all λ are not significantly different from zero after 2008. It suggests that unobserved factors that make the I/B/E/S forecasts are more likely to be associated with upwardly biased forecasts in the earlier sample years. Table 5.17 also reports the descriptive statistics of the valuation bias and inaccuracy based on the Heckman two-stage correction model. It shows that the magnitudes are similar to those reported in Table 5.14.

The above analyses are based on the 5-industry classification for grouping firms. The 5-industry classification can provide sufficient numbers of observations within each cross-section to alleviate the concern that finite-sample estimates from the generalized method of moments (GMM) may deviate significantly from their asymptotic values, but it may not achieve sufficient homogeneity. We replicate the above results using the Fama-French 12-industry classification to address this concern. The results are generally consistent with those based on the 5-industry classification.

5.6 Application of Synthetic Price Multiples

The investment professionals appear to prefer using price multiples in practical valuations. However, verifying the validity of a proxy for the target company's price multiple is challenging since there is no rigorous theoretical foundation to guide investors on how to identify comparable peers, select value drivers, and aggregate the peers' price multiples. The target company's price multiples disconnect from the popular discounted cash flow (DCF) valuation models introduced in the valuation textbooks. This section aims to bridge the gap between price multiples and DCF models by applying a "synthetic price multiple" introduced in Sect. 5.3.2.

5.6.1 Data Description

The sample includes all listed companies in NYSE, Amex, and Nasdaq. Data are extracted from the CRSP monthly returns file, the Compustat industrial annual file, and forecasts of earnings from the Institutional Brokers Estimate System (I/B/E/S) from 1979 to 2018.[23] The adjusted number of shares outstanding and adjusted

[23] Data in 2018 is one-year ahead forecasts, and data in 1979 is one-year lagged values over the sample period.

price of equity three months after the fiscal year-end are collected from CRSP. The cumulated adjustment factors for number of shares and stock price are collected from CRSP to calculate the adjusted number of shares outstanding and the adjusted price. The stock price three months after the fiscal year-end is used to ensure that information about the prior year's financials has been incorporated in the analysts' forecasts of earnings. Relevant accounting data are collected from Compustat. Firms with negative book values (CEQ) are deleted. Earnings are measured as net income before extraordinary items (IB). In this example, we use the one-year ahead analysts' forecasts of earnings ($feps_{t+1}$) as a proxy of the market expectation of firms' one-year ahead earnings ($E_t[e_{t+1}]$). The median consensus forecasts of earnings per share at the first month after the corresponding I/B/E/S-reported prior-year earnings announcements are used. All total variables used in the estimation are divided by the adjusted number of shares outstanding to reduce heteroskedasticity and increase comparability across time. In constructing the data set, 1% at the top and bottom of stock price, (price deflated) book value, (price deflated) earnings, dividends, number of shares outstanding, and (price deflated) analysts' consensus forecasts of earnings are simultaneously deleted to avoid the influence of extreme observations.

In Table 5.18, price (P) is the adjusted price per share. e, b, and d are, respectively, earnings per share, book value per share, and dividends per share based on the adjusted number of shares. Forward return on equity (ROE_1) is $feps$ scaled by book value. Return on equity (ROE) is net income before extraordinary items scaled by lagged book value. Table 5.18 shows the statistics of variables of interest in our analysis. For illustration in the application of value-to-forward earnings, we delete firm-year observations with negative consensus forecasts of one-year ahead earnings and divide the full sample into 12 industries using the classification from Ken French's website.[24]

5.6.2 Estimation of Industry-year Information Dynamic Parameters and Cost of Equity Capital

Based on 104,289 firm-year observations from the US sample between 1980 and 2017, we first estimate the relevant parameters that describe companies' economic and accounting characteristics for each industry year. The above sections provide a foundation on how we can simultaneously estimate valuation parameters ($\omega_1, \omega_2, R, \gamma$). From Eq. (4.3), the expected one-year ahead earnings can be written in terms of current earnings, current and lagged book values, and current stock

[24] https://mba.tuck.dartmouth.edu/pages/faculty/ken.french/data_library.html.

Table 5.18 Sample descriptive statistics

Panel A: sample statistics

	P	e	b	d	$feps$	$\frac{feps}{P}$	$\frac{e}{P}$	$\frac{b}{P}$	ROE_1	ROE
Mean	20.120	0.987	10.560	0.329	1.394	0.081	0.043	0.653	0.163	0.122
St.Dev	20.550	1.626	10.330	0.518	1.363	0.049	0.122	0.453	0.140	0.206
P_1	0.971	−3.60	0.404	0.000	0.030	0.004	−0.45	0.081	0.006	−0.47
$Q1$	7.273	0.241	3.840	0.000	0.490	0.050	0.028	0.340	0.093	0.058
P_{50}	14.250	0.758	7.643	0.083	1.000	0.071	0.055	0.552	0.140	0.126
$Q3$	25.560	1.572	13.810	0.462	1.830	0.100	0.085	0.839	0.196	0.189
P_{99}	104.40	6.302	50.960	2.362	6.800	0.250	0.225	2.309	0.630	0.666

Panel B: Pearson correlation matrix

	P	e	b	d	$feps$	$\frac{feps}{P}$	$\frac{e}{P}$	$\frac{b}{P}$	ROE_1	ROE
P	1									
e	0.530	1								
b	0.642	0.506	1							
d	0.389	0.450	0.497	1						
$feps$	0.769	0.692	0.709	0.521	1					
$\frac{feps}{P}$	−0.23	0.151	0.044	0.118	0.223	1				
$\frac{e}{P}$	0.049	0.564	0.112	0.158	0.192	0.266	1			
$\frac{b}{P}$	−0.28	−0.07	0.283	0.085	−0.06	0.449	−0.02	1		
ROE_1	0.085	0.094	−0.22	−0.01	0.194	0.256	0.061	−0.40	1	
ROE	0.126	0.459	−0.04	0.073	0.187	0.116	0.543	−0.23	0.328	1

value.[25] We use the one-year ahead analysts' forecasts of earnings as a proxy for the market's expected earnings and stock price as a proxy for the intrinsic value under the assumption of aggregate market efficiency. To reduce the effects of endogeneity, we can alternatively write it in the form of the forward earnings-to-price ratio in terms of the current earnings-to-price, book value-to-price, and lagged book value-to-price ratios as below:

$$\begin{aligned}\frac{e_{t+1}}{P_t} &= \frac{(R-\gamma)(R-\omega_1)}{R} + \frac{\omega_1\gamma}{R}\frac{e_t}{P_t} + [R-1-\omega_2 - \frac{(R-\gamma)(R-\omega_1)}{R}]\frac{b_t}{P_t} \\ &+\gamma[\omega_2 - \frac{(R-1)\omega_1}{R}]\frac{b_{t-1}}{P_t} + \epsilon_{e,t+1}.\end{aligned} \quad (5.51)$$

Note that Eq. (5.51) is exactly identified since there are four "instruments" and four "parameters": $(\omega_1, \omega_2, R, \gamma)$. We can use a jack-knifing procedure to simultaneously estimate firm-industry-year-specific parameters (Wang, 2018; Peng et al., 2024). Specifically, given the four parameters are connected in a nonlinear fashion,

25 Though using net incomes violates the clean surplus accounting assumption, it eliminates potentially confounding effects of one-time items or non-recurring items. We use net income as a proxy not only because dirty surplus accounting is not a first-order concern but also because empirical evidence shows that the earnings-based valuation model is robust to dirty surplus earnings (Isidro et al., 2006; Heinrichs et al., 2013).

we can run cross-sectional nonlinear regressions using data for each firm-year in the industry i without using the target firm's data to generate parameters, $(\omega_{it,1}, \omega_{it,2}, \gamma_{it}, R_{it})$. This allows the information parameters to reflect variations in economic and accounting environments across industries and over the years. This contrasts with most accounting-based valuation literature, which assumes a constant discount rate for all firms and all years in the model application. To capture the time trend and mitigate issues related to a limited number of observations in some industry years, we run regressions on a five-year rolling window basis.

Table 5.19 reports the average implied parameters in information dynamics (3.40) and (3.41), $(\omega_1, \omega_2, \gamma - 1)$ and the cost of equity capital $(r = R - 1)$ as well as their t-statistics on a year-by-year basis across 12-industry based on Eq. (5.51).[26] It shows that the mean and the median of the expected (nominal) long-term growth rates $(\gamma - 1)$ are 3.9 and 4.0%, respectively. The expected growth rates have a declining trend after the turn of the century, with a minimum value of 2.4% in 2007. The cost of equity capital has exhibited a clear trend of decline from a high of 15.1% in 1981 to 7.2% in 2016. Its mean and median are 9.8 and 9.3%, respectively. The last column displays the average annual risk premium (RP), calculated relative to the yield on a ten-year US government bond. The risk premiums (RP) of equity tend to increase over the years, with both the mean and median being approximately 3.6%. The persistence of abnormal earnings (ω_1) is between 0.059 and 0.366. It declines from 1980 to the mid-1990s, indicating that competitors may mimic innovations, so the persistence of abnormal profits is quickly diminishing. The persistence then stabilizes in a narrow range. The conservatism parameter (ω_2) is significantly positive in most sample years with a mean (median) of 0.03 (0.029).

Table 5.20 reports the average estimates on an industry-by-industry basis over 38 years. We use a nonlinear least squares procedure from 5-year rolling window regressions to simultaneously estimate four parameters, $\omega_1, \omega_2, (\gamma - 1)$ and $(R - 1)$ based on Eq. (5.51). As we would expect, industry #10 "Healthcare, Medical Equipment, and Drugs" has the highest growth rate $(\gamma - 1)$ of 4.9%. Industry #3 "Manufacturing" and industry #4 "Oil, Gas, and Coal Extraction and Products" have the lowest growth rate of 3.3%. Industry #7 "Telephone and Television Transmission" has the lowest cost of capital of 8.4% and the lowest risk premium of 2.1%. Industry #2 "Consumer Durables" has the highest cost of equity capital of 11.1% and risk premium of 4.9%. Industry #8 "Utilities" and industry #5 "Chemicals and Allied Products" have the highest persistence of abnormal earnings of 0.189. Industry #6 "Computers, Software, and Electronic Equipment" has the lowest persistence of abnormal earnings of 0.085 and the smallest accounting conservatism parameter of 0.019. These parameters reflect industry-specific effects.

---

[26] Since they are nonlinear regressions, we first use $(\omega_1, \omega_2, \gamma, R - 1) = (0.2, 0.05, 1.0, 0.09)$ as a starting point. These are parameter values similar to those reported or used in prior literature.

Table 5.19 Simultaneous estimation of information parameters and the cost of capital

	ω_1	t-stat	ω_2	t-stat	γ-1	t-stat	r_e	t-stat	RP
1980	0.366	10.17	0.07	3.36	0.047	9.38	0.15	40.89	0.036
1981	0.345	11.07	0.059	3.51	0.05	10.22	0.151	47.71	0.012
1982	0.336	11.96	0.059	4.24	0.055	11.81	0.145	49.83	0.015
1983	0.311	11.21	0.053	4.15	0.056	12.32	0.14	51.65	0.029
1984	0.233	9.92	0.037	3.08	0.056	13.00	0.131	56.52	0.007
1985	0.216	10.08	0.039	3.41	0.056	13.46	0.125	55.86	0.019
1986	0.173	9.03	0.036	3.24	0.051	11.83	0.113	52.91	0.037
1987	0.141	7.77	0.031	2.43	0.049	11.59	0.112	52.33	0.028
1988	0.137	7.78	0.032	2.64	0.044	10.33	0.108	50.66	0.02
1989	0.111	6.81	0.028	2.56	0.041	9.77	0.104	49.58	0.02
1990	0.112	6.56	0.024	2.01	0.041	10.52	0.105	51.01	0.019
1991	0.105	6.27	0.023	2.00	0.039	10.51	0.104	51.94	0.025
1992	0.099	6.41	0.019	1.95	0.041	11.66	0.101	51.68	0.031
1993	0.077	5.36	0.019	2.03	0.04	12.33	0.097	53.36	0.038
1994	0.092	5.88	0.017	1.82	0.04	13.12	0.096	56.04	0.025
1995	0.081	5.54	0.018	1.94	0.038	12.60	0.093	55.35	0.028
1996	0.069	4.56	0.02	1.89	0.037	12.30	0.092	55.05	0.028
1997	0.065	4.49	0.02	2.03	0.037	12.80	0.09	54.12	0.026
1998	0.059	4.65	0.015	2.01	0.038	14.24	0.09	56.14	0.038
1999	0.078	5.62	0.021	2.54	0.042	16.01	0.093	56.69	0.037
2000	0.068	4.98	0.021	2.75	0.043	16.32	0.094	56.07	0.034
2001	0.077	5.93	0.022	2.86	0.044	16.42	0.093	53.19	0.043
2002	0.084	5.89	0.024	2.90	0.042	15.28	0.094	53.14	0.048
2003	0.101	6.79	0.029	3.10	0.044	15.31	0.092	50.68	0.052
2004	0.091	5.91	0.028	2.75	0.038	13.30	0.085	47.62	0.043
2005	0.098	7.28	0.025	2.85	0.033	11.29	0.079	45.33	0.036
2006	0.115	7.90	0.024	2.74	0.034	10.85	0.08	44.16	0.032
2007	0.111	8.03	0.013	1.68	0.024	8.30	0.074	41.21	0.027
2008	0.092	6.93	0.034	4.12	0.032	11.10	0.081	47.67	0.044
2009	0.084	6.42	0.029	3.43	0.029	10.24	0.08	47.09	0.047
2010	0.092	6.63	0.032	3.35	0.03	10.10	0.081	46.84	0.049
2011	0.092	6.27	0.034	3.22	0.03	9.76	0.084	47.75	0.056
2012	0.087	5.85	0.034	3.22	0.031	9.88	0.083	47.24	0.065
2013	0.118	6.61	0.021	1.75	0.027	8.63	0.079	43.23	0.055
2014	0.145	7.95	0.033	2.90	0.03	9.59	0.079	43.65	0.054
2015	0.126	7.13	0.034	3.16	0.028	9.43	0.078	43.87	0.056
2016	0.116	7.11	0.039	3.81	0.025	8.13	0.072	40.76	0.053
2017	0.12	6.07	0.037	3.12	0.026	7.87	0.072	37.35	0.049

Table 5.20 Simultaneous estimation of information parameters by industry

	ω_1	t-stat	ω_2	t-stat	γ-1	t-stat	r	t-stat	RP
NoDur	0.099	5.87	0.023	1.82	0.039	12.50	0.101	49.3	0.039
Durbl	0.133	4.40	0.021	0.89	0.041	7.56	0.111	32.30	0.049
Manuf	0.131	9.63	0.022	2.40	0.033	12.7	0.101	62.81	0.038
Enrgy	0.13	4.84	0.027	1.48	0.033	5.09	0.092	25.28	0.030
Chems	0.189	7.12	0.03	2.08	0.044	8.18	0.103	31.86	0.041
BusEq	0.085	6.94	0.019	2.07	0.041	15.7	0.090	53.28	0.028
Telcm	0.132	3.16	0.054	3.08	0.035	5.3	0.084	22.13	0.021
Utils	0.189	8.43	0.041	4.60	0.040	11.58	0.099	69.46	0.037
Shops	0.118	7.80	0.029	2.67	0.035	15.15	0.096	62.33	0.034
Hlth	0.135	6.09	0.039	3.43	0.049	12.03	0.097	32.71	0.035
Money	0.143	13.46	0.038	6.64	0.044	20.35	0.107	97.46	0.045
Other	0.104	7.78	0.021	2.49	0.033	13.32	0.094	56.71	0.032

5.6.3 Synthetic Price Multiples: V/e_1, V/B and V/e

Equation (5.7) shows that vectors M and N jointly determine the synthetic price-to-forward earnings multiple and value premium over the capitalized expected one-period ahead earnings.

We first run cross-sectional regressions for each of the 12 industries to generate parameters $(\omega_{it,1}, \omega_{it,2}, \lambda_{it}, R_{it})$ over our sample period. We then calculate the coefficients of forward economic spread, current spread, and the abnormal growth in book value term in Eq. (5.7) for each firm-year. Finally, we estimate the synthetic price-to-forward earnings multiple for firm j in industry i at time t:

$$V/e_1 \equiv \frac{1}{(R_{it}-1)} + \frac{M_{1,i}N_{i,j}^T}{feps_{j,t+1}}, \tag{5.52}$$

where $M_{1,i} = [M_{11,i}, M_{12,i}, M_{13,i}]$, $M_{11,i} = \frac{R_{it}(\omega_{it,1}+\lambda_{it}-1)-\omega_{it,1}\lambda_{it}}{(R_{it}-\omega_{it,1})(R_{it}-\lambda_{it})(R_{it}-1)}$, $M_{12,i} = \frac{-\omega_{it,1}\lambda_{it}}{(R_{it}-\omega_{it,1})(R_{it}-\lambda_{it})}$, $M_{13,i} = \frac{R_{it}\omega_{it,2}}{(R_{it}-\omega_{it,1})(R_{it}-\lambda_{it})}$, and $N_{i,j} = [N_{i,j1}, N_{i,j2}, N_{i,j3}]$, where $N_{i,j1} = (E_t[ROE_{j,t+1}] - (R_{it}-1))b_{j,t}$, $N_{i,j2} = (ROE_{j,t} - (R_{it}-1))b_{j,t-1}$, and $N_{i,j3} = (b_{j,t}/b_{j,t-1} - \lambda_{it})b_{j,t-1}$. We also report the synthetic price-to-book multiple as in Eq. (5.8) for firm j in industry i at time t:

$$V/B \equiv 1 + \frac{M_{2,i}N_{i,j}^T}{b_{j,t}}, \tag{5.53}$$

where $M_{2,i} = [M_{21,i}, M_{22,i}, M_{23,i}]$, $M_{21,i} = \frac{R_{it}}{(R_{it}-\omega_{it,1})(R_{it}-\lambda_{it})}$, $M_{22,i} = M_{12,i}$ and $M_{23,i} = M_{13,i}$, and the synthetic price-to-current earnings multiple as in Eq. (5.9) for firm j in industry i at time t:

$$V/e \equiv \frac{R_{it}}{(R_{it}-1)} + \frac{M_{3,i}N_{i,j}^T}{x_{j,t}}, \tag{5.54}$$

where $M_{3,i} = [M_{31,i}, M_{32,i}, M_{33,i}]$, $M_{31,i} = M_{21,i}$, $M_{32,i} = \frac{-R_{it}(R_{it}-\lambda_{it}+\omega_{it,1}(\lambda_{it}-1))}{(R_{it}-1)(R_{it}-\omega_{it,1})(R_{it}-\lambda_{it})}$, and $M_{33,i} = \frac{R_{it}\omega_{it,2}}{(R_{it}-\omega_{it,1})(R_{it}-\lambda_{it})}$. We drop company observations with negative synthetic price multiples to generate meaningful price multiples.[27]

In Table 5.21, we report the average synthetic price-forward earnings, price-to-book, and price-to-current earnings multiples year-by-year in columns 2, 5, and 8, respectively, over our sample period. The mean and the median of synthetic price-to-forward multiples are 13.35 (with a standard deviation of 2.79) and 13.54, respectively. The mean and the median of synthetic price-to-book multiples are 2.41 and 2.51, respectively. The mean (median) of the synthetic price-to-current earnings multiple is 16.07 (15.62). The synthetic price multiples have the highest values in 2017 and the lowest in 1981. They became more volatile after the year 2000. We also report the percentages of average deviations of these synthetic price multiples from their "normal" counterparts to the synthetic multiples in columns 3, 6, and 9, and their standard deviations in columns 4, 7 and 10. The averages of the percentages for the synthetic price-to-forward earnings and price-to-book are 6.2 and 2.82%, respectively. The synthetic price-to-forward earnings multiples are less than their "norms" only in 1980–1981, 2002 and 2008. The synthetic price-to-book ratios are less than 1 in the first half of the 1980s, the beginning of the 1990s, the 2000s', and 2008–2009. Although these percentage values are small, the standard deviations of these percentages are relatively large. They are 0.75 and 1.64, respectively. It suggests that there are large cross-sectional variations of these deviations across firms. In contrast to the synthetic price-to-forward earnings, the average percentage deviation for the synthetic price-to-current earnings is 46.8%, and all deviations are positive except 1982, suggesting the adjustment component of this synthetic multiple is highly important if one insists on using the "normal" price-to-current earnings ratio in valuation.

In Table 5.22, we report the average synthetic price-to-forward earnings, price-to-book and price-to-current earnings multiples, and the cross-sectional variation in the synthetic price multiples for each of the 12 industries. The mean and the median of synthetic price-to-forward multiples are 13.51 and 13.17. The mean and the median of the synthetic price-to-book multiple are 2.47 and 2.45. The mean (median) of the synthetic price-to-current earnings multiple is 15.99 (16.04). Industry "Hlth" has the highest synthetic price multiples. As expected, the regulated industry, "Utils", the financial industry, "Money", and the industry "Durbl" have the lowest synthetic price multiples. The synthetic price-to-forward earnings multiple for the financial industry is close to its "normal" value. The synthetic price-to-book multiples are less than their "normal" value of 1 by about 13% for the financial

[27] There are about 4% of company observations that have negative synthetic price multiples.

Table 5.21 Synthetic price multiples and the percentages of deviation from their "normal" values by year

	V/e_1	$\frac{dev(V/e_1)}{V/e_1}$		V/B	$\frac{dev(V/B)}{V/B}$		V/e	$\frac{dev(V/e)}{V/e}$		N
	Mean	Mean	St.Dev	Mean	Mean	St.Dev	Mean	Mean	St.Dev	
1980	7.53	−1.82%	0.56	1.46	−24.29%	1.58	10.58	18.96%	5.38	1761
1981	7.44	−3.14%	0.74	1.44	−32.87%	1.76	10.06	14.45%	3.68	1837
1982	8.53	0.57%	0.75	1.61	−34.21%	1.85	11.41	−12.47%	11.64	2015
1983	9.35	11.29%	2.13	1.78	−11.24%	1.55	12.36	20.26%	7.92	2175
1984	9.51	1.94%	0.65	1.86	−13.09%	1.69	13.04	54.57%	9.76	2259
1985	10.31	3.20%	0.69	1.93	−12.97%	1.69	13.03	50.27%	4.58	2250
1986	11.45	5.78%	0.66	2.11	−4.47%	1.72	15.11	75.06%	11.75	2252
1987	11.31	5.84%	0.61	2.19	2.07%	1.63	15.31	52.77%	5.43	2290
1988	11.32	6.76%	0.53	2.23	9.43%	1.40	15.20	37.51%	1.67	2356
1989	11.40	5.11%	0.57	2.22	4.32%	1.59	15.56	24.75%	15.94	2373
1990	10.97	0.84%	0.64	2.02	−10.40%	1.78	15.04	43.85%	2.89	2232
1991	11.11	2.55%	0.67	1.93	−13.85%	1.82	14.47	50.00%	2.80	2335
1992	11.83	6.57%	0.61	2.19	2.37%	1.58	15.46	59.93%	5.84	2518
1993	12.54	9.03%	0.57	2.36	11.49%	1.47	15.32	52.41%	6.13	2777
1994	12.67	10.43%	0.50	2.44	19.01%	1.25	16.31	39.48%	4.51	3328
1995	13.21	9.60%	0.58	2.54	17.30%	1.42	16.23	59.88%	3.82	3566
1996	13.27	9.37%	0.54	2.51	18.40%	1.35	15.48	34.02%	11.94	3704
1997	13.81	9.40%	0.66	2.64	18.20%	1.51	17.98	45.92%	8.14	3703
1998	13.55	6.94%	0.72	2.56	9.96%	1.62	16.18	54.25%	10.49	3421
1999	13.72	7.50%	0.75	2.70	9.23%	1.71	17.33	65.27%	6.26	2960
2000	13.52	4.28%	0.80	2.63	0.02%	1.87	15.67	56.80%	6.35	2606
2001	13.68	0.87%	0.92	2.38	−13.19%	2.05	16.30	64.90%	6.24	2255
2002	13.20	−1.10%	0.90	2.30	−13.47%	2.01	15.47	48.75%	1.74	2292
2003	14.72	5.34%	0.94	2.56	−2.24%	1.84	15.45	67.89%	7.30	2548
2004	15.99	10.28%	0.78	2.76	14.42%	1.64	18.87	45.66%	3.05	2590
2005	17.66	16.66%	0.70	3.05	33.12%	1.20	20.42	18.90%	13.46	2631
2006	17.39	14.61%	0.57	3.00	29.09%	1.34	19.91	43.54%	2.80	2581
2007	17.17	9.26%	0.79	2.91	19.61%	1.49	18.69	66.25%	7.83	2419
2008	15.33	−3.38%	0.90	2.53	−18.26%	2.10	14.60	23.07%	10.43	1996
2009	15.62	2.60%	1.34	2.49	−13.78%	2.00	15.16	20.93%	32.51	2243
2010	15.27	4.78%	0.72	2.61	3.71%	1.71	18.40	50.16%	4.39	2255
2011	14.56	3.45%	0.67	2.52	1.25%	1.73	17.56	48.81%	9.52	2261
2012	14.72	3.68%	0.71	2.51	3.91%	1.68	16.36	57.14%	3.88	2154
2013	15.80	9.36%	0.58	2.63	15.06%	1.48	17.14	58.22%	3.85	2150
2014	16.27	11.79%	0.64	2.87	18.91%	1.46	19.10	40.72%	7.86	2025
2015	16.32	8.15%	0.73	2.89	13.87%	1.73	17.75	78.41%	9.16	1937
2016	17.30	11.49%	0.72	3.00	21.96%	1.48	19.63	75.01%	4.05	1896
2017	17.89	15.68%	1.10	3.31	28.95%	1.45	22.64	72.11%	5.60	1832

Table 5.22 Synthetic price multiples and the percentages of deviation from their "normal" values by industry

	V/e_1	$\frac{dev(V/e_1)}{V/e_1}$		V/B	$\frac{dev(V/B)}{V/B}$		V/e	$\frac{dev(V/e)}{V/e}$		N
	Mean	Mean	St.Dev	Mean	Mean	St.Dev	Mean	Mean	St.Dev	
NoDur	12.31	5.12%	0.74	2.51	3.15%	1.63	15.57	51.45%	8.11	5677
Durbl	11.28	7.94%	0.55	2.24	6.14%	1.45	12.88	54.09%	11.12	2831
Manuf	12	5.20%	0.78	2.24	−1.10%	1.65	15.19	27.49%	15.93	11,334
Enrgy	13.91	2.69%	0.82	2.38	−13.46%	1.99	16.11	48.26%	7.41	3333
Chems	13.23	16.54%	0.52	2.77	27.83%	1.19	16.06	43.39%	2.52	2549
BusEq	16.05	11.78%	0.78	3.04	15.69%	1.70	18.97	94.09%	7.65	15,475
Telcm	16.58	4.04%	0.83	2.74	−0.75%	1.81	16.82	41.54%	4.61	1777
Utils	11.54	3.00%	0.44	1.50	8.81%	0.91	13.16	1.36%	7.00	4668
Shops	13.11	6.59%	0.67	2.39	7.84%	1.60	16.02	53.03%	6.14	10,182
Hlth	16.97	23.39%	1.43	3.50	30.39%	1.46	20.38	73.61%	5.29	6245
Money	11.6	−1.11%	0.68	1.80	−12.62%	1.72	14.18	18.36%	7.72	17,882
Other	13.54	4.51%	0.76	2.53	2.40%	1.76	16.48	44.67%	9.75	10,830
Mean	13.51	7.47%	0.75	2.47	6.19%	1.57	15.99	45.95%	7.77	7732
Median	13.17	5.16%	0.75	2.45	4.64%	1.64	16.04	46.47%	7.53	5961

industry "Money" and the energy industry "Enrgy" over 1980–2017. We also report the percentages of average deviations of these synthetic price multiples from their "normal" counterparts to the synthetic multiples, as well as their standard deviation over our sample period. The averages of these percentages for the synthetic price-to-forward earnings, price-to-book and price-to-current earnings multiples are 7.47, 6.19 and 45.95%, respectively. Again, the standard deviations of these percentages are relatively large. They are 0.75, 1.57 and 7.77, respectively. Except for the utility industry "Utils", the synthetic price-to-current earnings multiples significantly differ from their "normal" values. It suggests that the "normal" price-to-current earnings multiple on "Utils" would work better than other industries.

5.6.4 The Synthetic Price Multiples and Actual Price Multiples

In Table 5.23, we report the averages of the synthetic price multiples and actual price multiples and compare these multiples on a year-by-year basis. The actual price-to-forward earnings are higher than the synthetic price-to-forward earnings for all sample years. The mean (median) of the synthetic price-to-forward earnings multiples is 13.35 (13.54), while the mean (median) of the actual price-to-forward earnings multiples is 16.80 (16.62). The actual price-to-forward earnings multiples are also much more volatile. The difference between these two multiples is statistically significant. The table also shows that the synthetic price-to-book (price-to-earnings) multiples are generally lower than the actual price-to-book (price-to-earnings) multiples. A few exceptions include turbulent periods in the financial markets surrounding 1987 and 2008. The differences between the synthetic and actual price multiples have their largest value during 2007–2008. It suggests that synthetic price multiples are more resilient, and valuation based on these synthetic multiples may better reflect a stock's intrinsic value, particularly during the global financial crisis.

While we can estimate a proxy for the intrinsic value (V) of a stock based on any of Eqs. (5.52)–(5.54), some may be more interested in whether the stock is over/underpriced more relative to other stocks. We can examine the extent to which the current stock price (P) deviates from our intrinsic value estimate by using $(1 - V/P)$ to measure the signed degree of over/underpricing. The last column of Table 5.23 reports the averages of over/underpricing of stocks. It documents evidence of mispricing from year to year. In particular, stocks are underpriced the most in 2008 by 37% and overpriced the most in 1982 by 18%. However, we find that the mean and the median of these mispricing are close to zero over our sample period. This is consistent with the assumption that aggregate markets are efficient.

In Table 5.24, we report the averages of the synthetic price multiples and actual price multiples, and compare the two on an industry-by-industry basis. It shows that the actual price-to-forward earnings are almost always greater than the synthetic price-to-forward earnings for all 12 industries. The mean (median) of the actual price-to-forward earnings multiples is 17.15 (15.72). Industry "Telcm" has the

Table 5.23 Synthetic price multiples, actual price multiples and V/P by year

	V/e_1	P/e_1	Diff	V/B	P/B	Diff	V/e	P/e	Diff	V/P
1980	7.53	9.61	−2.09	1.46	1.74	−0.28	10.58	12.60	−2.02	0.96
1981	7.44	8.05	−0.61	1.44	1.39	0.05	10.06	10.50	−0.44	1.12
1982	8.53	13.02	−4.49	1.61	2.11	−0.50	11.41	16.86	−5.45	0.82
1983	9.35	11.86	−2.51	1.78	1.94	−0.16	12.36	16.02	−3.66	0.96
1984	9.51	11.76	−2.25	1.86	1.98	−0.13	13.04	15.47	−2.43	0.97
1985	10.31	14.88	−4.57	1.93	2.35	−0.42	13.03	18.30	−5.27	0.84
1986	11.45	15.97	−4.52	2.11	2.46	−0.35	15.11	19.86	−4.75	0.90
1987	11.31	12.62	−1.31	2.19	2.06	0.13	15.31	17.06	−1.75	1.11
1988	11.32	12.53	−1.21	2.23	2.06	0.16	15.20	16.12	−0.92	1.12
1989	11.40	12.88	−1.48	2.22	2.14	0.08	15.56	16.78	−1.22	1.12
1990	10.97	13.38	−2.41	2.02	2.15	−0.13	15.04	17.82	−2.78	1.04
1991	11.11	16.09	−4.98	1.93	2.42	−0.48	14.47	19.87	−5.40	0.86
1992	11.83	16.14	−4.31	2.19	2.55	−0.36	15.46	20.01	−4.55	0.89
1993	12.54	16.08	−3.54	2.36	2.58	−0.22	15.32	19.02	−3.70	0.96
1994	12.67	14.70	−2.03	2.44	2.44	0.00	16.31	18.64	−2.33	1.07
1995	13.21	16.86	−3.65	2.54	2.79	−0.26	16.23	19.78	−3.55	1.00
1996	13.27	16.58	−3.31	2.51	2.70	−0.19	15.48	18.81	−3.33	0.99
1997	13.81	19.93	−6.12	2.64	3.28	−0.64	17.98	24.56	−6.58	0.86
1998	13.55	16.65	−3.10	2.56	2.70	−0.14	16.18	19.04	−2.86	1.11
1999	13.72	17.12	−3.40	2.70	2.90	−0.20	17.33	20.48	−3.15	1.19
2000	13.52	16.07	−2.55	2.63	2.64	−0.01	15.67	17.13	−1.46	1.15
2001	13.68	20.82	−7.14	2.38	2.94	−0.56	16.30	21.71	−5.41	0.87
2002	13.20	16.13	−2.93	2.30	2.33	−0.03	15.47	17.68	−2.21	1.04
2003	14.72	21.59	−6.87	2.56	3.05	−0.49	15.45	20.72	−5.27	0.83
2004	15.99	20.07	−4.08	2.76	2.89	−0.13	18.87	22.49	−3.62	0.95
2005	17.66	21.46	−3.80	3.05	3.18	−0.13	20.42	23.04	−2.62	1.00
2006	17.39	20.99	−3.60	3.00	3.07	−0.07	19.91	22.48	−2.57	0.99
2007	17.17	17.99	−0.82	2.91	2.57	0.34	18.69	18.51	0.18	1.19
2008	15.33	15.39	−0.06	2.53	1.96	0.57	14.60	13.86	0.74	1.37
2009	15.62	20.07	−4.45	2.49	2.47	0.02	15.16	17.36	−2.20	1.03
2010	15.27	19.31	−4.04	2.61	2.67	−0.06	18.40	21.54	−3.14	1.04
2011	14.56	17.55	−2.99	2.52	2.53	−0.01	17.56	20.70	−3.14	1.08
2012	14.72	18.69	−3.97	2.51	2.66	−0.15	16.36	19.84	−3.48	1.00
2013	15.80	21.95	−6.15	2.63	3.04	−0.42	17.14	22.43	−5.29	0.90
2014	16.27	21.40	−5.13	2.87	3.21	−0.34	19.10	22.39	−3.29	0.95
2015	16.32	19.50	−3.18	2.89	2.92	−0.03	17.75	19.99	−2.24	1.07
2016	17.30	22.10	−4.80	3.00	3.21	−0.21	19.63	22.94	−3.31	0.99
2017	17.89	20.57	−2.68	3.31	3.21	0.10	22.64	22.69	−0.05	1.14

highest value of 23.41 and industry "Utils" has the lowest of 12.95. These two industries also have the largest differences between the synthetic and actual price-to-forward earnings multiples. As expected, the utility industry, "Utils", has the

Table 5.24 Synthetic price multiples, actual price multiples and V/P by industry

	V/e_1	P/e_1	Diff	V/B	P/B	Diff	V/e	P/e	Diff	V/P
NoDur	12.31	15.32	−3.01	2.51	2.70	−0.19	15.57	18.54	−2.97	0.99
Durbl	11.28	13.80	−2.52	2.24	2.35	−0.11	12.88	15.56	−2.68	1.00
Manuf	12.00	15.01	−3.01	2.24	2.34	−0.10	15.19	17.80	−2.61	1.00
Enrgy	13.91	19.54	−5.63	2.38	2.36	0.02	16.11	19.55	−3.44	1.05
Chems	13.23	15.42	−2.19	2.77	2.88	−0.11	16.06	17.96	−1.90	0.99
BusEq	16.05	21.18	−5.13	3.04	3.31	−0.27	18.97	22.62	−3.65	1.03
Telcm	16.58	23.41	−6.83	2.74	2.98	−0.24	16.82	21.36	−4.54	1.00
Utils	11.54	12.95	−1.41	1.50	1.59	−0.09	13.16	15.03	−1.87	0.96
Shops	13.11	16.02	−2.91	2.39	2.58	−0.20	16.02	19.44	−3.42	1.01
Hlth	16.97	21.75	−4.78	3.50	3.70	−0.20	20.38	24.99	−4.61	1.05
Money	11.60	13.93	−2.33	1.80	1.89	−0.09	14.18	16.62	−2.44	1.01
Other	13.54	17.46	−3.92	2.53	2.72	−0.19	16.48	19.92	−3.44	1.03
Mean	13.51	17.15	−3.64	2.47	2.62	−0.15	15.99	19.12	−3.13	1.01
Median	13.17	15.72	−3.01	2.45	2.64	−0.15	16.04	18.99	−3.20	1.00

smallest difference between the two price-to-forward earnings multiples. The table also shows that the mean (median) of the actual price-to-book multiples is 2.62 (2.64). The actual price-to-book multiples are all greater than the synthetic price-to-book multiples except for the energy industry, "Energy", suggesting the industry is slightly underpriced with respect to its book value. Industry "BusEq" has the largest difference between the two price-to-book multiples and one of the highest actual price-to-book multiples. "Utils" also has one of the smallest differences between the two price-to-book multiples. While the industry "Utils" has the smallest actual price-to-current earnings of 15.03 and the smallest difference between the synthetic and actual price-to-current earnings multiples, the "Hlth" industry has the largest difference between these two price-to-earnings multiples. There is also considerable cross-industry variation in the price multiples. The last column of Table 5.24 shows that, on average, most industries are fairly priced, with the "Utils" industry being slightly overpriced.

For illustrative purposes, we also apply a synthetic price-to-forward earnings ratio in equity valuation on companies in four representative industries. The four industries have a relatively large number of observations: Consumer Non-Durables (#1), Manufacturing (#3), Business Equipment (#6), and Shops (#9).[28]

Table 5.25 compares the synthetic price-to-forward earnings ratios with the actual price-to-forward earnings ratios for the four industries over our sample period. In general, the actual price-to-forward earnings ratios are higher than the

[28] Industry "Consumer Non-Durables" include food, tobacco, textiles, apparel, leather, and toys. Industry "Manufacturing" includes machinery, trucks, planes, paper, and printing. Industry "Business Equipment" includes computers, software, and electronic equipment. Industry "Shops" include wholesale, retail, and some services (laundries and repair shops).

Table 5.25 Synthetic price-to-forward earnings ratio (V/e_1) vs. actual price-to-forward earnings ratio (P/e_1)

	Cons. NonDur.		Manuf.		Business Eq.		Shops	
	V/e_1	P/e_1	V/e_1	P/e_1	V/e_1	P/e_1	V/e_1	P/e_1
1980	6.854	8.35	6.824	8.695	9.373	13.65	7.384	8.408
1981	6.546	7.664	6.655	7.35	9.563	11.38	7.314	7.545
1982	7.133	10.58	8.085	13.03	11.4	18.53	8.298	12.95
1983	7.559	10.52	9.189	11.51	12.59	15.62	9.262	10.94
1984	8.097	10.96	9.248	11.27	12.43	12.91	9.499	11.61
1985	9.472	13.83	9.694	14.48	12.25	15.91	10.09	14.79
1986	11.37	14.74	11.29	15.9	12.8	17.11	11.59	15.71
1987	11.23	11.94	10.97	12.25	12.55	13.01	11.37	12.51
1988	11.39	13.22	11.19	11.58	12.09	12.5	11.72	13.39
1989	11.37	12.9	10.96	10.94	11.9	12.28	11.98	12.86
1990	11.04	13.53	10.21	11.45	11.28	13.4	11.82	13.75
1991	11.46	15.78	10.43	14.98	11.29	16.23	11.51	16.27
1992	12.33	14.98	10.97	15.78	11.75	16.42	12.29	15.98
1993	12.88	16.11	11.52	15.68	12.95	17.44	13.09	16.57
1994	12.96	13.6	12.31	13.14	14.05	17.58	13.04	13.95
1995	13.19	15.67	12.35	13.46	14.95	20.1	13.18	17.19
1996	12.89	16.5	12.06	14.16	14.96	19.31	13.45	16.47
1997	13.46	18.72	12.27	16.36	15.6	22.46	14.14	19.39
1998	13.12	15.04	11.63	13.08	15.39	21.07	13.73	15.86
1999	13.28	12.37	11.42	13.91	16.64	28.84	13.74	13.29
2000	12.76	14.42	11.19	12.67	15.81	22.35	13.57	14.72
2001	12.8	17.53	10.87	17.73	16.11	30.3	13.43	19.22
2002	12.11	14.46	11.06	14.49	16.91	21.86	12.19	14.2
2003	12.98	17.06	12.3	19.93	19.41	30.9	13.21	19.01
2004	14.26	17.04	15.03	17.71	20.63	25.83	14.98	17.94
2005	15.3	18.58	16.37	18.85	23.48	27.99	16.12	20.46
2006	15.83	20.39	16.46	17.57	22.65	26.17	16.42	19.69
2007	15.71	16.65	15.55	15.44	21.85	21.32	16.38	15.79
2008	14.69	13.78	13.08	11.27	19.05	19.02	15.15	14.16
2009	15.06	16.89	13.86	20.26	18.84	22.14	15.37	17.87
2010	14.37	17.36	14.59	17.38	17.92	22.15	15.24	17.02
2011	13.56	16.6	14.22	15.34	16.51	20.26	14.36	15.97
2012	14.02	18.28	14.28	16.72	16.45	21.05	14.63	17.77
2013	14.58	21.38	15.38	20.95	17.26	25.03	15.54	20.62
2014	16.22	21.93	15.58	19.12	18.14	24.18	15.96	20.74
2015	17.12	20.91	15.35	18.45	18.1	23.35	16.22	18.09
2016	17.51	21.34	16.97	21.04	19.83	26.44	16.7	19.64
2017	18.89	21.06	17.44	20.5	20.56	27.02	17.08	17.35

synthetic price-to-forward earnings ratios. The medians of the actual price-to-forward earnings ratios are 15.73, 15.16, 20.66 and 15.98 for industries "Consumer Non-Durables", "Manufacturing", "Business Equipment" and "Shops", respectively. The corresponding medians of the synthetic price-to-forward earnings ratios are 12.97, 11.85, 15.71 and 13.44 over 1980–2017. The actual price multiples are also much more volatile, as expected. The gap between the actual and synthetic price multiples is particularly larger for the industry of "Business equipment" from the 1990s to 2008. In fact, almost all actual price multiples are less than the synthetic price multiples for the four industries during the 2007–2008 global financial crisis. The synthetic price-to-book ratios and actual price-to-book ratios on a year-by-year basis for each of the four industries are reported in Table 5.26. A similar pattern emerges. The synthetic price-to-book ratios are generally lower than the actual price-to-book ratios. A few exceptions include turbulent periods in the financial markets surrounding 1987, 2000, and 2008.

Tables 5.25 and 5.26 show that the mean and the median of the synthetic P/e_1 are between 11.85 and 13.44, except for industry "Business Equipment", which is about 15.7. This industry also has the highest mean and median of synthetic P/B, which are 3.06 and 2.97, respectively. Otherwise, the mean and the median of the synthetic P/B are between 2.18 and 2.72, while the mean and the median of the actual P/B are between 2.42 and 2.85. On the contrary, the industry of "Manufacturing" has the lowest mean and median of synthetic P/e_1 and P/B. This should be expected since the industry "Business Equipment" consists of high-tech companies and "Manufacturing" is a traditional industry. There is considerable cross-industry variation in the price multiples. The two tables also indicate that synthetic P/e_1 and P/B generally have an upward trend for each of the four industries over our sample period. This upward trend is not inconsistent with empirical findings in capital market research, which document the failure of fundamental accounting numbers to fully account for value-relevant items, such as intangible assets and customer data, in the digital era.

5.6.5 *Valuation Bias and Inaccuracy*

Next, we apply the synthetic price-to-forward earnings multiples as an example to value equity shares. The value of a share equals the synthetic price-to-forward earnings, V/e_1, multiplied by its one-period ahead forecasts of earnings per share. To evaluate valuation bias and inaccuracy, we follow prior studies and define valuation bias as the difference between observable stock prices and the predicted values from the synthetic V/e_1 multiple, scaled by price. Valuation inaccuracy is defined as the absolute value of the difference between observable stock prices and the multiple predicted values, scaled by price.

For comparison, we also report valuation bias and inaccuracy by directly estimating information dynamics parameters, using the sequential approach as in

Table 5.26 Synthetic price-to-book ratio (V/B) vs. actual price-to-book ratio (P/B)

	Cons. NonDur.		Manuf.		Business Eq.		Shops	
	V/B	P/B	V/B	P/B	V/B	P/B	V/B	P/B
1980	1.322	1.437	1.221	1.474	1.913	2.74	1.268	1.444
1981	1.363	1.292	1.154	1.159	1.94	2.064	1.445	1.404
1982	1.367	1.868	1.252	1.702	2.634	3.496	1.643	2.262
1983	1.423	1.768	1.64	1.725	2.877	2.88	1.931	2.045
1984	1.582	1.941	1.57	1.703	2.586	2.362	2.022	2.193
1985	2.106	2.691	1.624	1.972	2.229	2.395	2.158	2.499
1986	2.508	2.897	1.771	2.101	2.624	2.61	2.131	2.562
1987	2.697	2.401	1.917	1.841	2.52	2.095	2.146	2.076
1988	2.517	2.527	2.139	1.926	2.487	2.07	2.248	2.255
1989	2.496	2.524	2.098	1.856	2.479	2.095	2.295	2.186
1990	2.448	2.544	1.972	1.797	2.098	2.203	2.28	2.461
1991	2.217	2.797	1.723	2.089	2.078	2.694	2.134	2.725
1992	2.315	2.639	2.205	2.521	2.569	2.852	2.353	2.697
1993	2.621	2.808	2.191	2.454	2.91	3.157	2.366	2.7
1994	2.661	2.567	2.493	2.405	3.391	3.514	2.288	2.196
1995	2.841	2.936	2.651	2.462	3.681	4.163	2.324	2.627
1996	2.478	2.798	2.442	2.498	3.392	3.707	2.224	2.46
1997	2.581	3.196	2.504	2.97	3.698	4.346	2.463	3.044
1998	2.702	2.838	2.321	2.243	3.759	4.027	2.351	2.533
1999	3.197	2.635	2.499	2.445	4.248	5.712	2.695	2.393
2000	3.247	3.112	2.154	2.103	3.219	3.546	2.575	2.643
2001	2.821	3.252	1.889	2.435	2.678	4.003	2.425	2.968
2002	2.621	2.793	1.861	2.014	2.768	2.85	2.176	2.213
2003	2.604	3.002	2.124	2.759	2.639	3.537	2.323	2.85
2004	2.649	2.906	2.928	2.913	2.97	3.157	2.672	2.837
2005	2.821	3.124	3.385	3.325	3.486	3.638	2.814	3.173
2006	3.162	3.486	3.601	3.373	3.519	3.445	3.056	3.134
2007	2.936	2.739	3.131	2.726	3.513	2.84	3.148	2.662
2008	3.561	2.584	2.411	1.652	3.221	2.358	2.455	2.038
2009	3.5	3.098	2.14	2.311	3.125	2.915	2.637	2.534
2010	2.978	2.961	2.734	2.8	3.342	3.482	2.784	2.75
2011	2.95	3.033	3.023	2.75	2.967	3.189	2.819	2.963
2012	3.193	3.466	2.978	2.927	2.967	3.245	2.935	3.161
2013	3.164	3.568	2.794	3.164	3.366	3.701	3.126	3.695
2014	3.583	4.275	3.124	3.278	3.661	4.024	3.269	3.96
2015	3.784	4.167	3.156	3.181	4.074	3.768	3	3.181
2016	3.64	3.701	3.338	3.544	4.3	4.63	3.208	3.374
2017	4.185	3.801	3.275	3.336	4.503	4.779	3.596	3.072

Dechow et al. (1999).[29] Specifically, we first assume a constant discount rate and use historical accounting data to run regressions to estimate information dynamic parameters (ω_1, ω_2) in a cross-section by ignoring growth G. We assume a discount rate of 9%.[30] Second, given the one-period ahead analysts' forecasts of earnings as a proxy for $E_t[e_{t+1}]$ and unconditional information dynamic parameters (ω_1, ω_2) from the first stage, we estimate the growth variable from Eq. (3.42): $G_t = E_t[e_{t+1}] - \omega_1 x_t - \omega_2(Rb_{t-1} - b_t)$ and then estimate the persistence of G_t from regressions on dynamic (3.41). Finally, equity value is given by valuation model (3.43).

Table 5.27 shows the valuation bias and inaccuracy for the four industries between 1981 and 2017. Panel A reports the valuation bias. It shows that the mean valuation biases from the synthetic V/e_1 multiple approach are between −0.006 and −0.057 across the four industries, while the minimum mean of valuation bias from the sequential approach is 0.267. It suggests that estimates from the multiple approach slightly overstate stock prices, but those from the sequential approach severely understate stock prices. The median valuation biases from the multiple approach are between 0.07 and 0.09, while the median biases from the sequential approach are between 0.362 and 0.518. The evidence of severe underestimation from the sequential approach is consistent in magnitude with the prior literature (Dechow et al., 1999; Choi et al., 2006). Panel B of Table 5.27 reports the valuation inaccuracy. The results indicate that the estimates from the synthetic V/e_1 multiple approach are more accurate than those from the sequential approach. The median valuation inaccuracy from the V/e_1 multiple approach is between 0.278 and 0.36, while the median from the sequential approach is between 0.413 and 0.532 across the four industries. Therefore, valuation biases and valuation inaccuracy are substantially improved by applying our synthetic V/e_1 multiples.[31]

5.6.6 *Prediction of Stock Returns*

If a company's actual price-to-forward earnings multiple is deviated from its synthetic price-to-forward earnings multiple, for example, we should be able to create portfolios based on the difference between the two multiples and generate

[29] Lo and Lys (2000) argue that this sequential procedure is problematic because the correlation between abnormal earnings and other information is important from an empirical standpoint.

[30] Dechow et al. (1999) assume a cost of equity capital of 12%. They also use 9% and 15% in their robustness test. Given the declining trend of risk-free rate over the last two decades, we assume a cost of equity of 9%. We also apply a 12% discount rate and find that the valuation errors are much higher. Note also that the sequential approach cannot estimate parameters in our sample in the first year, 1980.

[31] Our results, not reported, also outperform value estimates from models developed in Myers (1999) and Frankel and Lee (1998), as well as value estimates generated from the "warranted multiples" in Bhojraj and Lee (2002) and the "extended multiples" in Nissim (2013).

Table 5.27 Valuation bias and inaccuracy: using synthetic P/e_1 and using the sequential approach (SEQ) to estimate the LID

Panel A: valuation bias

	Consumer non-Dur.		Manufacturing		Business equipment		Shops	
	V/e_1	SEQ	V/e_1	SEQ	V/e_1	SEQ	V/e_1	SEQ
N	5429	5429	10,811	10,811	14,854	14,854	9856	9856
Mean	−0.01	0.275	−0.016	0.267	−0.057	0.439	−0.025	0.286
StDev	0.603	0.513	0.597	0.427	0.758	0.353	0.609	0.461
Q1	−0.2	0.118	−0.215	0.107	−0.316	0.290	−0.218	0.112
Median	0.090	0.398	0.076	0.362	0.071	0.518	0.075	0.400
Q3	0.332	0.590	0.317	0.549	0.390	0.677	0.318	0.594

Panel B: valuation inaccuracy

	Consumer non-Dur.		Manufacturing		Business equipment		Shops	
	V/e_1	SEQ	V/e_1	SEQ	V/e_1	SEQ	V/e_1	SEQ
N	5429	5429	10,811	10,811	14,854	14,854	9856	9856
Mean	0.390	0.464	0.390	0.421	0.484	0.506	0.390	0.455
Stdev	0.460	0.352	0.453	0.276	0.586	0.247	0.468	0.297
Q1	0.132	0.255	0.127	0.230	0.169	0.333	0.129	0.248
Median	0.278	0.454	0.279	0.413	0.360	0.532	0.279	0.451
Q3	0.501	0.623	0.505	0.579	0.622	0.686	0.501	0.625

a hedge return based on extreme differences if the synthetic price multiple is a better tool to value stocks (Sloan, 2002). Note that the synthetic price-to-forward earnings multiple incorporates both short- and long-term economic properties of a company and reflects its fundamental value. In contrast, the actual price multiple describes the contemporaneous price relative to the one-period ahead earnings. If actual price multiples of a portfolio are much bigger (smaller) than its synthetic price multiples, then the portfolio should have low (high) returns. Therefore, firms with high synthetic price multiples relative to their actual price multiples should outperform firms with low synthetic multiples relative to the actual multiples. For this purpose, we calculate the difference between the synthetic price multiple and the corresponding actual price multiple for each firm year. We group all firms into 10 deciles based on the difference each year and calculate the one-, two-, and three-year-ahead realized buy-and-hold returns. Firms in decile 1 have the smallest difference between the synthetic price multiples and corresponding actual price multiples, and firms in decile 10 have the largest difference. Therefore, firms in decile 1 should have lower returns than firms in decile 10. Firms in the middle deciles may be over- or under-priced relative to estimates based on synthetic price multiples.

Panel A of Table 5.28 indeed shows that the one-, two- and three-year buy-and-hold returns for firms in decile 1 are 0.13, 0.236 and 0.366, respectively, while those are 0.204, 0.376 and 0.575 for firms in decile 10 based on portfolios formed on the difference between the synthetic price-to-forward earnings multiples and actual price-to-forward earnings multiples. The return differences between these two

Table 5.28 Returns sorted on decile difference between synthetic price multiples and actual price multiples, and V/P

Panel A: on (V/e1 - P/e1) decile											
	1	2	3	4	5	6	7	8	9	10	10-1
$\frac{V}{e_1}$ - $\frac{P}{e_1}$	−29.720	−10.860	−6.113	−3.461	−1.710	−0.274	1.065	2.553	4.583	9.047	38.767
bhr1	0.130	0.140	0.152	0.157	0.150	0.154	0.169	0.169	0.168	0.204	0.074
bhr2	0.236	0.269	0.297	0.313	0.304	0.315	0.329	0.351	0.345	0.376	0.141
bhr3	0.366	0.441	0.451	0.477	0.474	0.482	0.513	0.520	0.558	0.575	0.208
beta	0.970	0.900	0.865	0.827	0.805	0.801	0.802	0.821	0.853	0.895	−0.075
mktcap	2533	2595	2711	3089	3416	3469	4005	4259	4127	3938	1405
Panel B: on (V/B - P/B) decile											
	1	2	3	4	5	6	7	8	9	10	10-1
$\frac{V}{B}$ - $\frac{P}{B}$	−3.069	−1.144	−0.677	−0.413	−0.217	−0.036	0.154	0.407	0.834	2.589	5.658
bhr1	0.129	0.131	0.155	0.157	0.153	0.160	0.169	0.168	0.176	0.195	0.066
bhr2	0.231	0.259	0.287	0.316	0.327	0.324	0.339	0.342	0.359	0.351	0.121
bhr3	0.350	0.412	0.446	0.502	0.501	0.501	0.526	0.538	0.532	0.553	0.203
beta	1.015	0.924	0.848	0.804	0.792	0.781	0.794	0.816	0.858	0.909	−0.106
mktcap	4172	3178	2372	2202	2583	3012	3517	3832	4236	5037	865
Panel C: on (V/e - P/e) decile											
	1	2	3	4	5	6	7	8	9	10	10-1
$\frac{V}{e}$ - $\frac{P}{e}$	−45.510	−11.980	−6.521	−3.779	−1.955	−0.401	1.171	3.111	6.403	28.540	74.050
bhr1	0.143	0.141	0.161	0.164	0.151	0.163	0.161	0.169	0.167	0.173	0.030
bhr2	0.249	0.271	0.310	0.324	0.319	0.326	0.329	0.343	0.344	0.321	0.071
bhr3	0.395	0.426	0.472	0.480	0.499	0.510	0.504	0.521	0.530	0.520	0.125
beta	0.960	0.898	0.854	0.820	0.804	0.791	0.801	0.828	0.873	0.910	−0.049
mktcap	2643	2861	3090	2913	3141	3437	4349	4340	4488	2879	236
Panel D: on V/P decile											
	1	2	3	4	5	6	7	8	9	10	10-1
V/P	0.244	0.512	0.670	0.788	0.887	0.984	1.093	1.234	1.467	2.240	1.996
bhr1	0.143	0.144	0.150	0.149	0.147	0.152	0.159	0.167	0.170	0.210	0.067
bhr2	0.272	0.270	0.287	0.304	0.296	0.301	0.319	0.345	0.347	0.396	0.124
bhr3	0.441	0.424	0.441	0.468	0.454	0.459	0.498	0.517	0.554	0.607	0.166
beta	0.899	0.909	0.877	0.842	0.825	0.817	0.816	0.828	0.848	0.880	−0.020
mktcap	1685	2599	3011	3117	3821	3741	4028	4471	4376	3294	1609

deciles are 0.074, 0.141 and 0.208, both statistically and economically significant. Furthermore, the returns exhibit an upward trend with deciles, and they appear to be unrelated to risk, as measured by Beta and firm size.[32] Portfolios formed on

[32] Market Beta (β) is estimated based on Welch (2021). It is the average beta for each stock, month by month, using daily stock returns with a rolling window of 60 months. Daily excess returns are winsorized at $(1 \pm 3) \times$ market excess return before the calculation. Older observations are given less weights based on a decay rate of 2/252 per day.

the difference between the synthetic price-to-book multiples and actual price-to-book multiples and on the difference between the synthetic price-to-current earnings multiples and actual price-to-current earnings multiples have similar properties, as shown in Panels B and C of Table 5.28. In particular, Panel C shows that portfolios based on the difference between synthetic and actual price-to-current earnings multiples generate the smallest hedge returns.

One may ask why we need to calculate price multiples if we can directly estimate a firm's value before we generate the synthetic price multiples. Instead of comparing the synthetic to actual price multiples, would we be just as well served by comparing the estimated value to actual price? To answer this question, we form portfolios based on the degree of the deviations of current stock prices (P) from their intrinsic value estimates (V). We group all firms into 10 deciles based on V/P each year and calculate the one-, two-, and three-year-ahead realized buy-and-hold returns. Firms in decile 1 have the smallest V/P, and firms in decile 10 have the largest V/P. Panel D of Table 5.28 shows that the one-, two- and three-year buy-and-hold returns for firms in decile 1 are 0.143, 0.272 and 0.441, respectively, while those are 0.21, 0.396 and 0.607 for firms in decile 10. The return differences between these two deciles are 0.067, 0.124 and 0.166. However, these hedge returns are all smaller than those reported in Panel A, but similar to those reported in Panel B, where portfolios are formed on the difference between the synthetic price-to-book multiples and actual price-to-book multiples. Collectively, portfolios generated from ranking the difference between the synthetic price-to-forward earnings and actual price-to-forward earnings multiples produce the most economically and statistically significant hedge returns.These results underscore the significance of synthetic multiples in practical applications.

5.6.7 The Synthetic Price Multiples of ESG Stocks

Since investors have prioritized environmental, social, and governance (ESG) goals in recent decades, we should be able to find that the footprints of firms investing in ESG are aligned with increases in shareholder value. The Bloomberg ESG disclosure score quantifies a company's transparency in reporting ESG information. It indicates the amount of ESG data a company has reported publicly from 2005. The score ranks from 0 to 100, where 0 indicates no disclosure about any ESG issues and 100 is the highest ESG disclosure level, with identical disclosure scores for some firms in a particular year. We refer to firms with high ESG disclosure scores as ESG firms. It is interesting to know whether the difference between the synthetic price multiples and actual price multiples differs between the ESG firms and other firms. Can we observe that the ESG firms have a high difference between the synthetic price-to-forward earnings (price-to-book) ratios and the actual price-to-forward earnings (price-to-book) ratios? Information in accounting disclosures, including ESG disclosures, is important input in equity valuation. Can ESG disclosures reduce valuation error and improve valuation accuracy? For firms with high ESG disclosure

Table 5.29 Price multiples, valuation errors and valuation inaccuracy from ESG disclosure score quintile sorted portfolios

	ESG	V/e_1	P/e_1	V/B	P/B	Error	Accur
1	11.3	15.930	21.130	2.788	3.009	0.081	0.328
2	13.01	15.370	19.370	2.358	2.460	0.039	0.280
3	14.45	15.830	19.380	2.778	2.870	0.053	0.277
4	18.15	16.020	18.720	2.988	3.003	0.034	0.245
5	37.46	16.900	17.000	3.735	3.387	−0.07	0.239

scores, we would expect an improved valuation accuracy. To answer these questions, we group all firms into 5 quintiles based on their ESG scores each year. Firms in quintile 1 have the lowest ESG scores, and firms in quintile 5 have the highest.

Table 5.29 shows that the synthetic price-to-forward earnings ratios (V/e_1) have an upward trend with the ESG scores, while the actual price-to-forward earnings ratios (P/e_1) decrease with the ESG score. The difference between the synthetic price-to-forward and actual price-to-forward earnings ratios reaches its largest value (-0.1) in quintile 5, from -5.2 in quintile 1 to -0.1. Not only is the difference between the two ratios the largest in quintile 5, but Table 5.29 also shows that the absolute difference between the two ratios decreases from 5.2 to 0.1 for the ESG firms. Both synthetic price-to-book ratios (V/B) and the actual price-to-book ratios (P/B) increase with the ESG score. Still, again, the difference between the synthetic price-to-book ratios and the actual price-to-book ratios is the largest in quintile 5. In addition, the table shows that the valuation biases (error) decrease, and the valuation accuracy (accur) improves when the ESG scores increase. It suggests that ESG disclosures can help in price discovery when applying the synthetic price-to-forward earnings ratio. If an investor buys firms with a high difference between the synthetic price-to-forward and actual price-to-forward earnings ratios, she will purchase firms with high ESG disclosure scores. It provides supporting evidence that firms investing in ESG also behave in the interests of their shareholders. Therefore, disclosing ESG-related information may help a company attract money from the capital markets, and ESG activities are not a waste of corporate resources (Lys et al., 2015; Ferrell et al., 2016).

In summary, a synthetic price multiple not only reflects the industry's common fundamental economic and accounting characteristics but is also determined by the future and current economic spreads, as well as abnormal growth in the book value of the target company, which drives cross-sectional variation across companies within its industry. In essence, a synthetic price multiple is built on the idea that the value premium is determined by risk and accounting policy. Unlike the commonly used price multiples that build solely on peers' inputs, a synthetic price multiple for the target company directly connects to its value drivers. Like conventional price multiples, synthetic price multiples rely solely on the one-period ahead forecasts of earnings and current period accounting numbers, and do not assume a company's dividend policy.

Chapter 6
Enterprise Valuation in a Unified Framework

The accounting for operating activities differs from the accounting for financial activities. To an approximation, the accounting for financing activities is at fair value, whereas the accounting for operating activities usually uses the (amortized) cost basis. Additionally, the fundamental origins of risk must be rooted in a firm's operations; most financing activities serve to attenuate operating risk, such as expanding operating activities by issuing more debt and adding leverage, or hedging operating risk by holding net cash and cash equivalents. In this chapter, we introduce a unified framework for forecasting operating earnings, valuing invested capital (or net operating assets), and determining the cost of capital at the enterprise level. Based on the intrinsic relationship between the value of invested capital and one-period ahead operating earnings, we can simultaneously estimate industry-level valuation parameters, including the weighted average cost of capital (WACC) and the expected long-term growth rate of operating earnings. This contrasts with conventional valuation analysis, which begins with forecasts of sales revenue. In an efficient market, macroeconomic conditions and industry trends are reflected in the current value of stocks, hence the value of invested capital. We can let the data reveal their intrinsic linkage, guiding the applications of machine learning in asset pricing. Using industry valuation multiples as proxies for individual firms' valuation parameters, we can estimate synthetic valuation multiples to value an enterprise and evaluate an individual firm's WACC.

6.1 Articulation Between the Valuation of Invested Capital and the Forecasting of Abnormal Operating Earnings

We make two standard initial assumptions. Assume that the invested capital is valued in an arbitrage-free market with

P. Wang, *Integrating Earnings Forecasts, Valuation, and Return Prediction*,
Contributions to Finance and Accounting,
https://doi.org/10.1007/978-3-032-05910-9_6

$$(1+\rho)MV_{IC,t} = E_t[MV_{IC,t+1} + FCF_{t+1}], \tag{6.1}$$

where $MV_{IC,t}$ and FCF_t are the market value of the invested capital and free cash flows at the enterprise level at time t, respectively. ρ equals the weighted average cost of capital, and $E_t[.]$ is the expectation operator based on information available at time t. This assumption leads to the well-known discounted free cash flow model (DCF).

We also assume that the firm-level clean surplus accounting relation (CSR) holds:

$$IC_t = IC_{t-1} + NOPAT_t - FCF_t, \tag{6.2}$$

where $NOPAT_t$ is net operating profit after-tax and IC_t is the book value of invested capital (or net operating assets) at time t. In the following analysis, we assume that payments of FCF reduce owners' invested capital on a one-for-one basis, $\partial IC_t/\partial FCF_t = -1$. Still, FCFs do not affect current operating profits, $\partial NOPAT_t/\partial FCF_t = 0$.

Equations (6.1) and (6.2) imply that the market value of invested capital equals the sum of the book value of invested capital and the present value of all expected future abnormal operating earnings or economic profits, i.e.,

$$MV_{IC,t} = IC_t + \sum_{i=1}^{\infty} \frac{E_t[X_{t+i}]}{(1+\rho)^i}, \tag{6.3}$$

where $X_{t+1} = NOPAT_{t+1} - \rho \times IC_t$ is the abnormal operating earnings.

To implement model (6.3), we need to connect future abnormal operating earnings to current accounting observables and future growth of operating earnings. A convenient approach is to assume an information dynamic to describe the evolution of future X_{t+1} in a linear dynamic. It is motivated by the parsimonious model (3.42), which describes the evolution of future abnormal earnings and establishes the basic theoretical constructs of equity value. Future X may come from three sources: the persistence of current abnormal operating earnings (X), accounting conservatism, and future nonzero NPV investment projects. We assume the following linear information dynamics:

$$X_{t+1} = \omega_1 X_t + \omega_2((1+\rho)IC_{t-1} - IC_t) + G_t + \epsilon_{1,t+1}, \tag{6.4}$$

$$G_{t+1} = \gamma G_t + \epsilon_{2,t+1}, \tag{6.5}$$

where $0 \leq \omega_1 < 1$, $0 \leq \gamma < 1+\rho$, and G_t is a variable that captures growth from future investments. $\epsilon_{1,t+1}$ and $\epsilon_{2,t+1}$ are mean zero random error terms. We assume that free cash flows do not affect the NPV of future investment growth, $\partial G_t/\partial FCF_t = 0$, which is consistent with a flat term structure of the required rate of return. The information dynamics describe how abnormal operating earnings evolve over time. To explicitly incorporate the firm's future growth opportunities and accounting conservatism, we allow for $1 \leq \gamma < 1+\rho$. The last inequality ensures the model's convergence. Note that G_t can be associated nonlinearly with accounting numbers and other non-accounting variables such as corporate governance and corporate social responsibilities. We can view $(\gamma - 1)$ as the expected growth rate in a steady state based on information available at time t. Assuming $\gamma \geq 1$ allows the firm to grow in free cash flows. The evolution of G is critical in forecasting future operating earnings, which in turn is one of the key factors in predicting the future cost of capital.

Assume Eq. (6.5) hold. We can show that information dynamic (6.4) holds if, and only if

$$MV_{IC,t} = IC_t + \lambda_1 X_t + \lambda_2 IC_{t-1} + \lambda_3 G_t \tag{6.6}$$

where

$$\begin{aligned} \lambda_1 &= \tfrac{\omega_1}{1+\rho-\omega_1}, \\ \lambda_2 &= \tfrac{(1+\rho)\omega_2}{1+\rho-\omega_1}, \\ \lambda_3 &= \tfrac{1+\rho}{(1+\rho-\omega_1)(1+\rho-\gamma)}. \end{aligned} \tag{6.7}$$

It demonstrates a one-to-one mapping between valuation and forecasting of abnormal operating earnings, given Eq. (6.5). Valuation model (6.6) can be expressed in an alternative form in terms of invested capital (IC_t), operating earnings $(NOPAT_t)$, free cash flows (FCF_t) and the value of future growth (G_t). Note that $FCF_t = NOPAT_t - (IC_t - IC_{t-1})$ and $X_t = NOPAT_t - \rho \times IC_{t-1} = (1+\rho)NOPAT_t - \rho(IC_t + FCF_t)$, valuation model (6.6) can be written as

$$MV_{IC,t} = IC_t + \alpha_1 NOPAT_t + \alpha_2(IC_t + FCF_t) + \alpha_3 G_t, \tag{6.8}$$

where

$$\begin{aligned} \alpha_1 &= \tfrac{(1+\rho)(\omega_1-\omega_2)}{1+\rho-\omega_1} = (1+\rho)\lambda_1 - \lambda_2, \\ \alpha_2 &= \tfrac{(1+\rho)\omega_2-\rho\omega_1}{1+\rho-\omega_1} = \lambda_2 - \rho\lambda_1, \\ \alpha_3 &= \tfrac{1+\rho}{(1+\rho-\omega_1)(1+\rho-\gamma)} = \lambda_3. \end{aligned} \tag{6.9}$$

It suggests that the cum-FCF market value of invested capital (IC) at time t can be written in terms of cum-FCF book value of IC_t, $NOPAT_t$ and the present value of future growth. Combination of FCF with IC makes sense since one dollar of FCF payments to capital providers will reduce IC by one dollar. Under our model set-up, it implies $\partial MV_{IC,t}/\partial FCF_t = -1$. That is, FCF is value irrelevant to enterprise valuation (see Penman and Yehuda, 2009). However, it does not rule out that FCF is useful for forecasting future abnormal operating earnings. This can be seen from information dynamic (6.4) and the clean surplus relation, $(1+\rho)IC_{t-1} - IC_t = FCF_t - X_t$. It is also not surprising that valuation weights α_i $(i = 1-3)$ reflect discount rate ρ and growth rate $\gamma - 1$. In practical application, since companies' valuation benchmarks each other, analysts often use industry-wide valuation parameters as if there are no potential effects of the industry-wide bubble. Estimating these industry-wide valuation parameters is a key issue we need to address. After we forecast future (operating) earnings, we can estimate simultaneously two value drivers, γ and ρ, together with book return on invested capital (ROIC) in an industry. Finally, we can estimate the market value of invested capital for firms within the industry.

6.2 Using a Proxy for Current Value of Invested Capital in Forecasting Future Net Operating Profits

Forecasting net operating profits (NOPAT) is of interest not only to shareholders but also to creditors. However, Eqs. (6.4) and (6.6) are not directly applicable since the present value of future investments G is unobservable. Existing literature does not provide any helpful guidance to identify G_t. To overcome this problem, we can first establish the relationship between future operating earnings and the intrinsic value of invested capital (IC).

Analogous to the equity level analysis, we can show that any two of the following three statements imply the third: (1) abnormal operating earnings dynamic (6.4) holds; (2) the market value of invested capital is given by Eq. (6.6) ; (3) abnormal operating earnings satisfy

$$E_t[X_{t+1}] = \delta_1 X_t + \delta_2(MV_{IC,t} - IC_t) + \omega_2(\gamma - IC_t/IC_{t-1})IC_{t-1}, \tag{6.10}$$

where $\delta_1 = \frac{\omega_1\gamma}{1+\rho}$ and $\delta_2 = \frac{(1+\rho-\omega_1)(1+\rho-\gamma)}{1+\rho}$.

Equation (6.10) establishes an important relationship between forecasting future operating earnings and the intrinsic value of net operating assets. Comparing with dynamic (6.4), Eq. (6.10) suggests that the present value of future investments can be inferred from accounting goodwill (the difference between enterprise value and book value of invested capital), current abnormal operating earnings and abnormal growth in book value of invested capital. It shows that the expected one-year ahead (abnormal) operating earnings can be written in terms of current (abnormal) operating earnings, book values of invested capital, and enterprise value. They link a firm's financial performance in its product market to the capital market, assuming that market value is a good proxy for the intrinsic value of invested capital (IC).

Given $X_t = NOPAT_t - \rho IC_{t-1}$, we can express Eq. (6.10) in terms of NOPAT as below:

$$E_t[NOPAT_{t+1}] = \delta_1 MV_{IC,t} + \delta_2 NOPAT_t + \delta_3 IC_t + \delta_4 IC_{t-1}, \tag{6.11}$$

where

$$
\begin{aligned}
\delta_1 &= \tfrac{(1+\rho-\gamma)(1+\rho-\omega_1)}{1+\rho} = \tfrac{1+\rho-\gamma}{1+\alpha_1+\alpha_2},\\
\delta_2 &= \tfrac{\omega_1\gamma}{1+\rho} = \tfrac{\gamma(\alpha_1+\alpha_2)}{(1+\alpha_1+\alpha_2)},\\
\delta_3 &= \rho - \omega_2 - \tfrac{(1+\rho-\gamma)(1+\rho-\omega_1)}{1+\rho} = \tfrac{\gamma-1-\alpha_2}{1+\alpha_1+\alpha_2},\\
\delta_4 &= \gamma(\omega_2 - \tfrac{\rho\omega_1}{1+\rho}) = \tfrac{\gamma\alpha_2}{1+\alpha_1+\alpha_2}.
\end{aligned}
\tag{6.12}
$$

Note Eq. (6.9) implies that $\omega_1 = \frac{(1+\rho)(\alpha_1+\alpha_2)}{1+\alpha_1+\alpha_2}$ and $\omega_2 = \frac{(1+\rho)(\alpha_1+\alpha_2)-\alpha_1}{1+\alpha_1+\alpha_2}$.

We can apply Eq. (6.11) to forecast future operating profits if we use the sum of the current prices of equity and debt as a proxy for the intrinsic value of invested capital ($MV_{IC,t}$). Specifically, we use historical operating earnings ($NOPAT_t$) as an explanatory variable and the market value of operating asset ($MV_{IC,t-1}$), operating profits ($NOPAT_{t-1}$), book values of invested capital (IC_{t-1}) and lagged invested capital (IC_{t-2}) as independent variables to estimate the coefficients, δ_i ($i = 1-4$). We then carry the coefficients forward to variables ($MV_{IC,t}$, $NOPAT_t$, IC_t, IC_{t-1}) to forecast $NOPAT_{t+1}$. Since aggregate accruals equal the change in invested capital, it suggests that accruals can be useful in forecasting (operating) earnings.

Given the clean surplus relation, we can replace the lagged invested capital IC_{t-1} by free cash flows FCF_t. Therefore, we can forecast one-period ahead operating earnings by regressing the market value of invested capital, operating profits, book value of invested capital, and free cash flows. We can use the model in cross-sectional or industry panel data to forecast out-of-sample one-year ahead or multi-period ahead operating earnings. In this analysis, we can also utilize the Jackknife technique by excluding information from the firm under investigation.

6.3 Incorporating Explicitly R&D, SG&A and Intangible Assets in Information Dynamic

We can extend the dynamic of future investment growth (G) to explicitly incorporate both tangible and intangible investments. For example, we can assume

$$
G_{t+1} = (1+g)G_t + \Gamma Y_t + \epsilon_G, \tag{6.13}
$$

where g is the expected steady state growth rate based on time t information. ΓY_t is a function of investments, such as a function of capital expenditure ($CapX_t$), research and development ($R\&D_t$), selling, general and administrative expense ($SG\&A_t$), and internal generated intangibles ($Intan$). Γ is a vector of parameters. That is, the NPV of future investments (G_{t+1}) depends on time t variables in Y_t:

$$
E_t[G_{t+1}] = (1+g)G_t + \lambda_3 CapX_t + \lambda_4 R\&D_t + \lambda_5 SG\&A_t + \lambda_6 Intan_t.
$$

Since G inherits growth and risk nature, we can also consider other variables, such as order backlog, accruals, return on assets (ROA), leverage, GDP, corporate governance, management remuneration, employee training, carbon emissions (ESG), or some risk proxies, in predicting G_{t+1}.

Given valuation model (6.6) and by scaling G, we can write the intrinsic value of invested capital in terms of two periods' book values of invested capital (IC), abnormal operating earnings (X), and the present value of future investments (G):

$$MV_{IC,t} = IC_t + \lambda_1 X_t + \lambda_2 IC_{t-1} + G_t. \tag{6.14}$$

It follows from Eqs. (6.1) and (6.2) that the abnormal operating earnings can be written as

$$\begin{aligned} E_t[X_{t+1}] = {} & \frac{(\rho - g)}{(1+\lambda_1)} MV_{IC,t} + \frac{(1+g)\lambda_1}{(1+\lambda_1)} X_t \\ & - \frac{\lambda_2 + (\rho - g)}{(1+\lambda_1)} IC_t + \frac{(1+g)\lambda_2}{(1+\lambda_1)} IC_{t-1} \\ & - \frac{\lambda_3}{(1+\lambda_1)} CapX_t - \frac{\lambda_4}{(1+\lambda_1)} R\&D_t \\ & - \frac{\lambda_5}{(1+\lambda_1)} SG\&A_t - \frac{\lambda_6}{(1+\lambda_1)} Intan_t. \end{aligned}$$

In terms of operating earnings, we have

$$\begin{aligned} E_t[NOPAT_{t+1}] = {} & \frac{(\rho - g)}{(1+\lambda_1)} MV_{IC,t} + \frac{(1+g)\lambda_1}{(1+\lambda_1)} NOPAT_t + \frac{\rho\lambda_1 - \lambda_2 + g}{(1+\lambda_1)} IC_t \\ & + \frac{(1+g)(\lambda_2 - \lambda_1\rho)}{(1+\lambda_1)} IC_{t-1} - \frac{\lambda_3}{(1+\lambda_1)} CapX_t - \frac{\lambda_4}{(1+\lambda_1)} R\&D_t \\ & - \frac{\lambda_5}{(1+\lambda_1)} SG\&A_t - \frac{\lambda_6}{(1+\lambda_1)} Intan_t. \end{aligned} \tag{6.15}$$

It establishes a link between future operating earnings and current tangible and intangible investments.

6.4 Valuation of Invested Capital

It has long been capital market practice that investors use currently observable companies' fundamental accounting statement information, such as net operating profits, invested capital, and free cash flows, to assess an enterprise market value. To estimate the intrinsic value of invested capital, we can explore the industry-level value drivers as discussed in previous chapters.

6.4.1 Estimating the Key Industry Value Drivers in a Unified Framework

The value of invested capital is expressed as the sum of the book value of invested capital and the present value of expected all future abnormal operating earnings in model (6.1). The linear information dynamic provides a simple way to facilitate the model. It effectively assumes that all future cash flows can be mapped into the current accounting fundamentals and non-accounting information, capturing future growth opportunities. The valuation weights attached to the current information variables must reflect the discount rate and future growth. In practical valuation, we need to estimate these valuation weights.

If we write the market value of invested capital in a linear combination of IC, NOPAT, and FCF as in Eq. (6.8), we have

$$MV_{IC,t} = IC_t + \alpha_1 NOPAT_t + \alpha_2(IC_t + FCF_t) + G_t, \tag{6.16}$$

where $MV_{IC,t}$ is the market value of invested capital, NOPAT is after-tax operating profits, IC is the book value of invested capital, and FCF is free cash flow at the firm level. If we assume future growth opportunities follow an AR(1) process as dynamic (6.5), we can then establish the relation between future operating earnings and the market value of invested capital as Eq. (6.17) below:

$$E_t[NOPAT_{t+1}] = \delta_1 MV_{IC,t} + \delta_2 NOPAT_t + \delta_3 IC_t + \delta_4 IC_{t-1}, \tag{6.17}$$

where $\gamma = 1 + g$ in equation system (6.12), and

$$\begin{aligned} \delta_1 &= \frac{(\rho-g)}{(1+\alpha_1+\alpha_2)}, \\ \delta_2 &= \frac{(1+g)(\alpha_1+\alpha_2)}{(1+\alpha_1+\alpha_2)}, \\ \delta_3 &= \frac{g-\alpha_2}{(1+\alpha_1+\alpha_2)}, \\ \delta_4 &= \frac{(1+g)\alpha_2}{(1+\alpha_1+\alpha_2)}. \end{aligned} \tag{6.18}$$

Suppose we use the sum of market capitalization and the book value of debt as a proxy for the market value of invested capital. In that case, we can apply model (6.17) to forecast one-period or multi-period ahead operating earnings. Note $FCF_t = NOPAT_t - (IC_t - IC_{t-1})$, forecasting Eq. (6.17) can be written as the valuation model:

$$\begin{aligned} MV_{IC,t} = {} & (1+\alpha_1+\alpha_2)\frac{E_t[NOPAT_{t+1}]-(1+g)NOPAT_t}{(\rho-g)} + (1+\alpha_2)\frac{IC_t-(1+g)IC_{t-1}}{(\rho-g)} \\ & + \frac{(1+g)FCF_t}{(\rho-g)}. \end{aligned} \tag{6.19}$$

It shows that the value of invested capital equals the discounted perpetual growth of the one-period ahead FCF adjusted for abnormal growth in NOPAT and the abnormal growth in the book value of invested capital. Note that the growth rate (g) appears in both the numerator and the denominator in each component, suggesting a nonlinear relationship between the market value of invested capital and future growth.

Alternatively, valuation model (6.19) can be written as a model of the cost of capital in terms of the company's fundamentals:

$$\rho = g + (1+g)\frac{FCF_t}{MV_{IC,t}} + (1+\alpha_1+\alpha_2)\frac{E_t[NOPAT_{t+1}]-(1+g)NOPAT_t}{MV_{IC,t}} \\ +(1+\alpha_2)\frac{IC_t-(1+g)IC_{t-1}}{MV_{IC,t}}. \tag{6.20}$$

That is, the weighted average cost of capital can be expressed as the sum of the growth rate of future free cash flows and the forward free cash flow yield, adjusted for abnormal growth of NOPAT and IC. Once we have forecasts of the one-period ahead NOPAT, and assuming the market value and book value of debt are equal, we can use observable stock prices and industry-wide information to infer industry-specific valuation parameters, including the long-term growth rate and the weighted average cost of capital, by regressing model (6.17).

Note that the same Eq. (6.17) can be used to forecast out-of-sample NOPAT in a consistent manner. If we run the following regression

$$\frac{NOPAT_{t+1}}{MV_{IC,t}} = \delta_1 + \delta_2\frac{NOPAT_t}{MV_{IC,t}} + \delta_3\frac{IC_t}{MV_{IC,t}} + \delta_4\frac{IC_{t-1}}{MV_{IC,t}} + \epsilon_{t+1}, \tag{6.21}$$

based on cross-sectional or industry panel data, equation system (6.18) can be used to infer the key valuation parameters for the cross section or industry as

$$\begin{aligned} 1+g &= \frac{1+\delta_2+\delta_3+\sqrt{(1+\delta_2+\delta_3)^2-4(\delta_2-\delta_4)}}{2}, \\ \rho &= g + \frac{(1+g)\delta_1}{1+g-\delta_2}, \\ \alpha_1 &= \frac{\delta_2-\delta_4}{(1+g)-\delta_2}, \\ \alpha_2 &= \frac{\delta_4}{(1+g)-\delta_2}. \end{aligned} \tag{6.22}$$

Noting the clean surplus relation, we can also use FCF to replace IC_{t-1} in regression Eq. (6.21) as

$$\frac{NOPAT_{t+1}}{MV_{IC,t}} = \delta_1' + \delta_2'\frac{NOPAT_t}{MV_{IC,t}} + \delta_3'\frac{IC_t}{MV_{IC,t}} + \delta_4'\frac{FCF_t}{MV_{IC,t}} + \epsilon_{t+1}, \tag{6.23}$$

where $\delta_1' = \frac{(\rho-g)}{(1+\alpha_1+\alpha_2)}$, $\delta_2' = \frac{(1+g)\alpha_1}{(1+\alpha_1+\alpha_2)}$, $\delta_3' = \frac{g(1+\alpha_2)}{(1+\alpha_1+\alpha_2)}$ and $\delta_4' = \frac{(1+g)\alpha_2}{(1+\alpha_1+\alpha_2)}$. The valuation parameters can be written in terms of the regression coefficients as

$$
\begin{aligned}
1+g &= \frac{1+\delta_2'+\delta_3'+\sqrt{(1+\delta_2'+\delta_3')^2-4\delta_2'}}{2},\\
\rho &= g+\frac{(1+g)\delta_1'}{1+g-\delta_2'-\delta_4'},\\
\alpha_1 &= \frac{\delta_2'}{(1+g)-\delta_2'-\delta_4'},\\
\alpha_2 &= \frac{\delta_4'}{(1+g)-\delta_2'-\delta_4'}.
\end{aligned}
\tag{6.24}
$$

Alternatively, we can use a nonlinear programming to estimate industry-level valuation parameters or cross sectional parameters $(\alpha_1^I, \alpha_2^I, g^I, \rho^I)$ directly from regression model (6.21) or (6.23). When estimating the industry-level parameters, we can also exclude firm j from the industry i portfolio in which firm j belongs (Jackknifing) if we use industry-level valuation parameters in firm j valuation. However, the impact of a single firm in the industry is likely to be minimal.

In summary, while conventional forecasts of earnings often start from forecasts of sales revenues, we can directly forecast (operating) earnings. We implicitly assume that the aggregate capital market is efficient, and macroeconomic conditions and industry trends are reflected in current stock and bond prices in the aggregate sense. We let historical data tell us the implied key value drivers. They include the net operating profits after tax (NOPAT), weighted average cost of capital (ρ) and future growth of NOPAT (g). The above suggests that we can estimate the key value drivers in a unified framework. Unlike applications of machine learning, we can establish the explicit structural relationship between future earnings, values, and the cost of capital.

6.4.2 *Estimating the Present Value of Future Investment Growth*

While growth rate g can be jointly determined from the regression coefficients, we need to estimate the present value of future investment growth (G), if we use model (6.16) to value invested capital. Given assumptions (6.1) and (6.2), valuation model (6.16) and information dynamic (6.5) imply that

$$(1+\rho)MV_{IC,t} = (1+\alpha_1+\alpha_2)E_t[NOPAT_{t+1}] + (1+\alpha_2)IC_t + (1+g)G_t.$$

The left-hand side equals $(1+\rho)(IC_t+\alpha_1 NOPAT_t+\alpha_2(IC_t+FCF_t)+G_t)$. When $\rho \neq g$, we reorganize terms and obtain

$$
\begin{aligned}
G_t = &\frac{(1+\alpha_1+\alpha_2)}{(\rho-g)}E_t[NOPAT_{t+1}] - \frac{(1+\rho)\alpha_1}{(\rho-g)}NOPAT_t - \frac{\rho(1+\alpha_2)}{(\rho-g)}IC_t\\
&-\frac{(1+\rho)\alpha_2}{(\rho-g)}FCF_t.
\end{aligned}
\tag{6.25}
$$

Since $FCF_t = NOPAT_t - (IC_t - IC_{t-1})$, we can write G in terms of the lagged invested capital, replacing FCF. We can rewrite it as:

$$G_t = \frac{E_t[NOPAT_{t+1}]-\rho IC_t}{(\rho-g)} + \frac{(\alpha_1+\alpha_2)(E_t[NOPAT_{t+1}]-(1+\rho)NOPAT_t)}{(\rho-g)} + \frac{\alpha_2(IC_t-(1+\rho)IC_{t-1})}{(\rho-g)}. \quad (6.26)$$

It suggests that the value of future investment growth is the present value of the perpetual growth of the expected one-year ahead abnormal operating earnings, adjusted for the abnormal increase in NOPAT and IC. Once we estimate the industry-wide or cross-sectional valuation parameters, we can use firm-specific fundamental variables, including forecasts of NOPAT, to estimate the value of future growth. For firm j in industry i, we have

$$G_t = \frac{E_t[NOPAT_{t+1}]-\rho_i IC_t}{(\rho_i-g_i)} + \frac{(\alpha_{1i}+\alpha_{2i})(E_t[NOPAT_{t+1}]-(1+\rho_i)NOPAT_t)}{(\rho_i-g_i)} + \frac{\alpha_{2i}(IC_t-(1+\rho_i)IC_{t-1})}{(\rho_i-g_i)}. \quad (6.27)$$

If we use industry valuation parameters $(\alpha_{1i}, \alpha_{2i}, g_i, \rho_i)$ as proxies for corresponding valuation parameters of firm j within industry i, we can then use valuation model (6.16) to estimate the value of invested capital for firm j, i.e.,

$$MV_{IC,t} = IC_t + \alpha_{1i} NOPATI_t + \alpha_{2i}(IC_t + FCF_t) + G_t. \quad (6.28)$$

6.5 Applying Valuation Multiples

A synthetic price multiple can also be constructed at the enterprise level. We can replace equity level book value, earnings, and stock prices in Sect. 5.3 by invested capital (IC), operating earnings ($NOPAT$), and the market value of invested capital (MV_{IC}), respectively. The persistence of abnormal net operating earnings, the conservatism parameter, the long-term growth rate, and the weighted average cost of capital can be simultaneously estimated on an industry-year basis. Based on model (6.11), the parameters in information dynamics (6.4) and (6.5) for industry i can be simultaneously estimated from the following regression model on a year-by-year basis:

$$\frac{NOPAT_{t+1}}{MV_{IC,t}} = \frac{(1+\rho-\gamma)(1+\rho-\omega_1)}{1+\rho} + \frac{\omega_1\gamma}{1+\rho}\frac{NOPAT_t}{MV_{IC,t}} + [\rho - \omega_2 - \frac{(1+\rho-\gamma)(1+\rho-\omega_1)}{1+\rho}]\frac{IC_t}{MV_{IC,t}} + \gamma[\omega_2 - \frac{\rho\omega_1}{1+\rho}]\frac{IC_{t-1}}{MV_{IC,t}} + \epsilon_{t+1}. \quad (6.29)$$

Therefore, given the one-year ahead forecasts of $NOPAT$ from the model-based forecasts or analysts' forecasts if available, the synthetic enterprise level value-to-forward earnings ratio ($MV_{IC}/NOPAT_1$) for the target company j in the industry i can be estimated similar to that in Sect. 5.3 as

$$\frac{MV_{IC}}{NOPAT_1} \equiv \frac{1}{\rho_{it}} + \frac{M_i N_{i,j}^T}{E_t[NOPAT_{j,t+1}]}, \tag{6.30}$$

where the vector of industry common parameters: $M_i \equiv [M_i^1, M_i^2, M_i^3]$,

$$M_i^1 = \frac{1}{(1+\rho_{it}-\omega_{it,1})(1+\rho_{it}-\gamma_{it})} \frac{(1+\rho_{it})(\omega_{it,1}+\gamma_{it}-1)-\omega_{it,1}\gamma_{it}}{\rho_{it}},$$

$$M_i^2 = \frac{-\omega_{it,1}\gamma_{it}}{(1+\rho_{it}-\omega_{it,1})(1+\rho_{it}-\gamma_{it})},$$

$$M_i^3 = \frac{-(1+\rho_{it})\omega_{it,2}}{(1+\rho_{it}-\omega_{it,1})(1+\rho_{it}-\gamma_{it})}.$$

The corresponding vector of firm j's value drivers are: $N_{i,j} \equiv [N_{i,j}^1, N_{i,j}^2, N_{i,j}^3]$, where

$$N_{i,j}^1 = (\frac{E_t[NOPAT_{j,t+1}]}{IC_{j,t}} - \rho_{it})IC_{j,t},$$

$$N_{i,j}^2 = (\frac{NOPAT_{j,t}}{IC_{j,t-1}} - \rho_{it})IC_{j,t-1},$$

$$N_{i,j}^3 = (\gamma_{it} - IC_{j,t}/IC_{j,t-1}))IC_{j,t-1}.$$

Once we estimate the company's synthetic value-to-forward operating earnings ratio, we can estimate the value of invested capital by multiplying the ratio by the company's one-period-ahead operating earnings.

A synthetic enterprise-level value-to-book ratio, MV_{IC}/IC, can also be similarly estimated and generate the identical value of invested capital as applying $MV_{IC}/NOPAT_1$. Again, these are, in essence, based on the intuition that the value premium is determined by risk and accounting policy. Accounting numbers, NOPAT and IC, are jointly in action in valuation. Accounting return on assets ($ROA = E_t[NOPAT_{j,t+1}]/IC_{j,t}$) conveys value and risk, including financial leverage. Higher expected future return on assets (current return on assets) relative to cost of capital (ρ) indicates high (low) risk.

The synthetic price multiples can, in principle, be used to estimate the value of a non-public company, although its price is not available. Vector M can be estimated based on common characteristics of the industry in which the company belongs, and vector N only relies on the company's accounting fundamentals and the industry's long-term properties. In practice, there are a number of variants on the $MV_{IC}/NOPAT_1$ ratio. We can estimate the synthetic valuation multiples such as value-to-EBIT, value-to-EBITA, value-to-EBITDA, and value-to-sales. They are the product of a synthetic $MV_{IC}/NOPAT_1$ (or MV_{IC}/IC) ratio and a measure of profit margin (asset turnover). For example,

$$\frac{MV_{IC,t}}{E_t[EBITDA_{t+1}]} = [\frac{MV_{IC}}{NOPAT_1}] \times \frac{E_t[NOPAT_{t+1}]}{E_t[EBITDA_{t+1}]}.$$

6.6 Estimating Directly the Weighted Average Cost of Capital (WACC)

There is no commonly accepted approach to directly estimating WACC since a firm's expected WACC is affected by the firm's various (un)known characteristics and macroeconomic factors. The absence of data on asset beta adds to the difficulties in determining a trustworthy estimate. In this section, we develop a method for estimating the weighted average cost of capital ex ante. Unlike the common practice of using the estimated cost of each capital component as an input, we estimate the WACC directly from the intrinsic linkage between forecasts of operating income and enterprise value as the implied cost of capital. Estimating the WACC directly is desired on both theoretical and practical grounds, such as capital budgeting, firm valuation, and investment decision making, as well as for regulatory purposes.[1]

When estimating the weighted average cost of capital (WACC) directly, the first step involves projecting future operating incomes, which are a fundamental determinant of firm value. To facilitate this, we develop a cross-sectional model aimed at forecasting operating income, an important and inherently interesting challenge in its own right. Leading valuation texts (e.g., Penman, 2013; Sloan and Lundholm, 2006) emphasize the importance of distinguishing between operating and financial activities for valuation purposes. Operating income tends to be more persistent than net income, as it is less affected by transitory accounting items. In addition, unlike net income, forecasts of operating income are of interest to all capital providers, including debt holders. Credit rating agencies often rely on projected operating incomes when assigning credit ratings. Following the estimation of operating income, we can investigate the relationship between the estimated cost of capital and corporate leverage, examining the existence of a U-shaped relationship between WACC and leverage, as well as an inverted U-shaped relationship between leverage and total market value, as often advocated in textbooks.

Assume that the market value of invested capital can be written as Eq. (6.16) and the NPV of future investments explicitly incorporates accounting conservatism similar to dynamic (4.6):

$$MV_{IC,t} = IC_t + \alpha_1 NOPAT_t + \alpha_2 (IC_t + FCF_t) + G_t, \tag{6.31}$$

[1] It is believed to be vital for regulatory purposes around the world. For example, the UK, Australia, New Zealand, and Germany all have regulatory regimes that require an estimate of the WACC. It has also long been argued in capital budgeting that the proper discount rate for a typical investment project in a company should be the WACC, even if it is financed by 100% of debt. This is because the company is using up some of its future borrowing capacity when financing with debt. Furthermore, the cost of bankruptcy is unobservable.

$$G_{t+1} = (1+g)G_t + \lambda(MV_{IC,t} + FCF_t - MV_{IC,t-1} - NOPAT_t) + \epsilon_{t+1}, \tag{6.32}$$

where g can be interpreted as the long-run average annual growth of the NPV of all future investments over the remaining life of the firm, as inferred from information available at time t. In order to make sure that the discounted present value of the future free cash flows is bounded, we impose the standard transversality condition, requiring that $\rho > g$. Similar to the weighted average cost of capital, the expectation of a new growth rate should be formed with the passage of time as a firm's operating environment or technology is expected to change, resulting in adjustments to the investment set. We measure accounting conservatism by the difference between economic income $(MV_{IC,t}+FCF_t-MV_{IC,t-1})$ and accounting income $(NOPAT_t)$. Note also, by clean surplus relation, $MV_{IC,t} + FCF_t - MV_{IC,t-1} - NOPAT_t = (\Delta MV_{IC,t} - \Delta IC_t)$, which is the change in the company's goodwill. Here, we accept the possibility that accounting may affect investors' expectations of future cash flows and impact expected growth rates. We refer to λ as the accounting policy parameter. Consistent with Miller and Modigliani (1961), we also assume that the NPV of future investments (and hence value of assets) is determined by its investment policy, not its distribution policy, and that $\partial G_t/\partial FCF_t = 0$.

We can show that

$$\begin{aligned} E_t[NOPAT_{t+1}] = {} & \tfrac{(1+g)\alpha_1+\lambda}{(1+\alpha_1+\alpha_2)} NOPAT_t + \tfrac{g(1+\alpha_2)}{(1+\alpha_1+\alpha_2)} IC_t + \tfrac{(1+g)\alpha_2-\lambda}{(1+\alpha_1+\alpha_2)} FCF_t \\ & + \tfrac{(\rho-g)-\lambda}{(1+\alpha_1+\alpha_2)} MV_{IC,t} + \tfrac{\lambda}{(1+\alpha_1+\alpha_2)} MV_{IC,t-1}. \end{aligned} \tag{6.33}$$

Applying the clean surplus relation, the expected one-period-ahead operating income can also be written in the form:

$$\begin{aligned} E_t[NOPAT_{t+1}] = {} & \tfrac{(1+g)(\alpha_1+\alpha_2)}{(1+\alpha_1+\alpha_2)} NOPAT_t + \tfrac{g-\alpha_2+\lambda}{(1+\alpha_1+\alpha_2)} \Delta IC_t + \tfrac{g(1+\alpha_2)}{(1+\alpha_1+\alpha_2)} IC_{t-1} \\ & + \tfrac{(\rho-g)-\lambda}{(1+\alpha_1+\alpha_2)} \Delta MV_{IC,t} + \tfrac{\rho-g}{(1+\alpha_1+\alpha_2)} MV_{IC,t-1}, \end{aligned} \tag{6.34}$$

where $\Delta MV_{IC,t} = MV_{IC,t} - MV_{IC,t-1}$ and $\Delta IC_t = IC_t - IC_{t-1}$ are two flow variables. This expression can be used in forecasting future operating earnings.

Equation (6.34) can also be rewritten as

$$\begin{aligned} \rho = {} & g + (1+g)\tfrac{FCF_t}{MV_{IC,t}} + (1+\alpha_1+\alpha_2)\tfrac{E_t[NOPAT_{t+1}]-(1+g)NOPAT_t}{MV_{IC,t}} \\ & +(1+\alpha_2)\tfrac{IC_t-(1+g)IC_{t-1}}{MV_{IC,t}} + \lambda\tfrac{(MV_{IC,t}-IC_t)-(MV_{IC,t-1}-IC_{t-1})}{MV_{IC,t}}. \end{aligned} \tag{6.35}$$

Once we know the market's expected one-period ahead NOPAT and individual company's valuation parameters $(\alpha_1, \alpha_2, g, \lambda)$, we can estimate the weighted average cost of capital ρ. The relationship implied by the first three terms of Eq. (6.35) can be rearranged to give $MV_{IC,t} = \frac{FCF_t(1+g)}{\rho-g}$, which is analogous to a cash flow growth model. Since g is the expected long-term growth rate of future operating earnings, ρ has to be adjusted for the abnormal growth in operating income, the abnormal growth in net operating assets, and accounting policy.

6.6.1 Forecasting of Firm-year Specific Operating Income

To estimate the weighted average cost of capital ρ, we need the one-period ahead forecasts of NOPAT and estimate the industry-level valuation parameters. Since the market expected one-period ahead NOPAT for a company is not observable, we can use model-based forecasts as a proxy for it. Fortunately, the variables in Eq. (6.33) consist of fundamental building blocks for forecasting future NOPAT. Because negative earnings are less persistent, we can introduce a dummy variable, Neg_t, which equals 1 if the firm has negative NOPAT at time t and 0 otherwise.

Given that financial professionals often use industry-level valuation parameters and value drivers, such as growth and discount rates, to estimate the value of individual firms within the industry, we can run time-series and cross-sectional regressions to forecast one-year-ahead operating income ($NOPAT_{ij,t+1}$) for each firm j in industry i:[2]

$$\begin{aligned}\frac{NOPAT_{ji,t+1}}{MV_{IC,ji,t-1}} &= \eta_{1,it}\frac{\Delta MV_{IC,ji,t}}{MV_{IC,ji,t-1}} + \eta_{2,it}\frac{NOPAT_{ji,t}}{MV_{IC,ji,t-1}} + \eta_{3,it}\frac{\Delta IC_{ji,t}}{MV_{IC,ji,t-1}} + \eta_{4,it}\frac{IC_{ji,t-1}}{MV_{IC,ji,t-1}} \\ &+\eta_{5,it} + \eta_{6,it}Neg_{ji,t} + \epsilon_{ji,t},\end{aligned} \tag{6.36}$$

where $\epsilon_{ji,t+1}$ is mean-zero error term. This implicitly assumes that parameters g, α_1, α_2 and λ are constant across firms within a particular industry portfolio but allow for annual variations. To reduce nonstationarity and minimize the effects of endogeneity, both sides of Eq. (6.36) can be deflated by the lagged value of invested capital. The model could be estimated using a rolling window regression, say, a rolling window of three years. For each forecast year τ, the model can be estimated using only data that is available in year τ -1 for firm j in industry i. The estimated coefficients from the panel regression are then multiplied by the independent variables as of year τ-1 to generate out-of-sample one-year ahead forecasts of operating earnings for firm j in industry i at year τ:

$$\begin{aligned}\widehat{NOPAT}_{ji,t+1} &= \hat{\eta}_{1,it}\Delta MV_{IC,ji,t} + \hat{\eta}_{2,it}NOPAT_{ji,t} \\ &+\hat{\eta}_{3,it}\Delta IC_{ji,t} + \hat{\eta}_{4,it}IC_{ji,t-1} \\ &+\hat{\eta}_{5,it}MV_{IC,ji,t-1} + \hat{\eta}_{6,it}Neg_{ji,t-1} \times MV_{IC,ji,t-1}.\end{aligned} \tag{6.37}$$

[2] Since operating accruals (ACC_t) are used to smooth (operating) earnings in accrual accounting, and the change in net operating assets ΔIC_t is equal to the sum of investment and accruals, one could include accruals in the NOPAT forecasting model.

6.6.2 Industry-year Specific WACC, Growth Rate and Other Valuation Parameters

Using the model-forecasted firm-specific $\widehat{NOPAT}_{ji,t+1}$ as a proxy for the market expected one-period ahead operating earnings of the firm, we run regressions based on Eq. (6.34) on an industry-year basis. Since the forecasts are out-of-sample, the parameters implied from the regressions can be viewed as expected values. By comparing the coefficients of Eqs. (6.34) and (6.38) below, we can infer average industry-year specific weighted average cost of capital ($\rho_{i,t}$), growth rate ($g_{i,t}$), valuation parameters ($\alpha_{1i,t}, \alpha_{2i,t}$), and accounting policy parameter ($\lambda_{i,t}$) from the regression coefficients. Here, we use a subscript t to indicate that these long-run parameters can be estimated annually based on updated annual information.

$$\begin{aligned}\frac{E_t[NOPAT_{i,t+1}]}{MV_{IC,i,t-1}} &= \delta_{1,it}\frac{\Delta MV_{IC,i,t}}{MV_{IC,i,t-1}} + \delta_{2,it}\frac{NOPAT_{it}}{MV_{IC,i,t-1}} + \delta_{3,it}\frac{\Delta IC_{it}}{MV_{IC,i,t-1}} \\ &+\delta_{4,it}\frac{IC_{i,t-1}}{MV_{IC,i,t-1}} + \delta_{5,it},\end{aligned} \tag{6.38}$$

where

$$\begin{aligned} g_{it} &= \frac{-(1-\delta_{1,it}-\delta_{2,it}-\delta_{3,it}+\delta_{5,it})+\sqrt{(1-\delta_{1,it}-\delta_{2,it}-\delta_{3,it}+\delta_{5,it})^2+4\delta_{4,it}}}{2}, \\ \rho_{it} &= g_{it} + \frac{(1+g_{it})\delta_{5,it}}{(1+g_{it}-\delta_{2,it})}, \\ \alpha_{1,it} &= (1+g_{it})[\frac{1+(\delta_{1,it}+\delta_{3,it}-\delta_{5,it})}{1+g_{it}-\delta_{2,it}} - 1], \\ \alpha_{2,it} &= (1+g_{it})[1 - \frac{(\delta_{1,it}+\delta_{3,it}-\delta_{5,it})}{1+g_{it}-\delta_{2,it}}] - 1, \\ \lambda_{it} &= \frac{(1+g_{it})(\delta_{5,it}-\delta_{1,it})}{(1+g_{it}-\delta_{2,it})}. \end{aligned} \tag{6.39}$$

Alternatively, we can use a nonlinear regression procedure to estimate directly the five parameters above.

6.6.3 Estimating the Firm-year Implied Weighted Average Cost of Capital

Given the one-period ahead firm-specific operating income and industry-year specific valuation parameters, we can follow industry practice and use the average industry-year parameters as common parameters for all firms in each industry-year portfolio to derive firm-year-specific weighted average costs of capital. For firm j in industry i, the firm-year-specific weighted average cost of capital (ρ_{jt}), according to Eq. (6.35), can be proxied by

$$\rho_{jt} = g_{it} + (1+g_{it})\frac{FCF_{j,t}}{MV_{IC,j,t}} + (1+\alpha_{1,it}+\alpha_{2,it})\frac{E_t[NOPAT_{j,t+1}]-(1+g_{it})NOPAT_{j,t}}{MV_{IC,j,t}}$$
$$+(1+\alpha_{2,it})\frac{IC_{j,t}-(1+g_{it})IC_{j,t-1}}{MV_{IC,j,t}} + \lambda_{it}\frac{(MV_{IC,j,t}-IC_{j,t})-(MV_{IC,j,t-1}-IC_{j,t-1})}{MV_{IC,j,t}}. \tag{6.40}$$

In summary, corporate valuation is central to numerous economic decisions taken by investors, creditors, corporate management, regulators, and policymakers. Classical finance approaches to valuation modeling focus on heroic assumptions about the cost of capital, derived at best from very low-powered, albeit theoretically elegant models such as the CAPM, in addition to difficult-to-forecast future cash flows. The question arises of whether we could improve on classical finance approaches to valuation and estimating the discount rate by bringing accounting insights to the table.

Accounting information is designed to inform economic decision makers, especially investors and creditors in companies. The principles used in measuring accounting numbers have evolved over a long period of time. Although accounting standards setters often do not clearly articulate the decision models that should be used by investors and creditors, accounting information displays properties linked to uncertainty in cash flows (earnings) resulting from economic transactions, conservative accounting principles, and hence risk. Cash flow (earnings) uncertainty and risk are central to valuation and the determination of the cost of capital or expected risk-adjusted returns.

In this monograph, we focused on accounting-based valuation models, which exploit the properties of accounting numbers to identify the drivers of future wealth creation, from which future cash flows to investors and creditors will be paid. The advantages of accounting numbers in both forecasting future earnings (cash flows) and valuation are now well-supported empirically. However, the links between accounting numbers and the cost of capital, or a proxy for expected returns, while well-known and often empirically robust, have only recently begun to be interpreted through a theoretical lens that exploits the properties of accounting measurement (see Penman, 2021). Understanding growth and its risk appears to be key to both valuation and reliable inference concerning the expected returns being made by investors in an aggregate efficient market. This monograph establishes a formal connection between accounting numbers and the intrinsic value of assets, as well as the cost of capital. It proposes approaches to forecasting future earnings, estimating intrinsic value, and predicting future returns in a unified framework.

Appendix

Proof of Valuation Eq. (6.6) The information dynamics (6.4) and (6.5) imply that the market value of invested capital (IC) can be written in terms of the book value of IC, abnormal operating earnings, the lagged book value of IC, and the present value of future growth opportunities in a linear form as described in Eq. (6.6). Now, we need to identify λ_i (i=1,2,3). The clean surplus relation relationship implies that

$IC_{t+1} + FCF_{t+1} = NOPAT_{t+1} + IC_t = X_{t+1} + (1+\rho)IC_t$. Hence,

$$\begin{aligned}&MV_{IC,t+1} + FCF_{t+1} = IC_{t+1} + FCF_{t+1} + \lambda_1 X_{t+1} + \lambda_2 IC_t + \lambda_3 G_{t+1}\\&= (1+\lambda_1)X_{t+1} + (1+\rho+\lambda_2)IC_t + \lambda_3(\gamma G_t + \epsilon_{2,t+1}).\end{aligned} \tag{6.41}$$

Given Eq. (6.4), we have

$$\begin{aligned}&MV_{IC,t+1} + FCF_{t+1}\\&= (1+\lambda_1)(\omega_1 X_t + \omega_2((1+\rho)IC_{t-1} - IC_t) + G_t) + (1+\rho+\lambda_2)IC_t + \lambda_3\gamma G_t\\&+(1+\lambda_1)\epsilon_{1,t+1} + \lambda_3\epsilon_{2,t+1}.\end{aligned}$$

Assumption (6.1) implies that

$$\begin{aligned}&(1+\lambda_1)(\omega_1 X_t + \omega_2((1+\rho)IC_{t-1} - IC_t) + G_t) + (1+\rho+\lambda_2)IC_t + \lambda_3\gamma G_t\\&= (1+\rho)(IC_t + \lambda_1 X_t + \lambda_2 IC_{t-1} + \lambda_3 G_t).\end{aligned}$$

Matching the coefficients, we have

$$\begin{aligned}&(1+\lambda_1)\omega_1 = (1+\rho)\lambda_1,\\&-(1+\lambda_1)\omega_2 + (1+\rho+\lambda_2) = 1+\rho,\\&(1+\lambda_1) + \lambda_3\gamma = (1+\rho)\lambda_3.\end{aligned}$$

That is

$$\lambda_1 = \frac{\omega_1}{1+\rho-\omega_1},\ \lambda_2 = (1+\lambda_1)\omega_2 = \frac{(1+\rho)\omega_2}{1+\rho-\omega_1},\ \lambda_3 = \frac{(1+\rho)}{(1+\rho-\omega_1)(1+\rho-\gamma)}.$$

On the other hand, given Eqs. (6.6) and (6.41), and $E_t[MV_{IC,t+1} + FCF_{t+1}] = (1+\rho)MV_{IC,t}$, we have

$$\begin{aligned}&(1+\lambda_1)E_t[X_{t+1}] + (1+\rho+\lambda_2)IC_t + \lambda_3(\gamma G_t)\\&= (1+\rho)(IC_t + \lambda_1 X_t + \lambda_2 IC_{t-1} + \lambda_3 G_t).\end{aligned}$$

Reorganizing the terms, we have

$$E_t[X_{t+1}] = \frac{(1+\rho)\lambda_1}{(1+\lambda_1)}X_t + \frac{\lambda_2}{(1+\lambda_1)}((1+\rho)IC_{t-1} - IC_t) + \frac{\lambda_3(1+\rho-\gamma)}{(1+\lambda_1)}G_t.$$

Note Eq. (6.7), we have Eq. (6.4). □

Proof of Eq. (6.10). From assumptions (6.1) and (6.2), and Eqs. (6.5) and (6.6), we have

$$(1+\lambda_1)E_t[X_{t+1}] + (1+\rho+\lambda_2)IC_t + \lambda_3\gamma G_t = (1+\rho)MV_{IC,t}.$$

Note from valuation Eq. (6.6), we have $\lambda_3 G_t = MV_{IC,t} - IC_t - \lambda_1 X_t - \lambda_2 IC_{t-1}$. It follows that

$$(1+\lambda_1)E_t[X_{t+1}] = (1+\rho)MV_{IC,t} - (1+\rho+\lambda_2)IC_t$$
$$- \gamma(MV_{IC,t} - IC_t - \lambda_1 X_t - \lambda_2 IC_{t-1}).$$

Reorganizing the terms, we have

$$E_t[X_{t+1}] = \frac{(1+\rho-\gamma)}{(1+\lambda_1)}MV_{IC,t} + \frac{\gamma\lambda_1}{(1+\lambda_1)}X_t - \frac{(1+\rho+\lambda_2+\gamma)}{(1+\lambda_1)}IC_t$$
$$+ \frac{\gamma\lambda_2}{(1+\lambda_1)}IC_{t-1}. \tag{6.42}$$

In terms of information parameters, the expected one-period ahead abnormal operating earnings can be written as

$$E_t[X_{t+1}] = \frac{\omega_1\gamma}{(1+\rho)}X_t + \frac{(1+\rho-\gamma)(1+\rho-\omega_1)}{(1+\rho)}$$
$$\times (MV_{IC,t} - IC_t) - \omega_2(IC_t - \gamma IC_{t-1}). \tag{6.43}$$

□

Bibliography

Alford AW (1992) The effect of the set of comparable firms on the accuracy of the price-earnings valuation method. J Account Res 30(1):94–108

Ashton D, Wang P (2013a) Valuation weights, linear dynamics and accounting conservatism: an empirical analysis. J Bus Finance Account 40(1–2):1–25

Ashton D, Wang P (2013b) Terminal valuations, growth rates and the implied cost of capital. Rev Account Stud 18(1):261–290

Ashton D, Wang P (2015) Conservatism in residual income models: theory and supporting evidence. Account Bus Res 45(3):387–410

Ashton D, Wang P (2025) Investment anomalies and the growth risk premium. Account Bus Res. https://www.tandfonline.com/doi/full/10.1080/00014788.2025.2533468

Ashton D, Peasnell K, Wang P (2011) Residual income valuation models and inflation. Eur Account Rev 20(3):459–483

Ball R, Shivakumar L (2005) Earnings quality in uk private firms: comparative loss recognition timeliness. J Account Econ 39(1):83–128

Barberis N, Huang M (2008) Stocks as lotteries: the implications of probability weighting for security prices. Am Econ Rev 98(5):2066–2100

Barney JB, Clark DN (2007) Resource-based theory: creating and sustaining competitive advantage. Oxford University Press, Oxford

Barth ME, Beaver WH, Hand JRM, Landsman WR (1999) Accruals, cash flows, and equity values. Rev Account Stud 4(3):205–229

Barth ME, Beaver WH, Hand JRM, Landsman WR (2005) Accruals, accounting-based valuation models, and the prediction of equity values. J Account Audit Finance 20(4):311–345

Basu S (1997) The conservatism principle and the asymmetric timeliness of earnings1. J Account Econ 24(1):3–37

Beaver WH, Ryan SG (2000) Biases and lags in book value and their effects on the ability of the book-to-market ratio to predict book return on equity. J Account Res 38(1):127–148

Beaver WH, Ryan SG (2005) Conditional and unconditional conservatism: concepts and modeling. Rev Account Stud 10(2):269–309

Bhojraj S, Lee CMC (2002) Who is my peer? a valuation-based approach to the selection of comparable firms. J Account Res 40(2):407–439

Boatsman JR, Baskin EF (1981) Asset valuation with incomplete markets. Account Rev 38–53

Botosan CA, Plumlee MA (2005) Assessing alternative proxies for the expected risk premium. Account Rev 80(1):21–53

P. Wang, *Integrating Earnings Forecasts, Valuation, and Return Prediction*,
Contributions to Finance and Accounting,
https://doi.org/10.1007/978-3-032-05910-9

Botosan CA, Plumlee MA, Wen H (2011) The relation between expected returns, realized returns, and firm risk characteristics. Contemp Account Res 28(4):1085–1122

Campbell JY (1991) A variance decomposition for stock returns. Econ J 101(405):157–179

Campbell JY, Cochrane JH (1999) By force of habit: a consumption-based explanation of aggregate stock market behavior. J Political Econ. 107(2):205–251

Campbell JY, Mankiw NG (1987) Permanent and transitory components in macroeconomic fluctuations. Am Econ Rev 77(2):111–117

Campbell JY, Viceira LM (2002) Strategic asset allocation: Portfolio choice for long-term investors. Oxford University Press.

Chenery HB (1960) Patterns of industrial growth. Am Econ Rev 50(4):624–654

Choi Y-S, O'Hanlon JF, Pope PF (2006) Conservative accounting and linear information valuation models. Contemp Account Res 23(1):73–101

Claus J, Thomas J (2001) Equity premia as low as three percent? evidence from analysts' earnings forecasts for domestic and international stock markets. J Finance 56(5):1629–1666

Clubb CDB (2013) Information dynamics, dividend displacement, conservatism, and earnings measurement: a development of the ohlson (1995) valuation framework. Rev Account Stud 18(2):360–385

Cochrane JH (2009) Asset pricing: revised edition. Princeton University Press, Princeton

Dechow PM, Hutton AP, Sloan RG (1999) An empirical assessment of the residual income valuation model. J Account Econ 26(1):1–34

Duffie D (2010) Dynamic asset pricing theory. Princeton University Press, Princeton

Easton PD (2004) Pe ratios, peg ratios, and estimating the implied expected rate of return on equity capital. Account Rev 79(1):73–95

Easton PD, Monahan SJ (2005) An evaluation of accounting-based measures of expected returns. Account Rev 80(2):501–538

Easton PD, Monahan SJ (2016) Review of recent research on improving earnings forecasts and evaluating accounting-based estimates of the expected rate of return on equity capital. Abacus 52(1):35–58

Easton P, Taylor G, Shroff P, Sougiannis T (2002) Using forecasts of earnings to simultaneously estimate growth and the rate of return on equity investment. J Account Res 40(3):657–676

Easton P et al (2009) Estimating the cost of capital implied by market prices and accounting data. Found Trends Account 2(4):241–364

Edwards EO, Bell PW (1961) The theory and measurement of business income. University of California Press, Berkeley

Elton EJ (1999) Presidential address: expected return, realized return, and asset pricing tests. J Finance 54(4):1199–1220

Epstein LG, Zin SE (2013) Substitution, risk aversion and the temporal behavior of consumption and asset returns: a theoretical framework. In: Handbook of the fundamentals of financial decision making: part i. World Scientific, Singapore, pp 207–239

Fama EF, French KR (1989) Business conditions and expected returns on stocks and bonds. J Financ Econ 25(1):23–49

Fama EF, French KR (1992) The cross-section of expected stock returns. J Finance 47(2):427–465

Fama EF, French KR (1993) Common risk factors in the returns on stocks and bonds. J Financ Econ 33(1):3–56

Fama EF, French KR (1997) Industry costs of equity. J Financ Econ 43(2):153–193

Fama EF, French KR (2006) Profitability, investment and average returns. J Financ Econ 82(3):491–518

Fama EF, French KR (2015) A five-factor asset pricing model. J Financ Econ 116(1):1–22

Fama EF, MacBeth JD (1973) Risk, return, and equilibrium: empirical tests. J Polit Econ 81(3):607–636

Feltham GA, Ohlson JA (1995) Valuation and clean surplus accounting for operating and financial activities. Contemp Account Res 11(2):689–731

Feltham GA, Ohlson JA (1996) Uncertainty resolution and the theory of depreciation measurement. J Account Res 34(2):209–234

Feltham GA, Ohlson JA (1999) Residual earnings valuation with risk and stochastic interest rates. Account Rev 74(2):165–183
Ferrell A, Liang H, Renneboog L (2016) Socially responsible firms. J Financ Econ 122(3):585–606
Fisher FM, McGowan JJ (1983) On the misuse of accounting rates of return to infer monopoly profits. Am Econ Rev 73(1):82–97
Frankel R, Lee CMC (1998) Accounting valuation, market expectation, and cross-sectional stock returns. J Account Econ 25(3):283–319
Frazzini A, Pedersen LH (2014) Betting against beta. J Financ Econ 111(1):1–25
García Lara JM, García Osma B, Penalva F (2011) Conditional conservatism and cost of capital. Rev Account Stud 16:247–271
Gebhardt WR, Lee C, Swaminathan B (2001) Toward an implied cost of capital. J Account Res 39(1):135–176
Givoly D, Hayn CK, Natarajan A (2007) Measuring reporting conservatism. Account Rev 82(1):65–106
Guay W, Kothari SP, Shu S (2011) Properties of implied cost of capital using analysts' forecasts. Aust J Manag 36(2):125–149
Hail L, Leuz C (2006) International differences in the cost of equity capital: do legal institutions and securities regulation matter? J Account Res 44(3):485–531
Harris RDF, Wang P (2019) Model-based earnings forecasts vs. financial analysts' earnings forecasts. Br Account Rev 51(4):424–437
Heinrichs N, Hess D, Homburg C, Lorenz M, Sievers S (2013) Extended dividend, cash flow, and residual income valuation models: accounting for deviations from ideal conditions. Contemp Account Res 30(1):42–79
Holthausen RW, Watts RL (2001) The relevance of the value-relevance literature for financial accounting standard setting. J Account Econ 31(1–3):3–75
Hou K, Van Dijk MA, Zhang Y (2012) The implied cost of capital: a new approach. J Account Econ 53(3):504–526
Hou K, Xue C, Zhang L (2015) Digesting anomalies: an investment approach. Rev Financ Stud 28(3):650–705
Hughes J, Liu J, Zhang M (2004) Valuation and accounting for inflation and foreign exchange. J Account Res 42(4):731–754
Ingersoll JE (1987) Theory of financial decision making, vol 3. Rowman & Littlefield, Lanham
Isidro H, O'Hanlon J, Young S (2006) Dirty surplus accounting flows and valuation errors. Abacus 42(3–4):302–344
Karolyi GA, Van Nieuwerburgh S (2020) New methods for the cross-section of returns. Rev Financ Stud 33(5):1879–1890
Khan M, Watts RL (2009) Estimation and empirical properties of a firm-year measure of accounting conservatism. J Account Econ 48(2–3):132–150
Kim M, Ritter JR (1999) Valuing ipos. J Financ Econ 53(3):409–437
Lee CMC, Myers J, Swaminathan B (1999) What is the intrinsic value of the dow? J Finance 54(5):1693–1741
Lee CMC, So EC, Wang CCY (2021) Evaluating firm-level expected-return proxies: implications for estimating treatment effects. Rev Financ Stud 34(4):1907–1951
Li KK, Mohanram P (2014) Evaluating cross-sectional forecasting models for implied cost of capital. Rev Account Stud 19:1152–1185
Lintner J (1965) Security prices, risk, and maximal gains from diversification. J Finance 20(4):587–615
Liu J, Nissim D, Thomas J (2002) Equity valuation using multiples. J Account Res 40(1):135–172
Lo K, Lys T (2000) The ohlson model: contribution to valuation theory, limitations, and empirical applications. J Account Audit Finance 15(3):337–367
Lucas RE Jr (1978) Asset prices in an exchange economy. Econ J Econ Soc 1429–1445
Luenberger DG (1998) Investment science. Oxford University Press.
Lyle MR, Wang CCY (2015) The cross section of expected holding period returns and their dynamics: a present value approach. J Financ Econ 116(3):505–525

Lyle MR, Callen JL, Elliott RJ (2013) Dynamic risk, accounting-based valuation and firm fundamentals. Rev Account Stud 18(4):899–929

Lys T, Naughton JP, Wang C (2015) Signaling through corporate accountability reporting. J Account Econ 60(1):56–72

Modigliani F, Miller MH (1958) The cost of capital, corporation finance and the theory of investment. Am Econ Rev 48(3):261–297

Mohanram P, Gode D (2013) Removing predictable analyst forecast errors to improve implied cost of equity estimates. Rev Account Stud 18(2):443–478

Myers JN (1999) Implementing residual income valuation with linear information dynamics. Account Rev 74(1):1–28

Nekrasov A, Ogneva M (2011) Using earnings forecasts to simultaneously estimate firm-specific cost of equity and long-term growth. Rev Account Stud 16(3):414–457

Nissim D (2013) Relative valuation of us insurance companies. Rev Account Stud 18:324–359

Nissim D, Penman SH (2001) Ratio analysis and equity valuation: from research to practice. Rev Account Stud 6:109–154

O'Hanlon J, Steele A (2000) Estimating the equity risk premium using accounting fundamentals. J Bus Finance Account 27(9–10):1051–1083

Ohlson JA (1995) Earnings, book values, and dividends in equity valuation. Contemp Account Res 11(2):661–687

Ohlson J, Gao Z (2006) Earnings, earnings growth and value. Found Trends Account 1(1):1–70

Pae J, Thornton DB, Welker M (2005) The link between earnings conservatism and the price-to-book ratio. Contemp Account Res 22(3):693–717

Peasnell KV (1982) Some formal connections between economic values and yields and accounting numbers. J Bus Finance Account 9(3):361–381

Peng Z, Wang P, Christodoulou D (2024) Bridging the gap between stock price and bottom-line accounting numbers. Rev Account Stud 29(1):701–735

Penman SH (1996) The articulation of price-earnings ratios and market-to-book ratios and the evaluation of growth. J Account Res 34(2):235–259

Penman SH (2013) Financial statement analysis and security valuation. McGraw-Hill, Columbus

Penman S (2016) Valuation: accounting for risk and the expected return. Abacus 52(1):106–130

Penman S (2021) Accounting for risk. Found Trends Account 15(4):373–507

Penman SH, Yehuda N (2009) The pricing of earnings and cash flows and an affirmation of accrual accounting. Rev Account Stud 14:453–479

Penman S, Zhang X-J (2020) A theoretical analysis connecting conservative accounting to the cost of capital. J Account Econ 69(1):101236

Penman S, Zhu J (2022) An accounting-based asset pricing model and a fundamental factor. J Account Econ 73(2–3):101476

Penman SH, Zhu JL (2014) Accounting anomalies, risk, and return. Account Rev 89(5):1835–1866

Petersen MA (2009) Estimating standard errors in finance panel data sets: comparing approaches. Rev Financ Stud 22(1):435–480

Pope PF, Walker M (1999) International differences in the timeliness, conservatism, and classification of earnings. J Account Res 37:53–87

Pope PF, Walker M (2003) Ex-ante and ex-post accounting conservatism, asset recognition and asymmetric earnings timeliness. Lancaster University/The University of Manchester, Lancaster/Manchester

Pope PF, Wang P (2005) Earnings components, accounting bias and equity valuation. Review of Accounting Studies, 10(4):387–407

Rubinstein M (1976) The valuation of uncertain income streams and the pricing of options. Bell J Econ 407–425

Sharpe WF (1964) Capital asset prices: a theory of market equilibrium under conditions of risk. J Finance 19(3):425–442

Sloan RG (2002) Discussion of who is my peer? a valuation-based approach to the selection of comparable firms. J Account Res 40(2):441–444

Sloan R, Lundholm R (2006) Equity valuation and analysis with eVal (2nd ed.). Irwin Professional Publishing.

Vuolteenaho T (2002) What drives firm-level stock returns? J Finance 57(1):233–264

Walker M, Wang P (2003) Towards an understanding of profitability analysis within the residual income valuation framework. Account Bus Res 33(3):235–246

Wang P (2013) The role of disaggregation of earnings in stock valuation and earnings forecasting. Account Bus Res 43(5):530–557

Wang P (2018) Future realized return, firm-specific risk and the implied expected return. Abacus 54(1):105–132

Wang P (2023) A modified ohlson (1995) model and its applications. Eur Account Rev 32(3):663–691

Wang P, Huang W (2015) The implied growth rates and country risk premium: Evidence from chinese stock markets. Rev Quant Finance Account 45:641–663

Watts RL (2003) Conservatism in accounting part i: explanations and implications. Account Horizons 17(3):207–221

Welch I (2021) Simply better market betas. Available at SSRN 3371240

Young S, Zeng Y (2015) Accounting comparability and the accuracy of peer-based valuation models. Account Rev 90(6):2571–2601

MIX
Papier aus verantwortungsvollen Quellen
Paper from responsible sources
FSC® C105338

If you have any concerns about our products,
you can contact us on
ProductSafety@springernature.com

In case Publisher is established outside the EU,
the EU authorized representative is:
Springer Nature Customer Service Center GmbH
Europaplatz 3, 69115 Heidelberg, Germany

Printed by Libri Plureos GmbH
in Hamburg, Germany